10/20

Praise for
CUBAN SON RISING

"Charles Gomez was young, gifted, Cuban, gay AND a closeted CBS network correspondent at the start of the AIDS epidemic which ultimately would ensnare him as well. Now a long-term survivor, the author has written a gut-wrenching memoir that captures the rollercoaster of horror and hope. From the homophobic corridors of network news, through the hospitals and health scares, this is a unique three-decade HIV journey to hell and back again."

—Sheley Ross
Former executive producer of *Good Morning America*

"Cuban Son Rising is a story of monumental personal courage. Not only did Chuck Gomez venture into Central American battle zones in his years as a TV network news correspondent, he also faced his own personal battles with HIV infection and a failing heart. He lays out his compelling memoir from the standpoint of one who is all too keenly aware of his own mortality, and he weaves an unforgettable tale of the people and places he's encountered in a remarkable journalistic career."

—George Lewis
Former NBC News correspondent

"Inspiring, thrilling and enriching! A coming-of age-memoir like few I have read! Charles (Chuck) Gomez is courageous, honest and determined. A man whose life is marked by tribulations and challenges that few can overcome. *Cuban Son Rising* is a testament to Mr. Gomez's will to live and a man's resilience in the face of death. A must read!"

—Conchita Sarnoff
Author, *TrafficKing*, and executive director, Alliance to Rescue Victims of Trafficking

"A revelatory, riveting account, by a seasoned television correspondent who takes you on an episodic journey through Cuba and war-torn Latin America, as he waged a more private struggle with his own mortality. We can all find strength in his courage and insights. His honest rendering of his monumental challenges is fascinating and inspiring."

—*Anne-Marie O'Connor*
Author, *The Lady in Gold: The Extraordinary Tale of Gustav Klimt's Masterpiece, Portrait of Adele Bloch-Bauer*

"As the father of a gay son, my heart ached as I read each page. I was drawn into his world, both as a father and as my father's son. I believe reading his story has helped me understand the mysteries and complexities of homosexuality. It has given me as a reader an opportunity to see a world I would never have known before. A must read."

—*Jeff Shaw*
Author, *Who I Am, The Man Behind the Badge*

"While the treatment of HIV is much improved, the stigma still prevails more deadly than the illness. Charles's courageous story will give others both the hope and the roadmap to survive HIV and its stigma."

—*Eric Sawyer*
AIDS activist

"Chuck Gomez's *Cuban Son Rising* is a compelling, well-written and fascinating autobiography. An unflinchingly honest look at a life filled with professional accomplishments, personal struggles, and a determination to not just survive, but triumph. A wonderful read!"

—*Tom Santopietro*
Author, *Why* To Kill a Mockingbird *Matters*

"*Cuban Son Rising* is a deeply fulfilling journey through the extraordinary life of one of the most prominent Cuban-American television journalists. He reported on the most significant social and political events of the mid-20th century. Gomez's personal life and relationships not only chronicle that history but also serve as a testimony to the spirit and strength of all immigrant families then and now. As a gay and Latino man diagnosed with AIDS, Gomez triumphs over discrimination and homophobia, with the grace and humility to heal family relationships. He opens our hearts and minds to what it means to be 'other' at a time when we need it the most."

—*Stanley Siegel*
Author, *The Patient Who Cured His Therapist*

"Gomez spans personal and political landscapes, and his internal struggles as a Cuban immigrant and a gay man diagnosed with AIDS and in search for his father's approval. Gomez's quest for personal and global truths guides this narrative."

—*Richard Blanco*
Inaugural poet, author, *The Prince of Los Cocuyos*

Cuban Son Rising

by Charles Gomez

© Copyright 2020 Charles Gomez

ISBN 978-1-64663-052-3

Published by

◤ köehlerbooks™

3705 Shore Drive
Virginia Beach, VA 23455
800–435–4811
www.koehlerbooks.com

CUBAN SON RISING

CHARLES GOMEZ

VIRGINIA BEACH
CAPE CHARLES

Special thanks to Stanley Siegel for lighting the path.
And to Karen Wilder, Joe Anson and Summer Brooke Gomez
for guiding me along the way.

and

in loving memory of
Cecilia Alvear
Bob Bergeron
Charles Romo
Coralee Harris
and
Angelina Sanz Gomez

For Papi

TABLE OF CONTENTS

A NOTE TO THE READER

AS A TELEVISION JOURNALIST, the terms *fast forward* and *rewind* are familiar ones. They are used in the editing room to let an editor know where a particular shot can be found. In this memoir, I frequently use the terms to take the reader forward or backward in the narrative. They are also used to make a point or clarify how I was thinking at a particular moment in time.

The names and other characteristics of certain individuals in this memoir may have been changed or omitted. Some persons are referred to with only initials.

MATTERS OF THE SEA

The sea doesn't matter
What matters is this
We all belong to the sea between us, all of us
Once and still the same child
Who marvels over starfish
Listens to hollow shells,
Sculpts dreams into impossible sand castles.

We've all been lovers holding hands
Strolling either of our shores
Our footprints,
Like a mirage of cells
Vanished in waves that don't know their birth
Or care on which country they break, they break
Bless us and return to the sea
Home to all our silent wishes.

No one is the other to the other to the sea
Whether on hemmed island or vast continent
Remember our grandfathers
Their hands dug deep
Into red or brown earth
Planting maple or mango trees that outlive them
Our grandmothers
Counting years while dusting photos of their weddings
Brittle family faces
Still alive on our dressers now.

PROLOGUE

The greatest glory in living lies not in never falling, but in rising every time we fall.
—Nelson Mandela

NO ONE LIFE IS more interesting than another. We're all unique and have lived through experiences that others would find fascinating. It's the details of one's life that make us different. The lessons learned. The roads traveled. I've been fortunate. As the son of immigrants from Cuba, I have lived in two worlds. Call me a *Cubanito*, but I'm an *Americanito*, too. My parents shaped me. Because of them, I learned to appreciate our new country. They left Cuba for opportunity and a better life. They inspired in me a fierce drive to succeed. They worshipped the American dream, and they lived to see us achieve our own dreams.

I've had a remarkable journey. I've covered stories around the world. I've had a grenade tossed my way in Nicaragua as the Somoza regime was about to crumble. I, along with my camera crew and producer, stared death in the face as government tanks rolled up a hill, their gunners pointing straight at us. I survived AIDS. I lived through a massive heart attack and quadruple bypass heart surgery. My heart was so damaged that tissue had to be grafted between my right and left ventricle. The surgeon told my brother to say his goodbyes. He wasn't sure I'd come through the ordeal. But I'm still here.

Others have no problem revealing the most intimate details

of their private lives. But, as a journalist (and as someone who has always focused on learning what makes others tick), it's scary to shine a light on one's own life. Is it an ego trip, or are there lessons here that could help others?

By the time I was twenty-six, I had covered civil wars where bombs were dropped on civilians. I saw bodies left burning in the streets, smoke rising in wispy columns, the smell left behind like burning tires.

I was told that I was the first Hispanic on-air correspondent to be hired by CBS News in 1979. That was four decades ago. Today there are dozens of Latino TV reporters on networks and local stations around the country. I'd like to believe that in some small way, I helped pave the way for them. Although my early years as a network correspondent were often dangerous, I had a guardian angel at my side watching over me. At least that's what my mother assured me. Indeed, for as long as I could remember, a small illustration of a celestial being guiding two children across a bridge hung above my bed.

As a journalist, I met some well-known leaders along the way: Bill Clinton, Fidel Castro, Baby Doc Duvalier, Nicaraguan dictator Anastasio Somoza, Salvadoran president José Napoleón Duarte, and Ferdinand and Imelda Marcos. I even interviewed Jamaican president Edward Seaga on *Face the Nation* when I was only twenty-five. I've also encountered my fair share of celebrities: Bianca Jagger, Elizabeth Taylor, Chita Rivera and a host of others. But those luminaries were hardly the most memorable. Regular folk touched me the most. There was the seven-year-old girl at a Salvadoran orphanage who handed me a tiny doll made out of twigs as a gift. There was the wizened Miskito Indian matriarch on the Nicaraguan-Honduran border wailing for grandchildren gunned down by government troops. They were trying to escape across a river to freedom. And in my personal life, I've been affected forever by the faces of my friends, visages etched in anguish as they waged war against a savage enemy: AIDS.

I was given a chance to live again. Now it's time to help others.

Whether working in a food pantry for the homeless, volunteering at a hospital or marching in the AIDS Walk, the life we live is only as rich as the lives we touch. In our narcissistic me-me-me world of Facebook postings, Twitter tweets and Instagram selfies, it's time to redefine our lives. We can offer hope. We can light a path.

I hope this memoir will move you. Perhaps it will even inspire you. I overcame all that I did for a reason. Most of you have faced your own personal demons. What was the reason you overcame what you did and triumphed? My reason was to write this book and spur on others to galvanize, to influence and to impel in their own lives. All of us can do the same. We can make it our motivation, our life's mission.

I'm my parents' son. A mother from Guines, Cuba, and a father from Havana. They fought to give my brother and me a better life in a new land. What is worth fighting for in your life? "*No te rindes*," my mother would always tell me. (Don't give up.) And I didn't. "*Tenga fe*," she'd also say. (Have faith.) And I do.

I hold on to faith, and so should you. No matter how many times I've fallen, I've always gotten back up. I'm standing now. I'm a Cuban son.

I'm a Cuban son rising.

CHAPTER 1
SHORTY'S WORLD

"Shorty" Gomez, a tangle of frost-covered stainless steel pipes above his head, is surveying a busy scene. Chug-chug-chug-bang! Hssss! Shorty smiles.
—*Miami Herald*, July 1984

I SEE THE CANDY canes from almost two blocks away. How could I miss them? They're lit up like candles and almost eight feet tall. I drive my rented Honda ever so slowly so as to not miss the driveway. My car hugs the right lane of Palm Avenue. And as I get closer I can count them: six, seven, and eight, lined up in a row on the front yard. They remind me of sentries standing at attention. I pull into a familiar garage. Then I see him. I can't help but grin. His white goatee-like beard is neatly trimmed, and he wears a stained white T-shirt tucked into a pair of baggy shorts. He's wearing those funny looking shoes with little holes in them. What are they called? Clogs? Crocs?

The old man stands to the left of the driveway. On the grass right in front of him stand the figures of Mary, Joseph and the Baby Jesus. A brightly lit star is affixed to a pole. Because of where he's standing, the star looks like it's sticking out of his head. An angel, almost as tall as the old man, stands beside him. I stop the car and get out. Only then does a smile break across a face etched with lines. He reaches out to me. "Charles, *mijo*," he says softly. We embrace. They call him Shorty. And I am Shorty's son.

Papi got the name Shorty when he started working in the dairy business in 1948. He was barely twenty. His first job was to shove sticks into ice cream bars as they came off the assembly line. That way one could eat ice cream on the go. One day the plant's manager, William Wilkerson, noticed Papi rummaging through papers in the garbage listing statistics and formulas.

"What are you doing, son?" Wilkerson asked.

"I want to learn how to make ice cream."

The manager told him he didn't have to look through the garbage anymore. "What's your name?" he asked.

"Guillermo or William," my dad answered.

"Well, we can't have two Williams here," Wilkerson said. "So, I'll call you Shorty."

It's been awhile since I last saw Papi's Christmas decorations. My mother died on Thanksgiving Day a year ago. This year he put up more lights with the help of Julio, his next-door neighbor. "I wanted to do something special in honor of your mother this year." He was like a little boy showing off his train set on Christmas Day. "Now I want you to see *el arbolito*" (the tree), he says, leading me inside.

On a console in the living room, a small artificial tree twinkles with tiny white lights. Santa ornaments and little glass hearts hang from the branches.

"Look, look," he says. "Do you remember these?" Beneath the tree he points to a nativity set with about a dozen red figurines. "These are the ones you brought me back that time," he says. And, indeed, on one of my trips to Mexico City for NBC News I had brought back the charming hand-painted characters. Mary's cheeks are rosy, and she smiles as she looks down at the child in the manger. Each Christmas, Papi would display my nativity set next to others given as gifts.

"Why do you like decorating for the holiday as much as you do, Papi?" I ask.

He pauses before replying, "I do it because it brings so much life into the house." With that he shakes his head, and his eyes well up with tears as if recalling a painful memory. "*Tu mami*" (your mother), he says.

For the next two weeks I stayed with Papi in our Hialeah home where I lived as a child from the age of eleven. Usually I stayed at a resort feet away from Fort Lauderdale Beach. But this year I wanted to be with Papi. He walked me to my room. There in the middle of the freshly painted bedroom was the bed I had slept on until I left home for college. It was a tiny twin bed outfitted with two thin mattresses. Papi had covered it in a beige bedspread with three satin pillows. Above my bed was a framed illustration of a guardian angel. To the right and left of it were framed photographs of my brother and me commemorating our First Communion. We were dressed in white suits, our hands folded in prayer holding a rosary. The photographer shined a light behind us that gave a halo effect. We were two of God's perfect little angels, piously praying the rosary. On the opposite wall was a photo of me lovingly holding my niece, Summer, shortly after she was born. I had just come back from Managua, Nicaragua, covering the civil war for CBS News.

"Here's your *camita* (cot)," my father said. "I washed the sheets just this morning."

Each day during my visit, I followed Papi's ritual. He woke me at 4 a.m. on the dot. He'd reheat *café con leche* from the refrigerator for us. We'd sit at the large wooden dining table. As I sipped, he would read morning prayers from a series of holy cards. He would study the illustration on the front of the card before flipping it over for the prayer. I sipped my café and watched him intently. At almost ninety, he was remarkably young looking. Yes, his white hair had receded and he had somewhat of a turkey neck (I was beginning to follow in his footsteps), but his eyes were clear and his complexion was rosy.

After he finished reading all the prayers, he made the sign of the cross. A little after 5 a.m. he'd get a call from Julio. For the last several years, Julio and his wife, Henaly, took it upon themselves to watch over my father. Julio would meet Papi at the fence that separated our yards. Sometimes his son-in-law, who lived in the same house, took over the duties. He would hand my dad two cups of *café con leche* and two pieces of slightly buttered toast. Papi would bring them to the table and we'd eat our breakfast together. He'd be dressed in his security guard uniform. It was covered with gleaming medals.

Papi was proud of being a security guard at Immaculate Conception Church. It was only a mile away, and volunteering there made him feel like he was part of a community. Among other duties, he opened the rectory in the morning. At some Masses, he would serve as an usher. Other times, Papi helped the priests give out Communion. Once a week he'd take cash from the offerings and deposit it in the church account at the bank.

But seeing Papi in his uniform brought up memories of my mother's strained relationship with the Church. When I was covering wars and revolutions for CBS News, she tried seeking guidance from priests at the church. I remember Mami telling me about a priest who looked her in the eye and said, "*Señora*, just go home and put your faith in God. There's nothing that we can do." She was so upset that she never returned. I felt that if the Church had turned its back on Mami, it could certainly turn its back on me. I had gone to Catholic school for five years and was even a choir boy. I knew that the Church considered it a sin to engage in homosexual acts. I had spent a lifetime worrying whether God would punish me for sinning. And I also spent a lifetime worrying that Papi would stop loving me if he learned his *hijo* (son) was gay.

I had flown to Miami from New York to be with my father and family for the Thanksgiving holiday. But the main reason was to start laying the groundwork for a trip to Cuba. And I wanted Papi to come with me. It had been almost six decades since he laid eyes on his homeland. Now, with my mother gone, he could go with me without worrying about having to take care of her day in and day out. But how would I bring up the subject without upsetting him? He had made it clear so many times before that Cuba no longer held a fascination for him.

For more than sixty years, I went out of my way to please my parents in general and my father in particular. From successes in school to my career in journalism, I tried so hard to make Papi proud. I had become my family's great Cuban hope. My father expected a lot from me. But I was a gay man, and somehow I always felt that I had disappointed Papi. I spent so much time seeking his acceptance. I dated women thinking that would please him. But the problem was I couldn't please *them*. I even asked a Cuban woman to marry me thinking Papi would be ecstatic that his son might one day give him a grandchild. She turned me down. I was fooling myself. I was gay. And here I was, a sixty-two-year-old gay man living with HIV. Did he love me less for it?

One day as I was writing at the dining room table, he brought over a stack of papers and scrapbooks and plunked them next to me. I looked up and said, "What are these, Papi?"

"These are things you need to look through," he said purposefully. First, he handed me a long piece of paper. I opened it. The heading read *Certified Copy*. It was a copy of my birth certificate. I was astounded. I thought it was lost. Years ago, I had called Jackson Memorial Hospital trying to get a copy, and I was told by a clerk that they couldn't find a record of my birth. But here it was. I had indeed been born at Jackson on September 2, 1953. But something else caught my eye. There was an affidavit next to the certificate. It read, "Guillermo Gomez being first duly sworn says that he is the father of Charles Gomez and that this affidavit is made for the purpose of correcting certain errors on the original certificate."

I asked my father what all this meant.

"When I came to this country and they asked me my name, I said William because Guillermo in English is William," he said. "But they told me they wanted the name on my birth certificate from Cuba, and that was Guillermo."

My birth certificate wasn't the only surprising thing my father produced. He kept the original certificate of my First Holy Communion as well as my high school diploma and the one from the University of Miami.

"Papi, why hadn't you ever told me you had all this?" I asked.

He just smiled and said, "I've been waiting to show you." I could only laugh.

In three other scrapbooks, my father showed me dozens of yellowed newspaper articles. Some were laminated in plastic. What were these? I had never seen them before. One by one he produced story after story in local newspapers about his success as an ice cream plant manager.

In the *Miami Herald* of Saturday, July 27, 1974, a banner headline reads "People Who Take Ice Cream Seriously: The Ice Cream Makers." The article reads,

> *It's difficult to take an ice cream cone seriously. Chocolate, strawberry, butter pecan or the ever-popular vanilla ice cream is something you associate with a carefree goodtime. It is, after all, a dessert, a treat. But if you make ice cream— four million gallons of the stuff annually as "Shorty" Gomez and his crew at The McArthur Dairy ice cream plant do—you take it seriously indeed. Because while eating ice cream may be a treat, making it is an exacting process complete with formulas, careful sterilization, quality control and yards and yards of shining steel pipes and tanks and machinery.*

I was amazed that my dad had been profiled by the *Miami Herald*. It continued:

"The first thing," says Gomez, who is production manager of the plant, "you have to start with fresh ingredients. A good combination or mix. And you have to have a good flavor. And if you freeze it fast, you have good ice cream."

The article took me back to when I was twelve or thirteen and my father drove me on weekends to the McArthur Ice Cream Plant in Fort Lauderdale. He would walk me into the ice-cold freezers where many of the mixes were kept. I remember thinking I was so proud of him and the work he did. I returned to the article.

Shorty takes great pride in making good ice cream. "We make all number one," he said (referring to the fact that no artificial flavor is used). "Mr. Mac always said, 'Nothing but the best for my customers.'"

As I read through the articles I learned that as a manager my father had increased production of ice cream from 2.2 million gallons to 4.2 million gallons per year. WOW! I read about his plant receiving perfect 100 scores by state inspectors. Many of the articles mentioned how at seventeen Papi slipped wooden sticks in ice cream bars eleven hours a day. I wondered how Dad felt performing such a tedious task day after day. But he was young, and part of living the American dream was to make enough money to put food on the table for his family. By 1987 a contraption was invented that inserted sticks into ice cream bars at a rate of 7,200 an hour. I enjoyed reading one description of Papi:

Gomez commands respect without aloofness or putting on airs. All of his people recognize that he knows the ice-cream production business in and out. He works as hard as anybody in the plant but he puts in much longer hours. Without the help of a secretary, he keeps his own log of production and at

*a moment's notice can provide information on any item made
in the plant—on a daily, monthly or yearly basis.*

I was tickled by another *Miami Herald* story commemorating
National Ice Cream Month in July 1984. I had never heard of a month
devoted to ice cream. As I read more, it was clear that Shorty was
the focus of the article:

*Shorty Gomez, a tangle of frost-covered stainless steel pipes
above his head, is surveying a busy scene. Chug-chug-chug-
bang! Hssss! Shorty smiles. The Vitaline is looking good. Three
clear plastic, three-inch pipes are squirting the frozen fluid
into molds at the end of a huge automated ice-cream bar
maker. A few steps down the assembly line, six wooden sticks
plunge into the mix. Kerplunk! They march a step down the
assembly line. Another six sticks drop into place.*

I read clipping after clipping while Papi stood right behind my
shoulder. I heard his heavy breathing. Sometimes he chuckled,
especially when he made me read the stories out loud. He relished
my reaction. It seemed like this Shorty Gomez was the stuff of legend.

On the front page of the Broward edition of the *Miami Herald*
from June 7, 1981, I came across a color photograph of my dad's
younger beaming face. He was all bundled up, holding an ice cream
bar to his mouth. I read, "Ice Cream Expert Finds His Calling at
40-Below." The story's first paragraph grabbed my attention: "Short-
sleeved Shorty Gomez strolled into the forty below cold and took a
deep breath. 'Relax,' the fifty-four-year-old ice cream expert advised."

I felt the irony. Here I was at sixty-two, just eight years older than
my father was then, reading a story about his accomplishments for the
very first time. I didn't know Papi as well as I thought I did after all.

That first night I slept like a baby in my childhood bed. Staying with Papi made me revert to those years of trying to make Papi like me and be proud of me. Our routine never changed. Every morning I'd hear Papi shuffle down the hallway. He'd go into the bathroom, shutting the door quietly so as to not wake me. But the sound of his steps were my alarm clock. I opened my eyes and listened. Sometimes I would hear a dog barking or rooster crowing in the distance. These were the sounds of Hialeah, the sounds that became so much a part of me, starting when I was just eleven years old. On this morning I heard Julio throw pebbles at the window. It was a signal that breakfast was ready.

We ate in silence, and when we finished I decided that it was time to bring up Cuba.

"Papi, I was hoping to do something special with you. Willie could be a part of it too," I said.

"Please don't tell me it's about Cuba." I could tell he was annoyed. "That chapter of my life is over. I don't even think of it anymore." With that, Papi got up and headed for the door. "I'm late for church," he said abruptly. Seconds later, I heard his car rumble out of the driveway. Damn! What could I say or do to convince Shorty to come to Cuba with me? Time was running out. Papi was almost ninety. What if he passed away before seeing Cuba one more time? I was anxious and impatient. Waiting calmly for something to happen wasn't a Gomez trait. Usually, we wanted answers and action *ahora* (now)!

That afternoon, after he came home from church, I happened to be taking a nap.

"Wake up," I heard him say.

"Hi, Papi," I said groggily. "I didn't hear you come in."

His eyes were wide open and he was grinning from ear to ear. It was clear he couldn't wait to tell me something.

"Let's go to the table," he said. Out of nowhere he began relating stories of his youth in Cuba. He knew I loved hearing his stories. He watched as I wrote in my journal each day. I couldn't understand why Papi had waited so long to tell me, but that didn't matter now. He wanted to share with me his childhood in Cuba, so as he began recounting his tales in Spanish, I scribbled it all down in English:

> *It was a regular school day, and during recess, I got together with my pals. But when recess was over instead of returning to class, we decided to escape. We went to see one of our teachers who was sick. When we got there, he was happy to see us, but then he started scolding us for playing hooky. After a while we all went on our way. When I got home, Mima called me over. It seems a policeman on a horse had come to our home. "Señora," he said. "A boy was seen entering this home who apparently left his classes in the middle of the day." Mima thanked him. Then she lit into me and screamed, "Never do that again!" With that she slapped me hard across the face and I've never forgotten it. Even at almost eighty-eight years old, it still hurts me today.*

Then Papi talked about his days at the *bodeguita* (small store). It was run by his mom and stepdad. Papi worked doing odd jobs along with another teen, a black kid named Felipe who lived nearby. As he talked about the *bodeguita*, Papi tugged at his earlobe as if doing so could magically summon details of memories from so long ago.

> *Each day at around 4 a.m. we would go to the main plaza to buy food we needed to sell at the store. We used to stick a knife into our pants. We carried a large sack to bring back items we had bought at the market. We had to walk about twelve long blocks and cross a large park. So, a police officer stops us and asks, "Where do you boys think you're going?" I told him that we were going to the market in the central plaza. Well, Felipe had a very aggressive way about him and screamed, "You don't have to tell him where we're going! That's none*

of his business." The police officer got angry and yelled, "I'm arresting both of you." He took us to the police precinct a block away. Well, I was beside myself and I blurted out, "Officer, my papi knows the captain of the precinct here. He goes to our bodeguita all the time." So, the officer calls the precinct and speaks to a higher-up. Whoever he spoke to told the officer, "No, those are good people. Let them go." So, he let us go and that was another day I'll never forget. When I got home I told the old man and he got angry.

Every day, Pipo would leave to drive his bus and leave Mima, my dad and Felipe to tend the store.

One day they brought us three or four bags of black beans to sell. And the beans in one sack were too hard, they couldn't be eaten, we would have to throw them out. But Felipe said to me, we can't do that. So, at night after we closed the bodega, we opened the sack and let the beans spill on the floor. Then we poured vegetable oil over them and with a towel we made sure to get every last bean. And the beans suddenly looked beautiful. They were actually shining. So then we took the beans and put them back in the sack and we'd sell them. When we'd sell three pounds of beans, we'd pour in good beans from two of the sacks and the bad beans from the other sack. We never had a problem. But sometimes a customer would say "Hey, the beans were great but some of them were a little hard." But that's what we would do so we wouldn't lose money on the bad beans by throwing them out.

And then Shorty told me about the yucca scam. Yucca root vegetable is popular in Cuban homes and often used as a substitute for potatoes. My dad explained that he and Felipe would buy dozens of yucca roots at the market and bring them back to sell at the *bodeguita.* When customers came to buy yucca, Papi and Felipe would ask if they wanted fresh yuccas, which would be sold for ten cents higher than the others. If they said yes, my dad would then go into the yard behind the store and bury yuccas in the soil. He told me that most customers almost always would say "Give me those fresh yuccas." My dad would pull the yuccas he had buried in the ground and bring them back into the store covered in dirt. "That was one of our better ideas," he said with a smile. But it was the cheese story that I found really surprising.

As Papi told it, one of the *bodeguita's* most popular items was goat cheese. But every once in a while tiny worms could be seen crawling out of the cheese.

"If we didn't sell it, we'd lose so much in profit," Papi said. And so a friend who worked with him came up with an idea. They pulled out the stopper in the sink, turned on the water and watched the tiny worms go down the drain. "Then we'd take the cheese and pour milk over it until it was fresh looking and beautiful again," Papi explained. "Customers would come into the store and comment on how white the cheese looked."

I then asked him, "Weren't you embarrassed doing this?"

He thought a moment and said, "No, because we found out all the *bodeguitas* would do things like this to make money."

And that little *bodeguita* was where my dad first laid eyes on Mami.

"We had a machine that would grind coffee by hand, and I'd have to turn the handle slowly when the coffee beans were put in. In the neighborhood there was a *muchacha* (girl) who would come in every single day to buy. She always wanted two pounds of ground coffee. So every time I'd see her walking toward the store, I'd think to myself, 'Oh no, now I have to grind all those beans. It'll take me fifteen or twenty minutes.' Mami would then take her freshly-ground coffee and saunter out of the store. One time after one of Mami's visits, a coworker said to me, 'You're always talking about her and complaining, but you know what? One day you're going to end up marrying that girl.'"

And that's exactly what Papi did. At this moment I turned to Papi, pleading my case for going to Cuba. This time he listened without cutting me off. I told him that we could visit the house where the *bodeguita* was. We could go to the church where he and Mami got married. We could walk the streets of Old Havana.

He paused before answering. "I'm not ready to go. I don't know how I'll feel if I go back there." I wouldn't accept that as his final answer and told him to think about it.

From there Papi skipped ahead to when he was seventeen and living in New York City. World War II was still going on, and he said there were still a lot of shortages, including sugar. And then, to my amusement, Shorty relayed this story to me:

A lot of times I'd slip into the Automat. [In the forties and fifties, Automats were the spots to go in New York City if you wanted to eat cheaply. Vending machines displayed sandwiches and desserts. If you put a coin in a slot you could open the door and remove the food.] At a counter there was this lady who would give out sugar from a bowl. But she would only give out a spoonful at a time. I had just come from Cuba, so of course I liked my coffee extra sweet. I tried to be like the Americanos and drink it their way but it tasted terrible. There was no way I could get it down.

One day I happened to hear the sugar lady speaking in Spanish. So, I went up to her and I said, "Please, señora, I just got here from Cuba and I'm so used to drinking my coffee sweet and this coffee tastes awful." So she says to me: "Don't tell anyone. Walk around the table as many times as you want and every time you walk by I'll put a little more sugar in your cup." So, I walked around the table at least ten times

and after the last time, the coffee finally tasted rico [sweet]
just the way Mima made it for me in Cuba.

From the "sugar in the coffee" story, Papi jumped to the end
of World War II. The day was May 8, 1945, when Nazi Germany
surrendered to the Allied Forces. Papi was only seventeen at the
time and like so many thousands that day ran to Times Square to
celebrate victory. It was less than ten blocks from the factory where
he worked with Pipo.

"Everyone was jumping up and down. People were hugging in
the middle of the street. Times Square was filled with people. You
couldn't walk through."

By now Papi had been regaling me with his stories for almost an
hour and I noticed his eyes begin to flutter. He was falling asleep.

"Papi," I said, "why don't you lay down for a while?"

"Okay," he said. As he went to lie down I realized that something
very special had happened. He had waited a lifetime to tell me stories
that I had never heard before. Some of them revealed a young man
with a mischievous streak who could get into loads of trouble.

The stories he told me were human stories, worms and all. He
had reached into his treasure trove of memories and gifted them to
me lovingly. He showed me his heart that afternoon. As I sat at the
dining room table, someone else was sitting right beside me. It was
the kid who played hooky from school. It was the culprit who buried
yucca in the backyard to make it appear fresh and charge customers
a dime more. It was the seventeen-year-old in New York City who
barely spoke English and wanted extra sugar in his coffee. And it was
the teen with hair flopping into his eyes who ran into Times Square
with thousands of others to celebrate the end of World War II.

And as I sat at the table that afternoon, so many images from
my own past flickered before me. There was Papi curling his tongue,
about to strike me as a kid after I did something wrong. I could still
hear Mami screaming, "*Guillermo, deja el niño.*" (Guillermo, leave the

boy alone.) There was Shorty yelling at my mom to stop coddling me. He was afraid that I might turn into the one thing all Cuban parents feared most: a *maricón*, a queer, a *pato.* GAY! But other memories came to me that day. There was the time Papi accompanied a scared fourteen-year-old to a country club for an oratorical contest, which I won! I realized, as I sat there with him asleep feet away, that I had spent a lifetime trying to earn Papi's approval. Despite all he did to prevent it, I had turned out to be a *maricón* after all. I had come down with HIV/AIDS. Did Shorty accept it? Or was he ashamed of me?

In Cuban families the façade that one presented to the outside world was critical. Appearances were everything. Harsh realities and dark secrets were never discussed publicly. For most Cuban families having a gay son wasn't something to cheer about. Now, after all these years later, I wondered what he expected of me. There was still so much that hadn't been addressed or resolved. Even though we had broken new ground, there was still a great deal I didn't know and wanted to know. Did I turn out to be the son Papi had hoped I'd be? Had my brother fulfilled all of Papi's expectations while I was just a big disappointment? Would Papi agree to go to Cuba with me? Was he proud of me?

I was going to have to wait to get my answers.

I was living in Shorty's world now. He had his routine. He had his timetable. Shorty's son would have to be patient. In Shorty's world, *ahora* (now) meant *mañana* (tomorrow). He'd think about it tomorrow. After all, *mañana* was another day.

CHAPTER 2
LIVING WITH AIDS

This disease will be the end of many of us, but not nearly all, and the dead will be commemorated and will struggle on with the living, and we are not going away. We won't die secret deaths anymore. The world only spins forward. We will be citizens.
The time has come.
—Tony Kushner, *Angels In America*

I GRABBED THE WOODEN crucifix off my bedroom wall. I stuck it in the left pocket of my jacket as I headed with my partner, B., for the doctor's office. It was 1992, almost a decade after the first wave of HIV/AIDS cases hit New York City, spreading a sense of doom and anxiety. In the eighties that gripping fear was felt not only among gay men. Many thought that even touching someone who might be infected could spread the virus. A decade later the stigma persisted. Oh, everybody professed not to be afraid. But they were lying. Lying big-time.

Gray clouds rolled across the New York skyline as B. and I walked into the Chelsea office to find out the results of our HIV tests. I touched the pocket of my jacket. Yep, the cross was still there. B. and I took our seats in the crowded waiting room. The patients all appeared to be gay. They ranged in age from their early twenties to their mid-sixties. How did they appear to be gay? I don't know. Maybe it was my *gaydar*. I spotted a trainer from my gym. Sandy blond hair and a sheepish smile were his calling cards. That and protruding pecs and bicep muscles. Guns, we called them. They popped out from a too-tight baby-blue spandex T-Shirt. Muscle Mary. Some read *Vanity Fair*, others read *Popular Mechanics*. Others listened to music through clownishly large earphones. Some looked our way. They had that perpetual look of surprise and curiosity many gays shared. It was a look that said, "Are you interested in me?" Could they possibly know why I was here? I studied their faces. Some were overly tanned, aficionados of the electric beach, suntan beds in salons with names like Portofino Sun Center or Future Tan. Others had the "AIDS look": gaunt faces with sunken cheeks and heavily etched marionette lines on the sides of their mouths. AIDS wasting.

I looked toward the receptionist, a kind-faced older woman who reminded me of Mima, my grandmother. She looked up at me. Then suddenly she looked away. Did she already know if I was a positive or negative? Was I being paranoid? Or did paranoia, as my friend Sheila Stainback was so fond of saying, border on perception? Although the room was silent, I felt I could hear the white noise of thoughts. *Rrrrrrr*. Who else might be here to find out if he or she had HIV? Was I the only one? *Rrrrr*. I touched my heart and felt my cross. My heart beat like a conga drum that only I could hear. *Bar-rump-pa-pa. Bar-rump-pa-pa.* As I looked out at the large picture window toward Nineteenth Street in Chelsea, the rains began. *Aguacero* (downpour), as my Cuban mother used to say. Thunderstorm. The rains beat against the window, casting latticelike shadows across the waiting room. We looked like prisoners behind bars.

I took the crucifix out of my pocket. My fingers clutched it tightly. I stared at the figure of Jesus. I looked into his face long and hard. What did I see? Grief? Resignation? How had I arrived at this moment? I had always tried to practice safe sex. But what about that time I slipped? It was before I met my partner, B. I had unprotected three-way sex. It was with a couple. Wait a minute. There had also been that sandy-haired entertainment reporter that time the condom broke. It rained harder. I tried to remember. It was the eighties and the AIDS epidemic was at its peak. Whispers that Rock Hudson had *the plague* reverberated through Hollywood. On *Dynasty,* his skeletal look shocked viewers. A sense of panic. Rumbling thunderclouds of fear.

I'd met a couple in their forties at a gay bar in Silver Lake, a section of Los Angeles. It had a name like Detour or One Way. One guy was tall and muscular with a walrus mustache and pork chop sideburns that met pouty lips. The other was shorter and blond, an eighties version of Tab Hunter (with blond locks that swept his forehead like an aging surfer). When he smiled, a snaggletooth peeked perilously from an otherwise perfect set of choppers. It was a quasi-leather bar where men wore distressed leather harnesses and smelled of cheap cigars and even cheaper gin. The stench of urine emanated from door-less bathrooms where communal latrines substituted for urinals. On the walls were hastily scrawled indecipherable messages, phone numbers and crude drawings of erupting penises; gay graffiti, homosexual hieroglyphics. I wondered if centuries from now anthropologists would try to decipher their meaning or simply give up. Outdated Donna Summer tunes blared from a rickety neon jukebox sitting atop a flock of dust bunnies. Throbbing red, blue and green lights crisscrossed brick walls reminding me of the El Morro lighthouse protecting Havana Bay. A mirrored disco ball twirled lazily from above, catching the rainbow-colored lights. *"She works hard for the money,"* Donna warbled. I had descended into the gay demimonde. I guzzled more drinks than I should have on that humid Silver Lake night.

I went home with them. It was my first three-way. Months later I learned that one of the guys was in the hospital. It was the Tab

Hunter look-alike. I visited him. His skeletal form lay like a piece of crumpled paper in a narrow bed connected to a switchboard of IV tubes. His once clean-shaven face was now adorned with a scruffy gray beard.

"Mark," I whispered. I stared at the purple marks that covered his body. The machines next to his bed made strange sounds. *Peep-peep-peep*. Mark half-opened his eyes. A faint smile crossed his sunken face. But he said nothing.

"It's Chuck," I whispered. "Remember?" He nodded. Then he closed his eyes. He kept opening and closing his mouth as if he were trying to say something. But no words came. "Get some rest," I said. I kissed him on the cheek as I left the room. I felt sad, like the day Mami told me that Mima had died. I wanted to cry. But no tears came. Later I learned Mark had passed away. I called his partner. I asked him if Mark had died from AIDS. There was silence on the other end of the line. And in my mind, I heard that *peep-peep-peep* of the machines in that tiny hospital room that day.

My new relationship was in the honeymoon phase. I had been seeing B. for about eight months. He was my golden boy. He had blond hair parted down the middle that fell into his eyes. He towered over me at over six feet. His eyes were a greenish blue that changed color depending on what he wore. He didn't so much laugh as he roared.

He was eleven years younger. I had left my prior partner for him. One winter night as we lay in our creaky bed, B. gave me an ultimatum. "You have to get tested for HIV," he said softly. He corrected himself. "We've got to get tested for HIV. We'll do it together."

The crackle of lightning outside the doctor's office snapped me out of my daydream. "Chuck," said the receptionist solemnly. When I got up I felt I was moving in slow motion. And when I walked it was like I was one of those astronauts I saw walking on the moon on TV in our little house in Hialeah. Each step was unhurried. Each movement deliberate. We were led to the second examining room on the right.

"I have good news and bad news," the doctor said.

The doctor was an impish and always jovial man who tilted his head before beginning a sentence. He reminded me of Richard Simmons, or Richard Simmons as a leprechaun. But on this day, he delivered the news without his usual crack: "When I see you, I always think of a drag queen covered in boas, feathers flying everywhere." Good news? Bad news? My partner and I exchanged confused looks. He said B.'s name. "You are negative." Then he lasered in on me. I knew what was coming. "But, Chuck, I'm sorry. You're HIV positive." I took a deep breath. I clutched the crucifix so tightly it broke in half. Jesus snapped off the cross. Anger, despair, rage. I felt the terrifying impact of what seemed to be a death sentence. I whimpered. My partner grabbed me. We embraced. I cried.

"It's going to be alright," he reassured me. I wasn't so sure. No event has changed my life more than finding out I was HIV positive. And in many ways, as strange as this may sound, HIV would transform me for the better. When one is faced with death, each moment of life tastes sweeter.

In 1984, when I came to New York City as a twenty-nine-year-old local television reporter, the whispers of a new killer virus were already reaching a crescendo. One stormy morning I was assigned to interview two men who had just come down with HIV. They agreed to talk about it at the offices of the Gay Men's Health Crisis (GMHC). As a gay man in the homophobic world of television news, I had kept my sexual orientation a closely guarded secret. Somewhere I had read a saying: "What you can't say owns you. What you hide controls you." It was certainly true on that gloomy day.

The Times Square that greeted me back then was an unforgettable, seedy demimonde. It consisted of live burlesque joints, porn theaters and XXX peep shows reached by climbing narrow stairways. Over on Forty-Second Street the marquee at the Victory flashed titles like *Secret Wet Dreams* and *All Night Orgy*. Channel 9 was in the middle of the maelstrom between Forty-Second and Forty-Third Streets.

In the early morning as I got to work, Broadway was still shrugging off the sleaze from the night before. Street walkers ambled groggily past the WOR-TV entrance, garish neon flickering across tired faces. They were in shades of lavender and chartreuse, reminding me of the ladies of the night from Toulouse Lautrec paintings.

"Chuck, do you have any problem interviewing two guys who got this AIDS thing?" my assignment editor asked.

"Of course not," I said. I watched as he talked to a member of the crew that would accompany me.

"They don't know how you get this fuckin' thing," the crew member shouted. "I want a Hazmat suit. I wanna be covered up and protected."

I was startled. I knew that you couldn't get HIV this way. But I kept silent. I was deep in the closet. I worried how my colleagues would react, not only to the fact that I was gay but also to the possibility that I might be carrying the virus myself. Finally, another camera crew agreed to go with me, provided the news station got us some masks. Rumors swirled that the AIDS virus was airborne. And even people who should have known better were petrified.

Just a few months earlier, a girlfriend invited me over to her apartment for coffee. She usually served it to me in a ceramic mug. On this morning when I walked in she had a funny look on her face. Her smile seemed forced.

"Oh, hi, Chuck, here's your coffee," she said. But instead of my usual mug, she gestured to a Styrofoam cup on the counter. "You know, with all this stuff going on, you can never be too safe," she said. I was crushed. The implication was apparent.

"I gotta go," I said. My exit line delivered, I followed it out the door.

In the eighties if you were even perceived to be gay, you were suspect. In 1989 the late CBS newscaster Andy Rooney said something on the air that stunned people living with HIV/AIDS. As Emmy Award-winning television producer Shelley Ross (with whom

I walked down the aisle at the University of Miami on graduation day so many years ago) wrote in *The Huffington Post* on October 4, 2011,

> *I always believe you can't judge a person by their worst moment and that certainly applies to the über talented Andy Rooney whose broadcasts offer nearly five decades of snapshots for a cultural yearbook. But there is a reason to revisit his, a December 1989 CBS Special "The Year with Andy Rooney," when the popular broadcaster, then 71, offered this:*

> *There was some recognition in 1989 of the fact that many of the ills which kill us are self-induced. Too much alcohol, too much food, drugs, homosexual unions, cigarettes. They're all known to lead quite often to premature death.*

> *"It wasn't as if they didn't bring it on themselves," he added.*

Gay leaders were outraged. Rooney was temporarily suspended. He later apologized.

In her article Ross added,

> *While these words wounded many, I knew of one secretly suffering the slings and arrows the most: Charles Gomez, the CBS News correspondent for Latin America who had recently been diagnosed with AIDS. Chuck, as I called him since our university days, was a smart and handsome Cuban-American journalist who, at the time, was best known for covering the dangerous "bang-bang" revolutions throughout Central America.*

I was in one of those "homosexual unions" Rooney was talking about. And ultimately I would come down with HIV myself. But I knew something that Andy didn't: AIDS wasn't a moral condemnation.

It was a virus that attacked indiscriminately. We, as gays, would never have chosen to bring "it" on ourselves. I wished I could have chatted with Andy Rooney. I wished he could have sat with me at the bedsides of friends in their final days. It may have changed his mind. The faces I looked into were emaciated, but the eyes flickered with hope. Those faces belonged to gays from all walks of life and economic circumstances. The movie *The Normal Heart* (based on the play by Larry Kramer) drove this point home powerfully. The scenes of lesion-scarred men with AIDS lying neglected in hospital beds (because nurses were too scared to treat them) were harrowing. I know because I was in hospitals visiting friends just like in the movie and witnessing similar scenes. These patients weren't pariahs; they were human beings cut down in their prime.

One of them was my friend Tom Morgan. I had known him for more than three decades. A reporter and editor for *The New York Times*, I had met Tom when we were both intern reporters at the *Miami Herald*. He suffered from pneumonia and other opportunistic infections. The combination of antiretroviral drugs Tom was taking weren't working. Tom died that winter, and as I sat at his memorial service, I thought of all my friends who were no longer alive.

There was Bill Flaherty, a chiseled Calvin Klein model who died before he turned twenty-eight. We met in Los Angeles when I was a network correspondent for NBC News. Tall, blond and blue-eyed, he looked like a model from the pages of an Abercrombie & Fitch catalogue. We became good friends. He developed HIV/AIDS when he returned to New York, and it was tough to see my handsome friend deteriorate. AIDS finally claimed him right before my eyes.

At Bill's funeral, I met Tom McBride, a fixture on the gay circuit. Tom was a model, actor, photographer and member of the gay "A-list"—they were invited to the most beautiful homes in Fire Island, Pines, and to the most fashionable parties in the city. Tall with a sculpted face, Tom was also living with AIDS. Tom had played the wheelchair-bound camp counselor in the movie *Friday the 13th*.

Tom developed toxoplasmosis, a parasitic disease that infected the brain. Tom soon began experiencing blackouts. In his final months, he was confined to his bed and I went to his apartment to see him. Tom no longer recognized me, but I took his hand and held it as tightly as I could. I wondered how long he had to live.

"During the AIDS crisis, I learned that people choose their moment of death," said my therapist Stanley Siegel. "Often when they felt others were prepared to accept it." Tom died on September 24, 1995, two weeks after my visit.

Rewind, 1992

I thought back to that morning when I was diagnosed. I couldn't look into the future and predict that I'd fall into a deep depression, turn to drugs and even seriously consider ending it all. I went to work that day determined to keep my secret to myself. Would cameramen now want to wear masks when they accompanied me on assignments? Would I be fired? All these thoughts swirled through my head. Suddenly, being in the closet seemed to make it all worse. I had cheered when CNN's Anderson Cooper came out, but in 1992 I couldn't do the same. I didn't have the guts. To use a more vulgar Cuban expression, I didn't have the *cojones*.

The times were so different. The homophobic corridors of network and local news weren't welcoming to reporters like me. In the seventies and eighties when I started, news was a macho game run predominantly by white males. Gay men and women in positions of power were few and far between. The same could be said for gays on the air. Being a Hispanic reporter in this environment was tough enough. Throw in being gay and it was even tougher. So gay reporters like myself laid low. Being "proud and out" wasn't an option.

In one of my first television jobs, I was befriended by a highly respected anchorwoman. She was in the closet at work, but to a select few she confided that she was gay. When I left for another station we had a heart-to-heart talk. "Whatever you do privately behind closed doors is your business, not your bosses' or your colleagues," she told me. "This is a tough business. Be careful." The implication was clear: being gay could cost me a future in TV news.

Two years later when I was hired by CBS News, I was promptly dispatched to cover the Nicaraguan Revolution. It led to the ouster of dictator Anastasio Somoza and the triumph of the Sandinistas. Like Cooper, being gay had nothing to do with the stories I was sent to cover.

Rewind, July 3, 1981

The New York Times reports on a "rare cancer seen in 41 homosexuals." It would be the first inkling of the impending AIDS crisis. In those first years of the epidemic I was petrified of being tested. I was worried that my results (if they were positive) could be made public and affect my job at CBS News. I bristled when I heard network news crews talk about "the gay cancer." It took years before I had the courage to find out my status. Network news was a "boys club," and I was trying desperately to fit in. Coincidentally, that same year Dan Rather was promoted to anchor of the CBS Evening News after Walter Cronkite stepped down. To me Rather was Mr. Macho personified. In my closeted mind I feared that he might try to get rid of me for not fitting the CBS mold. I was determined to be as buttoned-down as possible. Being gay could be perceived as a sign of weakness. I wasn't about to let myself be seen that way.

I'd cringe at the gay jokes made in the newsroom. But I kept silent. I butched it up. For all the world, I was a straight news correspondent. And now as the AIDS crisis churned around me, I paid the price for crouching in the back of the closet. I felt that I was nothing more than a gay coward. My conflicts ate away at me, and I'm sure I wasn't alone. The eighties and the early nineties were like that for us gay journalists.

Nowadays it's a different story altogether. Gay reporters post shirtless selfies with boyfriends and husbands on their Instagram pages, and their bosses couldn't care less. Yesterday's closet cases are today's "influencers."

Here I was this former Catholic choirboy. I was raised to believe that even thinking impure thoughts was a mortal sin. Being gay wasn't accepted by the Church. Now I wondered if having AIDS was somehow a "curse from God."

Fast Forward, 1992

The months after learning about my HIV status were professionally rewarding. But they were also personally traumatizing. I worried if I was doing the right thing by not taking a drug called AZT. It was one of the few medications that doctors were prescribing at that time to combat HIV/AIDS. In the early nineties, antiretrovirals weren't yet available. Doctors fought AIDS by treating complications as they arose, from opportunistic infections to cancer-like lesions. A year before joining WNBC in 1994, I won an Emmy Award for a piece called "Take Back the Village." I was working for WWOR-TV at the time. The night of the awards, I pinned a red AIDS awareness ribbon to my tux. My beaming parents (who had flown in from Miami) watched me accept the award. They never asked me what the red ribbon meant. The Emmy catapulted me to a job at WNBC-TV in New York City. I felt that I had made it, but I also lived in fear.

For the first two years of my diagnosis, I kept my status to myself and wondered when I would develop symptoms that would force me to tell my bosses that I had HIV. Just a year later, AIDS researcher Dr. David Ho called for a "hit hard, hit early" approach to fight AIDS. He believed in aggressive treatment with multiple anti-retrovirals. But my doctor was concerned that this path might increase side effects and multi-drug resistance. The uncertainty so early in my diagnosis led me to visit another doctor for a second opinion.

After looking at my bloodwork and reviewing my low T-cells (white blood cells that fight infection; when the CD4 count drops below 200, a person is diagnosed with AIDS) this doctor sat grimly in his windowless Chelsea office. Looking matter-of-factly at my chart, he told me that I might not have more than five years to live. With my T-cells below 50, I now had full-blown AIDS.

"You might think about getting your affairs in order," he said. What would I do now? I felt helpless. Thank God for AIDS activist groups like ACT UP. Founded by Larry Kramer, ACT UP pushed for the passage of drugs that weren't as toxic as AZT. They were called protease inhibitors. First approved in 1995, they seemed promising. It was then that I learned that almost every living cell contains protease, the digestive enzyme that breaks down proteins. The protease inhibitors slowed down the reproduction of the virus.

I came down with pneumocystis pneumonia (PCP), and my doctor considered sending me to the hospital. I begged him not to because I feared (given my low T-cell numbers) that I would come down with a staph infection or worse. He prescribed Bactrim, a strong antibiotic used to treat progressing infections in the lungs. I was allergic and broke out in hives. So, he tried something else. In the meantime, I was calling in sick and lying to my bosses about my condition. One week I said I had the flu—the next, a bad case of bronchitis. I was so afraid I'd lose my job if I took any more sick days. My suits hung off me as I lost more weight. At one point, I dropped to below 135 pounds on my 5'8" frame. I experienced AIDS wasting. I looked in the mirror, and staring back at me was someone I didn't know. I couldn't ignore the stares in the newsroom, the whispered conversations when I walked out of view. I covered my sunken eyes and cheeks with on-air makeup (Max Factor Pancake, Deep Egyptian #2), hoping nobody would notice. But I wasn't fooling anyone. Egyptian indeed.

I suffered from lipoatrophy, a loss of peripheral body fat. It was a common condition when CD4s (the number of cells fighting infection in the body) slipped below fifty. A friend of mine who had lipoatrophy, like I did, told me about a dermatologist on the East Side. For $1,000 he would inject silicone into my face in order to make me look more normal. I had no idea if the procedure was FDA approved. And frankly I didn't care. Some of my colleagues were already commenting on my gaunt appearance. One day, a friend at work, an older woman always ready with a wisecrack, pulled me aside.

"Chuck, what's wrong?" she asked. "You look like a walking skeleton. What is it?" She got louder and shrill. "Tell me. What is it?" She grabbed my arm and dug her long, manicured red nails into my arm. I thought she'd rip the fabric of my suit. And every time I saw her, she'd ask again, digging into my arm once more. In photographs from that time, I looked like a human hanger. My clothes were baggy and didn't fit.

I rushed to that East Side dermatologist my friend recommended. At first, I couldn't see a difference, but after three sessions I thought the lines began to disappear. Was it vanity? No, it was my livelihood. I didn't want anyone to suspect I had AIDS. The treatments helped, but I was still shockingly thin. I put on a brave face and got back to work.

Sometimes I'd put in as many as fifteen hours a day, especially when there was a breaking story like a plane crash or a fatal fire. I slipped into depression. My doctor prescribed anti-depressants, Wellbutrin, Zoloft (or "Go-Soft" as my gay friends would call it for its side effect of killing erections), and they made me feel loopy. I panicked that my colleagues would figure out I was sick. The depression got worse. I fleetingly considered suicide. How easy it would be to just jump off from my apartment's thirty-fourth-floor balcony. I'd fall on the street just a block from Broadway. "Reporter with AIDS plunges to his death," I imagined the headline would be in the *New York Post*. My parents would grieve, but they wouldn't have to live through the shame of their son having AIDS.

I was clearly in despair. I smoked pot. I snorted cocaine. It was usually during weekends when I felt I could control the behavior. I would drop ecstasy and hit circuit parties with names like "Alegria" and "The White Party." I would disappear into peep shows on Forty-Second Street with a bottle of poppers (amyl nitrate) and watch porn for hours on end. Sometimes I found myself wandering aimlessly through Times Square. The coke would sometimes trigger violent asthma attacks, but I didn't stop. I couldn't stop. On other weekends, I would flee to Fire Island and drink and drug myself into oblivion. My partner became alarmed at my reckless behavior.

"You've got to get this thing under control," B. would scream at me. "Look what it's doing to you!" My doctor recommended a psychiatrist. I balked. My father always believed depression was an excuse for the weak-willed. He believed it could simply be remedied by bucking up and acting like a man.

I was in denial about so many things: my gayness, my HIV and my drug addiction. I was living in two worlds. To the viewers who saw my reports on the 11 o'clock news each night, there wasn't even a hint of what I was going through. The camera was my shield, and when I was on the air, I felt invincible. But off camera my world was crumbling. My self-destructive behavior was hardly anything new for those living with HIV. We wanted to punish ourselves. We could die tomorrow, so why not live for today? Instead of nurturing ourselves, we wanted to annihilate ourselves. It was the epitome of self-destructive behavior. I made up excuses to avoid going to a psychiatrist.

"I can't afford it," I told my doctor.

"Quite frankly, you can't afford not to go," he shot back.

Soon I realized that it was time to tell my bosses I had HIV. I marched into the offices of the news director. As I laid it all out, I saw in his eyes that he was weighing the magnitude of what I was saying. He paused before reacting. "First of all I am terribly sorry you are going through all of this. You have our support," he said. "But let me also say this," he added. "To the extent you can carry out your duties, you don't have to worry." I understood what he meant without him having to say it. At the point that my work suffered, they'd have to let me go.

By this time, I had signed to a long-term disability policy. It would guarantee me a substantial percentage of my current salary. But it was up to my bosses whether I'd be allowed to take such a disability payout. The other alternative was not having my contract renewed. Then I'd be ineligible for the disability package. My head was reeling. I'd have to figure out a way to keep my head above water. I'd have to find a way to hold on to the job I'd worked so hard to get.

In July 1997, I was sent to cover the assassination of famed fashion designer Gianni Versace by serial killer Andrew Cunanan. It was a sweltering afternoon in Miami when police swooped down on a houseboat at 5250 Collins Avenue, about forty blocks north of the Versace mansion. Police fired rounds of tear gas into the boat. Police entered the houseboat, according to *Miami Herald* published reports. Witnesses heard a muffled shot from inside. Cunanan had apparently ended his life. Reporters, including myself, converged on Collins Avenue to report on the shocking development. Camera crews lined the street, and reporters took turns doing live shots sent back by satellite to local news stations across the country. The murder spree by a gay serial killer that ended with the execution of such a public figure as Versace had grabbed the public's attention. It was such a big story that local news stations sent their own crews rather than rely solely on network coverage. I remember finishing my live shot as sweat poured down my face. On July 24,1997, a national news correspondent ended his Cunanan report with a stand-up in which he stated,

> *What set off the killing spree? Some question if it was rage because Cunanan discovered he had the AIDS virus. The medical examiner will conduct an autopsy, but under Florida law, the AIDS test is confidential. Cunanan's motivation may remain a mystery forever.*

I was stunned. Here I was, a reporter with AIDS, listening to another journalist report that some questioned whether Cunanan's rage was fueled by an HIV diagnosis. In my opinion, millions of viewers were left with the impression that an HIV diagnosis alone could prompt someone to commit murder. The next evening the correspondent returned to the issue in his closing stand-up by saying,

> *Under Florida law, AIDS tests are a secret even to law enforcement. But [we've] learned the state attorney may ask a judge to make an exception in this case. That would make the AIDS result public knowledge. If Cunanan was HIV positive, the theory he was driven by rage could prove true.*

According to whom? The reporter? The "theory?" The "some" who questioned the source of Cunanan's rage? We never found out. I had kept my diagnosis secret. And now I felt I had made the right decision. A reporter on national television had tossed out a supposition that even the diagnosis of AIDS might prompt a murderous rage. In my view, not only was such reporting irresponsible, it was sensational. The public wasn't informed. It was made to feel afraid. Anyone with HIV could be suspect. Such was the attitude of "some" regarding AIDS in 1997 and among some journalists as well. No wonder so many of us in the public eye with HIV/AIDS had retreated into the shadows.

Fast-Forward, October 20, 2019, *Newsweek*
People with HIV should be quarantined, and the US would be safer if they "died more readily," according to Betty Price, a Republican state representative (Georgia) and wife of former health secretary Tom Price.

Rewind, May 1996
All this misinformed hysteria surrounding AIDS was on my mind as I wondered how to tell Mami and Papi that I was living

with HIV. Growing up in a strict Catholic household, I learned to compartmentalize my life. But it was getting more and more difficult.

I finally got the nerve to call my mother. "*Helllllooo*," she said in heavily accented English.

"Mami, it's Charlito," I said. "There's something I have to tell you."

She replied, "*Dime, dime*." (Tell me, tell me.) I explained that it wasn't such good news.

"*Mami, tengo esa cosa que está pasando a las gentes gay*." (I have that thing that is happening to gay people.) There was silence on the other end of the line. "Please don't worry, but I have *SIDA*." I heard her gasp.

"*Ay no, mi niño*" (Oh no, my boy), she whispered

"I wanted you to know in case I became very sick. But don't worry. I'm taking medicine and it's going to be all right." There was a long pause.

"I will pray to *la Virgencita de la Caridad del Cobre* [Cuba's Virgin of Charity] and *tu angelito* [your guardian angel] and I promise nothing, nothing bad will come to you," she said. We agreed to keep the news from my father, at least for now. Then she came up with a plan. "Charlito," she said in a conspiratorial little girl's voice, "if we can go to Lourdes, Our Lady can heal you."

Lourdes? I couldn't believe what I was hearing. Catholics believed that Lourdes, set in the foothills of the Pyrenees in Southwestern France, was the site where miracles could happen. In 1858 the Virgin Mary was said to have appeared to a peasant girl named Bernadette eighteen times. As legend goes, the grotto where the Virgin appeared flowed with healing waters. Six million people (including about 500,000 American Catholics) travel to Lourdes each year hoping to be healed from a variety of ailments. They believe Our Lady of Lourdes is responsible for miracles: cancers are reportedly cured, the crippled supposedly walk once more, the blind see again. It's called faith. "*Tenga fe*," my mother would tell me repeatedly as a boy. (Have faith.)

"You know your father is talking with the priest at church about a tour to the Holy Land and he said they also plan to visit Lourdes," she said excitedly. "Let's not tell your father about your *problemasito* [little problem], but maybe we can go on the tour and you can bathe in the waters. Let me see what I can do." Instead of crumbling, my mother rallied. And her faith gave me strength to persevere.

I began taking two new anti-retrovirals to fight the HIV and vowed to tackle my job with a renewed gusto. I was hopeful. But even as I willed myself to fight, I couldn't help but plunge into despair and suicidal thoughts. I got sick and couldn't go to work. I rallied and got better. But then the cycle would repeat itself. I felt that I was on a roller coaster and I couldn't get off.

In 1997 there was a sense of excitement in the WNBC newsroom. It was announced that Pope John Paul II would travel to Cuba. I was particularly thrilled because Cuba was my passion and my heritage. As a young reporter for WBBM-TV in Chicago, I had gone to Cuba in 1978. I began planning for the trip. I proposed a series of stories, from the renewed flourishing of Catholicism to more personal stories, including revisiting where my parents were born and where my relatives still lived. The trip to Cuba had given me a reason not to dwell on my health. I felt invigorated and renewed. I had already won one Emmy. Perhaps this trip would bring me another. But those who controlled my destiny felt differently. And I'd find out just how differently two weeks before the trip. A producer and close friend pulled me aside.

"Chuck, I want you to know something, but you must swear to me you can't say a word or I could lose my job," she whispered.

"Of course, you can tell me anything," I replied. She told me that at a meeting one particular producer was adamant that I not go on the assignment to Cuba.

"She said that given the fact you had HIV and were getting sick all the time, it might not be a good idea to send you. She said that if you got sick in Cuba, it might require a plane to fly you back home at an added expense to the station."

Under the guise of appearing compassionate and concerned, the producer was discriminating against me. I was being targeted as a health risk and liability before I had even stepped on Cuban soil. What could I do? Run into the news director's office and plead my case? Apparently, it was too late. The decision had been made. It couldn't be reversed.

Two days before the journey to Cuba, I pulled Michelle Marsh aside. She was a news anchor of great competence and even greater kindness. She had been selected for the trip.

"Michelle, can I ask you to bring me something from Cuba?"

"Of course," she replied.

"Don't bring me a gift. Just bring me something unique from Cuba, something that can't be duplicated anywhere else in the world."

She smiled a knowing smile. I didn't have to say more.

The Cuba trip was a resounding success for WNBC. New York Catholics watched the extensive coverage, and the ratings and critical reviews were a smash. On the day the pope visited Cuba, I was assigned to report from Union City, where thousands of devout Cuban-American Catholics lived. Instead of being in Cuba, I was in Jersey. As I reported on the pope's visit, I realized that my days at WNBC were numbered. True to her word, when Michelle Marsh returned from Cuba she handed me a gift bag. It was filled with Cuban soil. I couldn't go to Cuba, so she brought a bit of Cuba back home to me. I couldn't help but cry. This was soil from my parents' homeland. I'd treasure it forever. In October 2017 I learned that this sweet human being had passed away after a battle with breast cancer. I remembered Michelle's kind gesture on that day and I couldn't help but cry again.

I felt increasingly like a pariah. And I was treated like a reporter who might not be up to the task of covering the big stories. So I acted out. I drank too much. I smoked pot. I snorted coke. No wonder I triggered my own asthma attacks. I couldn't breathe. I would call in sick and spend days passed out on my living room couch. I was a mess. These were dark days. I desperately needed help. My psychiatrist recommended rehab. It worked. I tackled my demons. I confronted my HIV and my drug addiction. I felt reborn.

Months earlier, as a way to deal with my HIV, I had returned to a writing project that was dear to my heart. It was a musical called *Adios, Tropicana*. I wrote the play inspired by a story I covered for CBS News in 1980. It was the Mariel boatlift in which 125,000 Cubans arrived in the United States. I decided to set my story at the famed Tropicana Nightclub in Cuba. It was a project that brought light into my life at a time of despair.

Weeks later, when it was time for me to return to work, Paula (now the news director) called me and said she wanted to meet. She agreed to come to my apartment in the heart of Times Square. I felt so at ease with her. We spoke frankly about my HIV. She was sympathetic. I knew she was my boss. But I felt that at that moment, she was also my friend. I told her I was ready to come back to work. She smiled.

"Chuck, I listened to the CD you gave me and I loved the songs," she said. "Wouldn't you rather concentrate on something you love instead of returning to work and the stress that could affect your HIV?"

I realized Paula was giving me an out. Without telling me in so many words, she was giving me a blessing and an opportunity. She would pave the way for my getting long-term disability and keeping a percentage of my salary as a television reporter. If I insisted on returning to work, I realized there would be no guarantee that my contract would be renewed when it was up. The choice was a clear one. And to this day I love her for giving it to me.

Back at work I was told the newsroom was buzzing with rumors I was sick with HIV.

"People kept asking me, 'What's wrong with him?'" remembered Sheila, who was working as a freelance reporter at WNBC. "The assumption in the air was that you had AIDS."

When I didn't show up at work right away, a few people like Sheila called my home to check up on me. But many colleagues never contacted me again. One of them was the woman who strongly urged that I not be sent to Cuba to cover the pope's visit. Another "dear friend" called me to tell me that she "had heard the news." She expressed concern before adding, "I really want to be there for you." I never heard from her again.

A few weeks later I learned that I was to be honored by the New York City's comptroller's office for my contributions as a Hispanic reporter. On that day in 1998 I sat in a crowded room in City Hall with other honorees in other fields. Beside me sat Papi, who had flown in from Florida to be at my side. Paula was in the audience too. When it came my turn to speak, this is what I said:

> In 1945 my father packed his belongings and left Havana, Cuba, for a strange place—New York City. He lived in the shadow of Penn Station and, along with his father and cousins, traded guayaberas for winter coats, working in a factory that manufactured plastic parts for the war effort. A year later, he returned to Cuba, married my mother and returned to Florida where my brother and I were born.

> It's an immigrant story like any other and unique at the same time. Like many Hispanics, my parents came to this country and, through years of struggle, achieved their dream. I'd like to acknowledge my father, who flew in from Miami to be here. My father and mother instilled in us the quest for excellence, the belief that in this country, Cubans and Puerto Ricans, Dominicans and Cubans, Hondurans and Guatemalans, any Hispanic group, could find their share of the same dream as long as they were willing to work hard and make sacrifices.

> It was their encouragement that fueled my interest in journalism. There were very few Hispanic role models in the early seventies, among them Geraldo Rivera and a local

Cuban anchorman in Miami named Manolo Reyes. And every night he would go on the air and say (in heavily accented English) "My sources tell me that Castro may have already been assassinated."

It was the first time I realized that journalists make mistakes. I followed in my dad's footsteps and moved to New York City myself, receiving a master's degree in journalism from Columbia School of Journalism when I was twenty-one. It led to a career that has enriched and rewarded me. As a Latin-American correspondent for CBS News, I covered wars and revolutions and met presidents and dictators. As a local news reporter in this market for fourteen years, I've covered everything from water-main breaks to the Yankees, from the Washington Heights disturbances to the rising number of cases involving Latinos and AIDS.

And what I've learned is that Hispanics, as you may know, are sometimes judged by harsher standards. As much as our uniqueness is valued, it can often lead to stereotypes, which is why we struggle to not only be competent, but outstanding, not only accepted, but respected.

There are still too few Hispanics on the national scene covering Capitol Hill and the White House and, on the local scene, too few Hispanic anchormen and women in a city where our numbers continue to grow every day. Today's tribute underscores the importance of our contribution as Hispanics, not only in the media but in every competitive field where our resumes, our educational and professional achievements can be proudly compared to the finest candidates anywhere.

I remember the words my father whispered to me as I left for

New York for the first time so many years ago: "Believe you can succeed and you will. Make me proud." Today, Dad, I hope I have.

Papi received a thunderous ovation. The city comptroller said, "That applause isn't for Chuck; it's for his dad." My father basked in the attention. As the applause continued I wondered if Mami had told Papi the news that I had AIDS. If she did, he never asked me about it. I had always been so proud to be his son. Every day I look at the photo of my father sitting beside me at the City Hall ceremony. It gives me strength. And as I look back I'm reminded of my mother's faith. On the dresser the statue of our Lady of Lourdes reminds me.

Less than a year after I first call Mami with the news that I have HIV, her wish comes true. I travel with Mami and Papi to the Holy Land in a tour organized by the local Catholic church. We take a plane and fly to France. From there we take a bus to Lourdes. My parents and I stroll through the picturesque town. It's been transformed into a kind of Disneyland for the faithful. On every corner we spot stores selling statues of the Virgin Mary, some as tall as ten feet high. Some even glowed in the dark. The cobblestone streets wind through the town and we come upon a large plaza. It's magnificent, sprawling before us almost as far as we can see. I learn that it's called the Sanctuary of our Lady of Lourdes or "the Domain." It surrounds the shrine or grotto with twenty-two separate places of worship. "*Que lindo,*" Mami says. (It's beautiful.)

We climb hundreds of steps to see the plaza from above. Suddenly, dozens of buses drive up. It's almost nightfall. Ominous gray clouds fill the sky, and it looks like a thunderstorm is about to erupt. And then from the buses hundreds of men and women begin to emerge. Some are placed in wheelchairs by attendants. Others maneuver crutches, hobbling up the plaza. Behind them we notice a procession of the faithful holding flickering candles. Tiny flames illuminate the grounds like the glow of thousands of fireflies. The crowds grow larger. Their faith has brought them here. Mami and Papi stand closer to me and Mami grabs my hand tightly. As we stand there transfixed by the spectacle, I can't help but feel that my mother is willing a miracle to happen.

That next morning, I meet her in the lobby of the hotel where we're staying and we rush off to breakfast. Papi goes sightseeing with the pastor. At the table, Mami moves her face right up to mine.

"Charlito, something happened last night," she says.

"Are you all right?" I ask, concerned that she's ill.

She shakes her head. "I fell asleep but then I woke up and I saw her," she says. "I saw the Virgin Mary. She had light coming from inside her and her hands reached out like this," she says, demonstrating. "And then *la Virgen* told me, 'Don't worry about Charlito, nothing will happen to him.'" Then, my mother says, the beautiful lady disappeared. "*Mi hijito* [my son], you're in her hands." My mother believes. And because she believes, I believe it too.

The next day, Papi's doing more sightseeing with the pastor, and so Mami accompanies me to the communal bath. I stand in line with dozens of men and wait my turn. Mami waits just outside. Attendants help us take off our shirts. One by one, we dunk our heads into a pool of cool water. I pray for Our Lady of Lourdes to heal me. When I emerge, Mami's waiting for me. She holds me tightly and I hear her say softly, "*Gracias, Señora.*" (Thank you, our Lady.)

At that moment I feel that my prayers have been heard. I'm also so grateful. HIV is not my death sentence. Faith has brought me to a different place. My fear of AIDS and the terror I've lived through because of it seems to vanish. In its place, I find something that's been missing these last few years. I've finally found hope.

Fast-Forward, October 2, 2019

The New York Times reports, "After decades of fearsome infection rates, the state had just 2,481 new diagnoses of the virus that causes AIDS, a drop of 11 percent from the previous year. . . . Governor Andrew M. Cuomo declared that New York is on track to meet its goal to end the AIDS epidemic in the state by 2020."

✷

Rewind, July 31, 2019

According to UNAIDS, there were approximately 37.9 million with HIV/AIDS in 2019. Of these, 36.2 million were adults and 1.7 million were children. An estimated 1.7 million individuals became newly infected with HIV.

CHAPTER 3
AMERICAN DREAM

*There are those who will say that the liberation of humanity,
the freedom of man and mind is nothing but a dream. They
are right. It is the American Dream.*
—Archibald MacLeish, Poet

IT WAS JULY 1959. Willie was six. I was just five. Here we were, two brothers at a kiddie park, strapped snugly into a little car about to zip around a miniature race track on a blazing Havana afternoon. We were wearing matching striped short-sleeved shirts and sporting matching shorts. Why did Mami dress us this way? Just that morning I had screamed bloody murder when *mi cosita* (little thing) got stuck in the *shortzito* (little shorts) zipper. Mami had to come to the rescue. My brother just laughed and laughed.

A ray of light from the rising Cuban sun bathed our faces as we squinted and smiled our forced smiles for the camera. Young girls screamed in delight as they descended on the musical Ferris wheel. What song was it playing? To our right we could make out the graceful undulating *caballitos* on the pink-and-blue fairytale carousel. Could we ride that next? We also heard someone's voice (was it Mami's?) urging us to smile widely as she snapped photo after photo of us in the *carritos* (little cars). A red '52 Buick inched by us and parked on the street. Our *carrito* took off. We lurched forward.

Castro's revolution was taking off too. The regime wasn't even a year old, and there were many who held out hope for this "revolution of the people." Would it usher in a new democracy? But it was not to be. Castro would embrace communism. We would get older. The park would close and the little *carritos* would turn from gleaming marvels into rusty relics. Only the old car parked on the street would stay the same. In the frozen smiles of a photograph, Cuba would always stay the same for us, two *hermanitos* (little brothers) having fun at *los caballitos* as the Cuban sun blazed above us.

May 1945, La Víbora, Cuba

It was the middle of May in Havana and it was another scorcher of a day. Though the temperatures were in the high nineties, a sweet breeze blew off the ocean, as it often did, making the blazing heat almost bearable. The palm trees swayed like Hawaiian hula dancers in Havana's La Víbora neighborhood. And the hibiscus bushes, filled with fiery orange-red blooms that looked like tiny suns, lit up the block like fireworks in the Havana sky. La Víbora—that's where Papi lived with Mima and brothers Peter and Eddie at 206 Avellaneda, between Josephina and Gertruda Streets. It was 1945 and World War II had cast an ominous shadow even over this tropical paradise. Cuba declared war on the Axis Powers in December 1942. It was one of the first Latin-American countries to do so. My father, all of seventeen, rushed home from his construction job hardly able to contain his enthusiasm. He was a skinny, gangly young man with a narrow face, a long nose and a mop of black hair that fell into his face like a Cuban Dennis the Menace. Papi was going to the United States. He'd be on a plane to Miami *mañana*. From there he would take a train to New York to meet up with Pipo and his brother Catalino. It would be the start of his American dream. And it would be a *sueño* (dream) my mami and my brother, Willie, would be a part of as well.

For years the two Gonzalez brothers (and their first cousin Everardo) owned a small fleet of *gua-guas* (buses) in Havana. They operated three popular routes that chugged noisily from the dusty barrio of Mantilla along 10 de Octubre all the way into La Habana Vieja (Old Havana). The last stop was Havana Cathedral in the Plaza de la Catedral. My father would ride along on the sweltering, packed *gua-guas*, taking in the hustle and bustle of Havana at its most frenetic. But those happy days on the bus would soon be ending. The war had made bus parts scarce.

Catalino had flown to New York to buy new parts and tires with the idea of bringing them back to Cuba. But once there, Catalino was dazzled by the bright lights of Nueva York and enticed by the opportunity to make "moola" in the US. This was true of so many Cubans who left the Island before 1959. They left for opportunity, not freedom or to escape communism. These were not the rich plantation owners or rum barons who fled as Castro assumed power. These were working-class Cubans like my dad's stepfather. An older brother, Eliseo, had already paved the way, working for Sears Roebuck in New York City. Now Catalino and Pedro worked in a factory in New York's garment district making leather carrying cases for soldiers in the war effort. Cousin Everado decided to stay behind in Havana. Catalino and Pedro's sister, Berta, left Cuba for New York City as well. Now Pedro (Pipo) wanted Guillermito (Papi) to join them. "Yuma" (the US) was calling.

Papi could barely sleep the night before the trip. He spent hours packing what he could into a small hand-me-down suitcase.

"I was so excited," he told me. "I couldn't wait to leave." That hadn't been the case just three years earlier. Papi had caught the eye of Cuban president Fulgencio Batista (the first non-white Cuban in that office) during a visit to a hospital. Batista offered to help Papi with his studies as an electrician's apprentice. But by 1944, another president (Ramón Grau San Martín) had come into power. And positions for electricians (especially without Batista's patronage) were tough to come by. So, my papi turned to construction.

In Cuba, the winds of change were already blowing. In 1943, Batista had legalized Cuba's Communist Party. In 1944, Fidel Castro, a student about to enter a Jesuit high school in Havana, was voted the best high school athlete. By the time he was in college, Castro's sympathies with socialist movements were becoming evident. The head of the Bus Cooperative, which controlled Cuba's *gua-guas*, would soon develop socialist leanings as well. When my dad was twelve, Cuba's constitution had established a National Assembly. The new constitution struck a balance between the rich and the working class. It protected individual and social rights, supported full employment and a minimum wage, extended social security and called for equal pay for equal work. Socialism was in the air. It was against this backdrop that Papi packed his tiny blue *maleta* (suitcase).

"I had all these little papers I had to take with me," my father told me. The notes were instructions from Pipo on where to go and what to do. "I had to stay in Miami for fourteen days because the trains were being reserved for soldiers and there were only a limited number of seats for everyone else." Pipo had instructed my dad to stay in a hotel in downtown Miami about a block away from Biscayne Boulevard. But it was booked and the clerk told him to try another hotel. As my dad didn't speak a word of English at the time, the clerk arranged for someone from the hotel to assist my father.

"This man took me by the hand and walked me to another hotel," my dad said. "I was so scared, because I didn't know anyone and I only spoke Spanish." For a week, my father didn't eat. He only drank water. Papi was petrified of ordering anything on a menu he didn't understand. Finally, he encountered two Colombians chattering in Spanish in the hotel's lobby. My father was ecstatic as well as relieved.

"Please, can you take me to get something to eat because I've been starving this last week," he said to them. The young men took him to the hotel restaurant. For the next week, the hotel manager would take a sandwich to Papi's room at noon each day. This was my dad's first taste of "life in the United States."

Papi got a call that his train was scheduled to leave for New York. He boarded it a terrified seventeen-year-old. He sat down, and as he looked out his tiny window, the memories of Mima and Havana faded and his new future came into view. A day later, Pipo met him at Penn Station and whisked him to the tiny walk-up apartment that would be his home for almost the next two years. The very next day he began his new job in a leather factory located off Ninth Avenue a few blocks from Penn Station.

Living in New York City was strange and exciting to say the least. The skyscrapers were intimidating, as was the constant rush of thousands on the street. "*Como hormigas*" (like ants), my father said. My dad loved the Automat and the local pizza joints of this new land. Eventually he came to love the crazy pace too. By day he worked in the factory with Pipo and Catalino, and by night, he learned English. It was a year of firsts. His first snowfall. The first time he got lost in the subway. His first meatball hero. His first bedbug attack.

"We lived on the first floor of this walk-up, but in the basement, there was a factory where they made coats," Papi said. "It was infested with *chinchas* [bedbugs] and those damn *chinchas* would climb up the walls like soldiers from the basement right up to my apartment." He remembered, "It was like a parade of bedbugs. I'd hit them with my shoes but I couldn't kill them." As my dad tells it, one of the bedbugs bit him in the worst place a bedbug could bite a guy. *Ay Dios mio!* Within a day, his private part was terribly swollen and inflamed. Cousin Berta rushed him to a doctor.

Eyeing the bite, the doctor exclaimed, "Young man, have you been with a woman? One of those women?"

Papi assured him that wasn't the case. "Doctor, a bedbug bit me THERE!"

The physician started laughing and gave my dad a shot and

sent him home with a prescription for antibiotics. A few days later my dad, Pipo and Catalino hastily moved out of the bug-infested tenement. *"Hasta luego, chinchas!"* (Goodbye, bedbugs!)

About a year later, as my dad remembered, Pipo decided to go back to Cuba. He had brought to the US his wife, Edermira, and Papi's two stepbrothers, Peter and Eddie, but New York proved too cold for Edermira, so Pipo bought a small home in Miami. Dad stayed in New York about another six months and then joined the family in Miami. He worked odd jobs before working in a hotel on Miami Beach. Pipo worked in a shop that made women's purses on Washington Avenue. Sometime later, a cousin told Papi about a job at Foremost Dairies in Miami. So, at eighteen, my dad was hired to stick plywood handles into frozen ice cream bars. Soon Papi was working a variety of jobs at the plant, and eventually through his hard work and drive, he was promoted to manager of Foremost Dairies. His American dream was becoming a reality.

My dad lived with Pipo and Mima in the Little River section of Miami. It was an exciting time for Papi. He was learning to love this new place called America, and the best part was that Miami reminded him of Havana. But something was missing in his life. He wanted someone to share his new life and his American dream. He always recalled that dark-haired beauty from Havana with her swiveling hips. Where was she? Would he ever see her again?

At twenty-two, my mother, Angelina, left her family's farm in Guines for the big city of Havana. She got a job in a local factory where they manufactured socks and women's nylon stockings. She was now no longer a farm girl; she was a working woman in the bustling capital of Cuba.

Like many young Cuban women, my mother had rhythm in her hips. And when she strolled down a Havana street, the guys in the neighborhood would notice her, and Papi was no exception. When

I got older, Mami told me the men would whistle and say, "*Que pechuga tiene ese pollo.*" (What breasts that chicken has.) Of course, Mami would ignore them and continue on her way.

In 1950 (when she was twenty-eight), Mami decided to travel to Miami on a short visit. She stayed at the home of a couple that she knew from Havana. Coincidentally, they happened to be related to my father. One scorching Miami day, the wife pulled my dad aside and said, "Why don't you ask Angelina to marry you? I think you two would make a perfect pair."

To skinny Shorty, voluptuous Angelina was a goddess. Before her trip to Miami ended, my papi told me, he fell to his knees and handed her a sparkling engagement ring.

"I want you to be with me in Miami forever," he said. "I want us to start a new life here. *Por favor*, China, will you marry me?" ("China" was an endearment many Cuban men called the women they loved. It was inspired by the wave of Chinese immigrants who first came to Cuba in 1847 to work the sugar fields. After their contracts ended, many Chinese immigrants settled permanently in Cuba.)

My mom simply smiled and whispered coquettishly, "*Bueno, vamos a ver.*" (Well, let's see.) Years later when my mami would recount the story, she'd say that she loved the ring but wasn't too sure about Papi.

"He eventually wore me down. I thought at first I'd just take the ring and return to Cuba, but he was very persistent." Who knows if my mother was telling me the truth. I think she was as madly in love with Papi as Papi was with her. So determined was Papi that less than a year later they married in the same Havana neighborhood where they had first met.

My father brought his new bride back to Miami, and just a year later, my brother, Willie, was born. My mother insisted on giving my brother a distinctly American name, in honor of the new land where their lives were about to begin. A year later, it was my turn. My dad had a pal at work named Larry, and that's what he wanted to call me. But Mami couldn't pronounce the double r's.

"*Larrrrry*," she would demonstrate with difficulty for me. "Too much trouble pronouncing." She told me that she called me Charles because that was the name of a young man a girlfriend of hers was dating in Cuba. My mother pronounced it *Char-lesss*. Now, Charles was hardly a Cuban name, and how a Cuban man came to be named *Char-less* seemed a mystery to me. I imagined that a Cuban Carlos had fancied the name Charles from British royalty and perhaps appropriated the name himself. "Don't call me Carlos. Now my name is Charles." In any event, Charles I became. And for the rest of my life, people would say to me, "But your real name is Carlos, right?"

We moved to a little house in Little River. And from there we moved to another home in a new section of Miami, Allapattah. It had a huge front yard and lots of trees. We lived next door to the DeCarions. I was the same age as their daughter Lillian, and as little kids, we played games in the yards. Sometimes she let me play with her Barbie doll. My brother was more of a boy's boy, and he always seemed to get into trouble. One day he got his arm stuck in the roller of one of those old-fashioned wringer washing machines.

"My arm went through the roller all the way up to my shoulder," he remembered. "I was screaming and Mami ran out and started going crazy." My mother's screams were so loud she attracted the attention of three Hell's Angels types riding their motorcycles. They tore down the street, right into our backyard. The guy on the first bike jumped off and pushed down the latch release on the washing machine, releasing my brother's arm. Willie was rushed to the hospital, his arm placed in a cast. Catastrophe avoided. *Gracias*, Hell's Angels.

Another time, on a Christmas Day, my brother was given a box of sparklers from a woman in the neighborhood. He rushed into my mother's bedroom where she kept a candle lit in honor of la Virgen de la Caridad del Cobre, Cuba's patron saint. He took one of the sparklers and lit it but then panicked, and instead of tossing it outside, he threw it under my parents' bed. My mom kept all the wrapping paper for presents under the bed. The sparkler ignited the paper and soon their bedroom was in flames. The firemen came and they were finally able to put out the blaze. My brother ran under my next-door neighbor's home and hid in the crawl space. Nobody could find him. Finally, my neighbor ratted him out. The firemen tried to scare Willie, calling him an arsonist and telling him that they might have to haul him off to jail. My father promised to teach him a lesson. The firemen left and my father curled his tongue and swatted Willie's behind. My brother never threw a sparkler under the bed again. My brother likes to remember I was the favored son. But it might have had a lot to do with the fact that I was asthmatic from a very young age. While my brother ran around the neighborhood playing with friends, I retreated to my world of books.

We lived an uneventful life in Little River, then later Allapattah. My dad worked long hours at the ice cream plant. When he got home, the last thing he wanted was two screaming kids. So, in his presence, we were like the sphinxes of Egypt, silent and unmoving. When Dad went to bed, my brother and I watched television, turning the volume down low. We watched *Lassie, I Love Lucy, The Lone Ranger* and the variety shows. I loved *The Loretta Young Show* where she would burst through double doors, swishing a long couture gown.

My brother and I also loved the horror movies, like *Mothra* and *Rodan*. *Rodan* was especially scary because it featured a giant, flying, prehistoric insect-type creature that destroyed Japan. We also watched *Godzilla*, the fire-breathing dinosaur who could destroy buildings in a single blow. We grew up speaking Spanish at home but only English when we were outside playing with the neighborhood kids. We were bilingual but never thought it was anything special. We didn't really think of ourselves as the Cuban kids on the block. Even at a young age we considered ourselves American.

But around Christmas time, we'd turn Cuban again. That's when Pipo would roast a pig in the backyard. *Ahhhh. Puerco asado*. Such a Cuban tradition. It can be traced back hundreds of years to the Cuban *campesinos* who perfected the art of killing a wild pig and serving it with all the trimmings on a holiday, most notably Christmas. To many of our American neighbors, it seemed somewhat of a primitive tradition—that is until they were invited to a Cuban feast like ours and felt the roasted pork melt in their mouths like warm butter. My brother remembers going with my dad to West Miami to a farm where pigs were raised.

"I'd watch as they'd shoot the pig in the head with a .22 rifle," he said. "They'd then take the pig and throw it in boiling water and, with a sharp razor, take all the hair off the pig until it was completely hairless."

As part of the process, the twenty-five-pound pig would be gutted. Papi would bring him back to Pipo's house and hoist him on a tree in the backyard. The next day, they'd lay the pig on a grate of sorts made from the coils of a mattress. Then they covered it with banana leaves. Under the grate, Pipo would empty bags of coals. The roasting of the pig began early in the day and would last eight or nine hours. Before the pig was roasted it would marinate in a special *mojo* sauce Mima (my grandmother) and sometimes Mami would prepare the night before. *Mojo* was a secret Cuban concoction. A pitcher or bowl would be filled with the juice of bitter oranges and limes. Next Mami would add lots of minced garlic, pepper and olive oil. Sometimes she added cumin or whatever spices suited her. Using a spoon or a mixer, the liquid was stirred repeatedly. The resulting *mojo* would be poured over the pig and basted over and over again to make the skin succulent and tasty. Finally, after all those hours cooking, the *puerco* was served with white rice and black beans and plantains, or sometimes *con gris* (rice mixed with black beans). The taste was indescribable. When Americans tried to cook pig, it often tasted dry and tough. Not Cuban *puerco*. It was truly heaven for the taste buds.

It was a Gomez family tradition that on Christmas Eve Mami would hide all our beautifully wrapped gifts in a hallway. She would tell us not to wake up because *Santi Clo* was coming. So, just like all the other American boys and girls, Willie and I would pretend to fall asleep and then peek through the door to see how big our bounty might be. My brother remembers that weeks before Christmas our mom would have us go through the "Western Auto Christmas Catalogue" and copy on paper word-for-word descriptions of any toys we wanted. We were told to place our lists on a wooden window in the Florida room. Mami said Santa would read them and deliver the gifts we asked for on Christmas morning.

"But we never ever got any of the toys we asked for," Willie told me. Mami apparently just threw the papers away and got us what she thought we wanted. But one Christmas Willie got a surprise he wasn't expecting. It was a bow and arrow just like the ones Tonto used in *The Lone Ranger*. He took his new toy out into the yard where I was playing. Suddenly I watched in horror as Willie drew back the bow. The arrow (with a rubber suction cup at the end) flew through the air. It hit me smack dab in the middle of my forehead. "*Aaagh!*" I screamed at the top of my lungs. Papi ran out of the house and I thought he was going to kill Willie.

Willie discovered that Santa wasn't real way before I did. When my brother blurted out to me "*Santi Clo no es de verdad*" (Santa Claus is made up), I wanted to cry. He was Debby Downer even back then. But I didn't want to act like a little girl. I kept Willie's shocking disclosure to myself. I didn't want to get him angry. And I didn't want to get hit by another arrow.

On most Christmases, my parents loved to invite lots of people to our home. During one such gathering, Willie, me and cousin Catalanito (the son of Catalino, who came to the US right before my dad) crawled under the dining table as the adults dined above. Beneath the cover of the long tablecloth, we convinced two girls to "play doctor." We instructed them to lift their little skirts and show us their private parts. And we showed them ours. We were astonished when we saw that the girls didn't have "pee-pees" like us. Well, the girls told their parents, and Mami and Papi, of course, were furious.

"They say they'll never set foot in our house again, because it is not their custom to go to homes where little boys exhibit themselves to little girls," Mami screamed at us. The ban didn't last long. A year later the girls were back for our next Christmas party, but now we stayed in our chairs and above the table.

I always thought I was a "different" kind of little boy. But I certainly didn't know I was gay (as so many friends of mine claimed they knew at an early age). I do remember watching Shirley Temple movies on weekends. The local station would run a marathon, and I couldn't get enough of *Little Miss Marker* and *Heidi* and of course *Bright Eyes*, in which she sang *On the Good Ship Lollipop*. There was a scene when Shirley's mother bought her a beautiful birthday cake at a bakery. She began walking with the cake down a city street with lots of traffic. Suddenly she steps into an intersection without looking. The next scene shows the destroyed birthday cake on the street. The implication was clear: Shirley's mom had been killed. I started to cry and couldn't stop. My mother came running from the kitchen.

"*Que te pasa?*" (What's wrong with you?) she screamed.

"The mommy died," I tried to say through my torrent of tears. My mother comforted me.

"It's only television," she said. "Don't worry, I'm right here."

Once a year, like all the kids in the neighborhood, we watched *The Wizard of Oz*. After the black-and-white opening of the movie, Dorothy's house landed in Oz. She got up and opened the door and everything turned into beautiful color. But because we still had an old black-and-white set, we couldn't enjoy the color dynamics of the movie. We kept begging Papi to get a color TV like a lot of the neighborhood kids had. One day he brought something back from the hardware store in a paper bag.

"Well, kids, you've been talking about a color TV, right?" he announced dramatically.

"Yes, Papi, yes," my brother and I shouted. Finally, our color TV dreams were coming true.

"OK, turn on the TV," he said. We did as he said. I felt tiny goosebumps race up my arm and on the back of my neck. From the bag, he pulled out four large sheets of colored plastic in green, blue, yellow and red. He took the first sheet in green and scotch-taped it to the set. He then took the other sheets and taped those over the TV set as well.

"There's your color TV," he said, laughing. Now we could barely make out what was happening on the screen. So much for our new color TV.

After watching the *The Wizard of Oz*, we would pretend we were in the movie. Lillian from next door played Dorothy. Willie played the Lion, and I was the Tin Man. Sometimes I'd play the Scarecrow. But secretly I wished I were Dorothy because she had the best lines ("There's no place like home") and the coolest shoes. We fantasized that a local mean lady who sat on her porch and watched us ride by on our bikes was the Wicked Witch of the West herself. Emerald City was a huge cardboard box that originally housed some neighbor's washing machine (no doubt a Christmas gift from a hubby to an Allapattah housewife). Anyway, we'd reenact scenes from the movie from noon to almost sunset. Lillian sang like Dorothy in the sweet voice of an angel:

> *Someday I'll wish upon a star*
> *And wake up where the clouds are far behind me*
> *Where troubles melt like lemon drops*
> *Way above the chimney tops*
> *That's where you'll find me*

I had no idea why that song touched me so. I didn't know then it would one day be referred to as the gay national anthem. All I knew then was that it made me feel uneasy inside, like watching Shirley Temple's mother dropping Shirley's birthday cake on the street after getting hit by a car.

We enjoyed our life in Miami, but beneath the surface I sensed something brewing with Mami. Whatever it was seemed to be tearing her apart. She had uprooted herself from the Cuba she knew. And she was bringing up two children in this strange land. I think the responsibilities overwhelmed her. My father told me later that my mother seemed to experience *un ataque de nervios.* In modern-day terms, it could best be described as a nervous breakdown. Years later, Mami would tell me that her world was crumbling.

"I'd try to bathe you in the bathtub, but I couldn't bring myself to grab the soap." She told me her sudden attack of nerves came after she visited a doctor who told her she had a mysterious malady. He said she had six months to live. The news terrified her. She felt powerless to take care of us.

As my mother's mental state deteriorated, our grandmother took care of us. Later Mami claimed that Mima tried to convince my father that it might be best to put her in a Cuban mental institution. But Papi denied that. He said he spoke to friends and soon found a doctor that would treat Mami with medication. In the sixties, taking pills for depression or other mental issues was not common. And it wasn't talked about either. Mental illness was considered taboo in the Cuban culture. And I think my grandmother thought it might bring shame upon our family. Mami started taking the antidepressants, and soon she was herself again.

So many of my friends talk about the defining moments when they realized they were gay or were attracted to the opposite sex. It wasn't until I was in junior high school that I think I began noticing boys in too-tight khaki shorts playing in gym class. They were the "banana hammocks" of their day. Until then I was a Catholic school kid who was taught sin was bad and to stay away from impure thoughts. I attended Corpus Catholic School and we were taught by Franciscan nuns. They were very strict. We took our religious lessons seriously. By the time I was seven, I had already served in the church choir and my brother was an altar boy. During the Cuban Missile Crisis, we participated in drills where we hid under our desks. Castro was now considered evil, and we were told by the nuns that the

Cuban Missile Crisis was his fault. It didn't seem possible that this man we heard Mami and Papi talk about was now a bad guy.

The year that Castro had come to power, my brother and I traveled with our mother to Havana, Cuba. Mami was going for a mysterious medical reason, and Willie and I were excited about going to this place where Mami and Papi were born. It was summertime and we stayed at a relative's home in the very neighborhood where Mami met Papi. The *milicianos* (militiamen) who had fought with Castro in the mountains came in caravans to Havana. And they were greeted enthusiastically by Cubans. My brother and I wore fake beards and waved toy machetes just like the real *milicianos*. I loved our stay in Havana. They dubbed *I Love Lucy* in Spanish, and we would sit on the floor in front of the TV laughing. The commercials and the jingles popped up during breaks: "*Con jabon Blanco Rina, tus ropas quedan divina.*" (With White Rain, your clothes will come out divinely!) How gay! After Lucy, we would watch cartoons. My favorite was one called *Cucarachita Martina*. It was about a sexy cockroach who wanted to lure a man. She'd powder her face with a big fluffy puff until she looked white as a ghost and then sashay through the streets of Havana looking for a date.

There's a picture I treasure of Mami washing clothes in a backyard sink in Havana. In the foreground we stood beside a handsome *miliciano*. He didn't look threatening at all. And he certainly didn't look evil. The *miliciano* is wearing a straw hat and holding a cigarette tightly between his lips with a long machete dangling from his belt, looking a lot like Clark Gable or Victor Mature. He holds the top of the machete tightly. To the left, my brother in a short-sleeved shirt and shorts is holding a tiny gun. I'm to the right of the *miliciano*, dressed almost exactly like my brother. We're wearing straw hats too, and if you look very closely, you see we had tiny photos of Fidel pinned to our hats.

My mom, smiling broadly in the background, may have been washing clothes in a backyard sink, but she was no washer woman. She's sporting a black pencil skirt, a white short-sleeved blouse and gleaming white heels—the Loretta Young of Havana, perhaps? I hold my fingers up to my face, pretending I'm holding a little gun just like Willie. Posing with one of Castro's *milicianos*. How shocking? Not really. People forget that Castro had yet to declare himself a hard-boiled communist, although some suspected.

The revolution was still in bloom. There was a sense of excitement and promise in the air. *The New York Times* had published breathless stories of the charismatic Fidel and his *revolucion*. Little did I realize then that exactly eighteen years later, as a young television reporter from Chicago's WBBM-TV, I would be interviewing Fidel Castro.

In 1959, the mass exodus of Cuban refugees had not yet begun, and the US embargo had yet to be declared. There was no hint a Cuban Missile Crisis would loom and threaten our very existence. No idea the Soviets would begin bankrolling Cuba and hiding missiles just ninety miles from the Florida coastline. And certainly no one could imagine there would be a failed Bay of Pigs Invasion launched by Cuban exiles to overthrow Castro. That summer we spent in Havana with our Mom was a time of innocence for two American boys. We cheered Castro's *milicianos* on the porch in La Víbora, singing "Adelante Cubano." We waved and blew kisses as the men rode by in a cavalcade of jeeps and cars. Only two short years later "Adelante Cubano" would be labeled a communist anthem. It was forbidden to be sung in any respectable Cuban-American home in Miami.

Around the time of the Missile Crisis drills, my mother began taking an interest in my friendship with one little boy in school. His name was Felipito and he was effeminate. I had no idea that it was wrong for me to play with Felipito. I knew he acted a bit like a girl, but he was funny and I enjoyed his company.

One day my mom pulled me aside and asked, "Why do you play with Felipito so much?"

I thought a moment and replied, "Because he's my friend."

"You should play with other boys," she said. But I didn't understand why. Did my mom even then fear that her child might grow up to become another Felipito? Not too long after that, Felipito stopped attending Corpus Christi.

When I asked Mami if she knew what had happened to him she just said, "Felipito and his mom and dad moved away." She frowned and averted her eyes. Mami never said where Felipito had moved, and I stopped asking. My friend was gone. I think that was the first time I felt the painful jab of loss.

My mom coddled and protected me. And I believe she knew that I was different from the other boys. My brother loved rough-and-tumble horseplay. But I lived in my own world.

One day when I was about five I spotted some beautiful red high heels in my mom's closet. Without giving it a second thought, I put them on and stood in front of the mirror. First, I smiled. Then I started laughing. The giggles brought my mom in from another room. Instead of scolding me, she laughed too.

"Better take those off before Papi comes home," she told me. My mother treated me like I was a special child. She kept me indoors, fearful that playing in the dirt would trigger my asthma. I remember my papi telling her that she was *mimándome*. (*Mimándo* meant treating someone like a baby.)

As I grew up, I became a bookworm, and my father bought my brother and me an encyclopedia for children called *The Book of Knowledge*. The volumes, bound in wine-colored leather, still sit on a bookshelf in my father's home in Hialeah. In these books of knowledge I would escape into fanciful tales of kings, queens, princes and princesses. I wanted to be like them.

I was about eight when I discovered a poem by Robert Louis Stevenson. It was called "The Swing." I felt it opened a door. It made me incredibly happy but also made me wonder if I was different in a way I couldn't yet understand.

How do you like to go up in a swing,
Up in the air so blue?
Oh, I do think it the pleasantest thing
Ever a child can do!

Up in the air and over the wall,
Till I can see so wide,
Rivers and trees and cattle and all
Over the countryside—

Till I look down on the garden green,
Down on the roof so brown—
Up in the air I go flying again,
Up in the air and down!

Was I the gay boy in the swing?

Around that same age my mother invited Manolo, a friend from Cuba, to our Allapattah home. It was a hot summer day. The gardenias my mother had placed in a cobalt-blue glass (after plucking them from a bush in our front yard) had already begun to turn yellow. Sweating profusely, Manolo announced theatrically that he would soon be performing in a recital in the *Co-co-no Gro* (Coconut Grove) section of Miami. Manolo was a somewhat flamboyant man in his mid-forties with dyed jet-black hair he slicked back on his head. He was over six feet tall and, until then, the tallest man I had ever laid eyes on. Manolo tried to look like a movie star from the forties, Tyrone Powers perhaps. He always wore a suit and tie. On this hot summer day, he carried into our home what appeared to be a tape recorder. At that time, they were quite large contraptions, outfitted with huge reels of tape. Manolo placed it on the table.

"And now I am going to sing to you *una canción bella* [a beautiful song] from a show on Broadway, 'Saw-Pa-cee-feek' [*South Pacific*]." With a flourish and a flick of his wrist, Manolo pressed the play button and the most beautiful music began to play. Manolo closed his eyes and placed his hands over his heart. The many rings on his fingers sparkled like Mami's diamond wedding ring. Then Manolo began to sing in heavily accented English: "*Some enchanted evening, you may see a stranger, you may see a stranger, across a crowded room.*" For the next few minutes I sat mesmerized. I knew this was something very beautiful and very special. It was my first introduction to Broadway and my first introduction to a real homosexual. I felt a connection.

For the next several years, Dad relished living his American dream. From sticking handles into ice cream bars, he moved up the ladder at Foremost Dairies. He worked long hours. And Mami took care of Willie and me at home. On weekends, we'd join relatives (who had also come from Cuba), to beach outings at Crandon Park. It was the first time I remember being introduced to and experiencing racism. My mom would talk about us going to the "white section" of the beach. I had no idea what she meant. I would later learn that blacks had their own beach. I didn't quite understand why. Did we think that they somehow might contaminate the ocean? It seemed so strange to a little boy growing up in Miami.

In 1959 when I was five years old, I remember Mami taking us to Sears, Roebuck & Co. in downtown Miami. Ironically it was just a few blocks from the hotel where my dad first stayed when he came to this country in 1945. My brother and I were thirsty, so she walked us to the back of the store where the water fountains were located. One was labeled "White" and one "Colored." A pipe ran from the "white" fountain to the "colored" one. Did the water change on the way to the "colored" fountain? Without paying too much attention, I remember running up to the "colored" fountain and trying to take a sip.

"No, no, no," my mother said firmly. *"Ese es para los Negros. Nosotros tenemos el otro."* (That's for the Negroes. Ours is the other one.) I asked her why. "That's just the way it is," she explained.

Florida was still considered the South, even though Miami was somewhat of a more cosmopolitan (and tolerant) urban oasis. But the harsh reality of racism was as true in Miami as in Selma, Alabama. Segregation of public facilities, including water fountains and restrooms, was officially outlawed by the Civil Rights Act of 1964. In 1959, Sears, Roebuck & Co. on Biscayne Boulevard remained segregated. It's impossible to measure how such a thing affected a child growing up. We acquire our parents' fears and attitudes. But my mom would always insist she wasn't racist.

"In Cuba," she would tell us proudly, "there was no racism. The whites would go their way and the coloreds their way. We lived together but we didn't mix together." It was a strange logic, but as a child, I didn't question its wisdom. (It wasn't until the 1960s when the term "black" and "African-American" replaced the word "colored" and "negro.")

I'll never forget my mother telling me the story of the time she boarded a bus in Havana. She was wearing a beautiful new dress she had saved up for from her salary at the sock factory and had just bought at El Encanto. El Encanto was Havana's Saks Fifth Avenue. It was a store of sparkling waxed floors and gleaming glass vitrines. El Encanto was filled with beautiful things sold by beautiful women. They looked less like clerks and more like long-necked graceful models that adorned the fashion magazines. Or so my mother said. Mami bought a white dress cinched at the waist that flared outward, falling just below the knees. The white background of the frock was punctuated by a sea of beautiful red roses. She wore the dress with red shoes that a family friend, Esperanza (Hope), had bought for her. She boarded the bus proudly, confident in how beautiful she looked. Her lustrous brunette hair fell to her shoulders in waves as soft and rolling as those who danced to the shore of Guanabo Beach where she honeymooned with

Papi. As she sat contentedly in her seat, she suddenly noticed a rotund black woman in her forties boarding the bus.

As the woman reached the driver to pay her fare, Mami noticed she wore the exact same dress Mami was wearing.

As a child, my eyes popped open wide and I asked, "What did you do?" I should have asked, "How did you feel?"

She paused and said, "I didn't do anything." She continued, "But when I got home I took the dress off and never wore it again." She didn't explain. She didn't need to. My mother was not racist. She was a product of her times and of her environment. She grew up during Fulgencio Batista's presidency. I don't believe that in Cuba there was the level of racism and violence against blacks that prevailed during the Jim Crow days of the South. But perhaps there was a more subtle kind of discrimination. Whites held the top jobs. Blacks held the others. That's why when Batista (who was of mixed race) came to power as president of Cuba, there was racial as well as social tension.

The slave trade had brought Africans to Cuba starting in 1762. More than a million African slaves were seized and brought to Cuba by both Britain and Spain. Cuba didn't end its participation in the slave trade until 1867. Africans intermingled with Spaniards, so a large proportion of Cubans descended from slaves. They now outnumbered Cubans of European origin. A new race was forming. Many Cubans were now mixed. There were still pure white-skinned Spaniards in Cuba, but mixed-race Cubans were multiplying, adding to the diversity of *los Cubanos.*

My brother and I continued going to Catholic school during that time we lived in Little River. I was always chosen as the hall monitor. My job was to keep the other kids standing in straight lines as we waited to enter a room or go out to play in the schoolyard. I remember the nuns would stamp little angels on my papers noting "Job Well Done." My brother was another story. He was always getting in trouble. One day, he was working on his penmanship. The nuns were sticklers for cursive writing. Every loop and crossed *t* had to be executed just so. The principal, Mother Thomas Rose, walked into the class. The third-grade pupils stood up like soldiers, intoning in unison, "Good morning, Mother Thomas Rose, and God bless you." Mother Superior walked up and down the rows, examining the penmanship as if the lesson were as critical as learning how to repair a torn heart valve. When she got to my brother, she winced. Obviously, his penmanship was not up to par, and Mother Superior was hardly amused.

"No, like this," she said as she took my brother's hand and guided him into writing the letters to her liking. She then continued walking like a general inspecting troops.

Once again, she stopped at my brother's desk. Her eyes widened like two golf balls popping out of her head. She did not like what she saw. She pulled a ruler out of her habit, a ruler with a metal edge.

"She whacked me across the knuckles," Willie remembered. "She said, 'You're just not doing it right.'" With that she hit him across the knuckles again. As she raised her arm to smack him a third time, Willie jumped from the desk and kicked Mother Thomas Rose squarely on the shin.

The nun screamed bloody murder and my brother took off running. He ran through the hallways. I stood like the good little hall monitor. The pupils, standing in line like little angels, began cheering as if my brother were running a race. I started cheering too. "Go, Willie, Go!" Behind my brother, Mother Superior ran too. But she couldn't catch up with Super Willie. He dashed up a stairway, then down another before finally being wrestled down by the cafeteria cook, a stout and muscular Italian woman. She held him down until Mother Thomas Rose could catch up. Mother Superior dragged my brother by the ear down the hallway to her office. She promptly called Papi. He arrived twenty minutes later from work. He had that look in his eyes, and my brother thought he saw him curl his tongue.

"I thought Dad was going to kill me," he said. Mother Superior told him about his escapade. Papi began apologizing to the nun and spanked my brother right in the office. "I'm so sorry," he kept repeating.

Mother Superior explained that Willie was suspended for the day. My brother rode home in silence with Papi. Halfway home he asked Willie to recount the tale. This time my brother explained about the whacks and how the ruler made him bleed. And he told my dad about kicking Mother Thomas Rose as hard as he could. My brother waited for my father to explode. But instead Papi began to laugh. It was a small laugh at first, but then it crescendoed. Papi the disciplinarian was now Papi the soft-hearted. No matter how tough he could be, he had a special place in his heart for his *hijos* (children).

Each day, my brother and I would take the bus to Corpus Christi from our home. And each afternoon we would take it back. We loved watching people who weren't Cubans like us getting on the bus. One afternoon the Beatles from London were in town to perform at the Deauville Beach Club. The bus was filled with teenage girls screaming and carrying on. I couldn't understand why. Just a few years earlier, girls just like these were dancing on the sidewalk as they waited for our bus. They moved up and down and shook their hips to a dance called the Twist. A black guy named Chubby Checker was behind the dance craze: "*Round and around and up and down we go (Yeah, oh, baby) making with the shaking to and fro*," he'd sing on TV. When I watched him I wished that I was a teenager too.

By this time the Cuban refugee kids had begun to arrive in droves at Corpus Christi. I was assigned to help them and translate. Soon we were far from the few Cuban kids in school. There were new faces in class every day. By the time I was in fifth grade, my mom told me that they could no longer afford to keep us in Catholic school. Tuition was too high. Papi was already thinking of moving the family to a new and strange place called Hialeah. At that time, Hialeah was still mostly farm fields, and there was little housing development. That was about to change. Hialeah would become a new Cuban mecca.

Before moving to Hialeah, we lived in a house across the street from the new expressway. I'd sit on the front porch for hours watching the cars whiz by. Life was good and I remember thinking I was a lucky kid. We had chickens and roosters in the backyard. It wasn't uncommon in a Cuban household, as they reminded them of the *campo* (countryside). My grandparents, Mima and Pipo, grew up near farms to the sounds of roosters "*kree-kree-kreeing*" at dawn. One day Papi brought home a black rooster we promptly named Blackie. He was a funny pet who hobbled from side to side like Charlie Chaplin in one of those old movies. About two weeks later, I saw Blackie eat a huge lizard. It got caught in his throat. Mami used an eye-dropper, trying to force water down Blackie's throat so he'd stop choking. Soon after, Willie and I noticed Blackie had disappeared. We asked Mami and Papi where he had gone, but they kept strangely silent. A few days later, we were at Mima's house lamenting Blackie's disappearance. A sly smile crossed Mima's face. We asked her if she knew where Blackie had gone. She let out a loud laugh before delivering the news.

"You had him for dinner last week," she guffawed. We were mortified! I thought I was going to throw up.

In 1963, when I was ten, I began understanding my place in the world. I started following current events and watching news programs. And I'll never forget one special day that seemed to change everyone's life. Mother Superior swept into our classroom at Corpus Christi Catholic School. We stood like little soldiers and recited our mantra: "Good morning, Mother Superior, and God bless you!" We quickly took our seats. Mother Superior's chocolate-brown Carmelite habit billowed ominously. Her brow was scrunched. She clenched her hands into fists in front of her. Then she whispered something into Sister Agnes Bernadette's ear.

Mother fled the room, and Sister turned to us and delivered the news: "Children, the president has been shot in Dallas." A collective gasp. We looked at each other in wide-eyed horror. The scene seemed to play out in slow motion. Sister Mary Agnes Bernadette spoke again: "Pick up your things, children. You may go home early."

We scrambled from class and I remember feeling shaken and frightened. I also felt for some reason the need to deliver the terrible news to whomever would listen. My brother ran toward the bus stop as a strong wind whistled through the bending palm trees. As we crossed the highway, and as the cars whizzed by, I screamed at the top of my little lungs, "The president has been shot! Did you hear!? The president has been shot in Dallas!" The cars sped by and the drivers looked at me through their opened windows like I was a crazy child. "The president has been shot!" I kept screaming. My brother was crying as he held my hand tightly. But I just kept shouting: "Did you hear!? The president has been shot!" That day was the turning point in my life. That was the day I became a reporter.

As I waited for the bus, I felt an incredible sense of sadness. I loved John F. Kennedy because he was *Católico* (Catholic). That night I sat with Mami, Papi and Willie and watched television. We watched Walter Cronkite ("The most trusted man in America") talk about what had happened. There was something comforting in the way he spoke. Earlier in the day, as I was shouting at traffic, it was Cronkite who delivered the sobering words that made history: "From Dallas, Texas, the flash apparently official, President Kennedy died at 1 p.m. Central Standard Time, 2 o'clock Eastern Standard Time, some thirty-eight minutes ago." Then the veteran newsman stifled tears. His were the tears of a nation.

On that day, I wished I could fly away just like little Dorothy in *The Wizard of Oz*. Something had been taken away from me. But it had also been taken away from our country. The sixties bubble of perfect lives with beautiful color televisions had been burst. Nothing would ever be the same. As I got on the bus and headed home, I looked out the window and I remembered Dorothy singing that song about birds flying over the rainbow. Little did I know then that for the Gomez family "over the rainbow" would be a place called Hialeah.

CHAPTER 4
HIALEAH

You squint your eyes at the empty places between the frames,
the spots we've taught each other to ignore.
—Jennine Capó Crucet, *How to Leave Hialeah*

IN 1963, PAPI DECIDED we were moving from Allapattah. Our cousin Julia had moved to a new home north of Miami. It was a place called Hialeah. I thought it was a funny name. It was pronounced Hi-a-lee-uh. I had no idea what it meant. I only knew that we were leaving the home I had grown to love. I later learned the funny-sounding name was Indian in origin (either Muskogee or Seminole) and that it meant "pretty prairie." Julia told Papi that they would be constructing five new homes in Hialeah right next to hers. She wanted Papi and Pipo to buy the homes so we could live close to each other. Papi said we would go to a public school in Hialeah. I wasn't convinced it was a good idea.

I had come to love being taught by the Franciscan nuns in their flowing brown habits. I enjoyed eating the glazed donuts after Mass in the dining hall. I had grown accustomed to the ritual surrounding Christmas. That's when all of us choir boys filed down the main aisle

of the church, hands clasped in prayer, to the hymn "O Holy Night."
We literally had to fall to our knees (ouch, that really hurt) at the
precise moment when we sang *"Fall on your knees, oh hear the angels'
voices."* All I could hear was the collective sound of knees hitting the
floor. *Thump. Thump. Thump.*

But I later learned there was another reason we were leaving
Allapattah. In fact, we weren't so much leaving as escaping. Allapattah
had been a white enclave into the sixties (Cuban-Americans fleeing
the Castro regime had settled here in large numbers) when black
Americans began buying homes in the area. They had been displaced
in their neighborhoods by the construction of the North-South
Expressway (I-95). The white flight to suburban Miami, Dade County
and Broward County had begun.

Were we as children receiving a subtle message regarding racism?
Why was it a bad thing to have blacks as neighbors? We didn't quite
understand, and explanations weren't forthcoming. The issue had
cropped up years before at the "white" and "colored" water fountains.
And now, in 1963, it was coming up again. My parents were afraid
of the unknown, but they were hardly racist. Papi worked closely
with many blacks at Foremost Dairies. They were not only colleagues
but friends. But perhaps there was something about dozens of black
families moving into the neighborhood that seemed to trouble them.
Why? We never found out for sure. My mother would always say
there was no racism in Cuba. But then she'd add, "They would go
their way and we would go ours."

One day we set out to Hialeah to see the block where our homes
were about to be built. Julia's house was right on the corner. There
was a huge empty lot behind her house. I remember Julia (who
reminded me of Anna Magnani in the film *The Rose Tattoo*) laughing
that full-throated laugh and telling my father, "Isn't it great? We'll be
neighbors, *primo!*" I wondered how I'd grow accustomed to this new
and mysterious place.

Hialeah at that time was just beginning to transform itself from cow pastures to a booming city. It would become home to tens of thousands of Cubans wanting a place to call their own. Just to the west of where our new home would be built were fields where farmhands baled hay. The entire area west of Twelfth Avenue (we were on Palm) between Fifty-Third and Sixtieth Street (our house would be on Sixty-Second Street) was part of the huge White Bell Dairy Farms owned by John G. DuPuis. Most people, of course, associated Hialeah with the Hialeah Race Track. It opened in 1932 as one of the grandest horse-racing parks in the country.

What Papi didn't realize when he brought us to look at the lot was how much Hialeah would change. He didn't know it would become the sixth largest city in the state with a population of 224,669 people. Nor could he imagine our new city would turn into one of the largest Spanish-speaking and Cuban-American communities in the country (with 92 percent of households speaking Spanish).

In 1964, we finally moved into our new home. I thought we had moved into a palace. Our home was the next to last on our block. Papi decided to paint the house canary yellow, the same shade his friend René had painted his. The color reminded me of the canaries my grandfather kept in a Rococo cage, the same canaries which each day sang their sweet morning hymns. Pipo ended up moving next door to us.

Soon it was time to start public school. My brother was off to Hialeah Junior High, and I would be a sixth-grader at Palm Springs Elementary. I was eleven years old and feeling confused and worried. How would I adapt to this new school? I had no friends. Everything was scary.

Although I was book smart, I lacked physical prowess. I wasn't interested in a lot of "boy" things. And my father seemed to notice that. One day he asked me to take the garden hose and screw it to the faucet in the front yard. Try as I might, I couldn't quite attach it. I remember him shouting at me, "What's wrong with you! Don't you have any common sense?"

My brother seemed to excel in all the areas that I didn't. Every time I attempted to perform a chore Papi assigned me, the same thing always happened. I was helpless. "Your brother is going to get ahead, but if you don't get some common sense, you're going to end up on the street." What I realized years later is that he meant I would end up not only homeless but, far worse, a failure. This feeling of not being good enough was something I felt long after I couldn't screw on the garden hose.

Besides lacking any sense, I was a first-class nerd. I wore Coke-bottle glasses and looked like Don Knotts when he turned into a fish in *The Incredible Mr. Limpet.* I was also chubby, with chipmunk cheeks, and wore ugly clothes that Mami bought at Sears. What a sight I was.

I decided that I'd find another way not to "end up on the street." I'd be successful and prove my father wrong. Sometime during sixth grade, Mr. Leventhal, my homeroom teacher, assigned us to write a short story. Reading was my passion, and I loved everything from the *Adventures of Huckleberry Finn* by Mark Twain to *To Kill a Mockingbird* by Harper Lee. But I also read all the Hardy Boys books and Nancy Drew, too. I began to write for hours at a time. When I finished, I had produced a 150-page Hardy Boys–type detective novel. I called it *The Curse of the Hidden Treasure.* A few days later Mr. Leventhal pulled me aside and praised my work, saying, "Charles, this is excellent." Soon I found myself sitting in the principal's office. He loved it too.

"You're going to grow up to be a famous writer," he said, beaming. That afternoon when the school bell rang, I ran home feeling euphoric. Papi's words no longer bothered me. Who needed common sense when you could be an author? But despite the momentary feeling of being on top of the world, the bullies still made fun of me.

"There's the sissy who throws like a girl," they jeered. I would try to ignore them.

"Don't listen to those morons," my friend Susan would tell me. Susan Bracewell was a pretty girl with long, brown hair who sat beside me in sixth grade. I walked her home every day after school. "Just pretend they don't exist," she'd say. "Don't give them control over you."

When it came time to climb a rope, I could only hold on to the bottom of the rope, unable to move up even an inch. "Try, Gomez," the macho gym teacher would say. "Use your legs, for God's sake." His exasperation only made it worse. I couldn't move.

Later, when I started junior high school, I'd dread doing the 600-yard run. I dashed as fast as I could, but soon I'd collapse. I was having an asthma attack. "Poor Gomez," the boys would shout. "Don't cry now, you little baby." I was always the kid picked last for the teams. I became withdrawn. I had no idea then how this negative reinforcement would shape my future sexual identity. All I knew then was that I wanted to be one of the guys.

During the summer before I entered junior high, something happened that changed me forever. A slightly older neighborhood boy invited me to his house. No one was home and I didn't know where his parents were. While there he said, "Hey, come here. I want to show you something. Pull your pants down," he said.

Was I hearing him correctly?

"Pull them down. Don't be afraid. Everyone in junior high's doing it."

I was confused and scared.

"Come on, pull them down and I'm going to kiss you down there!" He kept nodding, trying to encourage me. But I recoiled. I may have been confused, but I knew even at eleven that this just wasn't right.

"No, no, no. It's a sin."

I never told Mami. And if Papi ever found out, well, I couldn't even contemplate that possibility. I never mentioned it to the priests during confession. I certainly didn't tell Susan Bracewell or the kids at Palm Springs Elementary. I always wondered why that kid approached me. Had he seen something strange or unusual in the way I acted? Or was it just random? Were all the kids in junior high doing it? Or was it a phase that kids went through before moving on to their girlfriends? I was so confused. Because I could never entirely dismiss what happened, it made me ask myself more questions. Who was I and what sex was I attracted to? Was it OK to play with other boys *down there*? I kept these thoughts to myself.

One day in class, I met a peculiar teen named Evelio. He was a tall, gangly Cuban-American boy with dark skin and an infectious laugh. Like Felipito in Catholic school, Evelio was effeminate. Evelio and I were in the same grade in junior high. We were both bookish. But where I was reserved, Evelio (who soon started referring to himself as Dennis) was extroverted. He was the smartest kid I knew and totally comfortable in his own skin. Already in junior high school, he was better read than most adults. Dennis was a cinema aficionado at twelve years old. He knew which movies were cutting edge and must-sees. Unlike my family, which was devoutly Catholic, Evelio's believed in an Afro-Cuban religion called Santeria.

One day, Dennis invited me to his home. I was startled. There were statues of saints on display everywhere with tiny votive candles flickering around them. Some were adorned with plates of fruit. Were the saints supposed to snack on them? I would come to learn that Evelio's sister was a Santera and the entire family were followers. As a child, I occasionally heard Mami refer to Santeria, but only in the most derogatory way. "That is *brujería* [witchcraft]," she'd say. "We don't believe in that because we believe in God."

> *You wanted chicken blood, people wearing burlap, goats maybe, statues eating fruit and drinking bottles of beer. You want zombies.*
> —Jennine Capó Crucet, *How to Leave Hialeah*

Santeria mixed elements of Yoruba mythology brought to Cuba from West-African slaves and borrowed greatly from Catholicism. That explained why there were so many saints in Dennis's home. The

Catholic saints (the Virgin of Charity, St. Barbara, Saint Lazarus) corresponded to African deities. Santeros or Santeras (like Dennis's sister) engaged in dances, trances and sacred drumming rituals to conjure the gods. The gods, in turn, would help humans ward off bad luck, find romance or get rich, among other things. When my mother found out that I was friends with a boy whose family believed in Santeria, she begged me to cut it off. "You'll attract the devil. Be very careful," she warned.

But while I was friends with Dennis, his family never tried to get me to participate in any rituals or become a follower. In fact, they never talked directly about their devotion. They'd only allude to it. In Dennis, I found a friend who exposed me to a wealth of knowledge beyond the borders of Hialeah. And his vibrant mother, Berta, would become a second mother to me. Berta drove us to see films that kids our age would never see on their own. They were adult fare and required that we be accompanied by a grownup. Berta would drive us to theaters in Miami and Coral Gables that showed such sophisticated fare as Francois Truffaut's *Fahrenheit 451*, *Is Paris Burning?*, Claude Lelouch's *A Man and a Woman*, Ingmar Bergman's *Persona*, and even such provocative fare as *The Killing of Sister George*, a British drama with lesbian undertones. After the movies, Dennis would offer his interpretation and ask my opinions. His mother listened intently, and in her eyes you could tell she loved her son very much.

Dennis told me that when he was younger a close relative forced him to have sex. The abuse started at age five and continued until he was eleven. When Dennis told his mom, she was devastated. She had no idea. The relative was banished, and Berta made it up to Dennis by becoming a mother hen and fierce protector. Instead of being scarred by the experience, Dennis never dwelled on the abuse. Instead he excelled in school and extracurricular activities. And his friendship became more and more important to me. Felipito was gone, but Dennis was right here.

In junior high, the teasing by bullies continued. "Am I a sissy?" I wondered. My friendship with Dennis made me think twice. I admired him for being himself, but I didn't want to act like him. I didn't want to be a *pájaro*. *Pájaro* meant bird, and to many in the Cuban culture being a bird meant being gay. I wanted to be like the other guys. In a strange way, I wanted the bullies to like me. So, in a desperate attempt to fit in, I joined Speech Class. There I learned to speak in a lower register. By doing that and controlling my mannerisms, I hoped I'd be able to gain the respect of the swaggering boys. I signed up for oratory contests and entered a string of them. Surprisingly I won first place in two.

My speeches were about overcoming obstacles. I cited examples from the history of civilizations and spoke about leaders triumphing against the odds. I listened to the speeches of past oratory winners. Their voices sounded so deep. I began to imitate them, and in time I sounded just like them. In my mind I even sounded like the newsmen on TV that I so admired. Finally, the illusion of masculinity was complete. My voice would never give me away as a *pájaro*.

In my middle year of junior high school, I joined the Special Education Service Club. We helped kids with Down syndrome, cerebral palsy and other afflictions get to class. We pushed their wheelchairs, pretending they were race cars. They gleefully laughed as we whizzed down the hallways. We wanted them to feel the same as all the other kids.

One day, some of the jocks began to make fun of one of the kids with Down syndrome. The bullies began to grunt and flip their wrists, mocking them. I felt a rage building inside me. In a crowded hallway between classes, I found my voice.

"You guys think you're so tough," I said. "But anyone who would make fun of these kids has a big problem. Why don't you pick on each other? You should be ashamed of yourselves." There was silence. In fact, I thought I might have seen the faint sign of some grudging respect from one of the bullies. I finally stood up to them. I felt empowered.

The taunts came less and less now, and my confidence grew. One day my hip English teacher tried to talk me into running for Student Council president. Miss Host wore her light-brown hair in a flip like Patty Duke. I told her I thought I was too much of a nerd to run for president.

"You're not a nerd; you're cool. From now on, you're no longer Charles. Now you're Chuck." I hated the name at first, but I got used to it and it caught on really fast. I won the election, and the following day the headline in the student newspaper read, *"Go Go with Gomez" was the winning slogan and the Student Body went!* I was still a big nerd, but now I was Chuck, the president of the Student Council. I had finally arrived. In fact, I not only won the respect of my classmates, but more importantly I was gaining Papi's respect.

When I broke the news to Papi, he said, *"Así es como tiene que ser. Siempre seas el mejor."* (That's the way it should be. Always be the best.) But despite my victory, there was still a distance between us. I think he intuitively sensed that I was gay even before I admitted it to myself. He could never embrace that part of me no matter how many awards or achievements I received.

Meanwhile, Hialeah was undergoing a huge transformation as more Cuban families moved in every day. Instead of being one of the few Cuban faces at Hialeah Junior High, I was one of several. The new immigrants forced the schools to change their curriculum to include more classes that reflected the community. I studied Spanish literature and learned to write in Spanish. Before that I spoke in what we called Spanglish, a mixture of English and Spanish. It was a shortcut slang we *Cubanitos* used to communicate. "Cornflakes" was *conflei.* "Hamburger" was *jamberger.* "To hang out" was to *janguear.*

My friendship with Dennis intensified. We were very close, and I considered him to be my best friend. Although Mami didn't seem very pleased, she grew to accept it. We saw more and more daring movies. *The Killing of Sister George* was condemned by the Catholic Church, deemed not suitable for children under eighteen. Dennis said that was all the more reason why we should see it. So off we went with Berta driving us to the only theater where it was playing in Miami. There on the screen I watched the two female characters kiss. I don't think I fully understood the concept of lesbian sex, but the movie showed me that if two women could kiss, perhaps two men could as well. My Catholic upbringing had taught me it was wrong, but Dennis explained it was part of what happened in the world. It shouldn't be hidden and it shouldn't be a secret.

I eventually came to conclude that Dennis's outlook on life was influenced by the painful abuse he'd suffered. But rather than turn away from the idea of homosexual sex, he comfortably embraced it. Dennis believed that it didn't matter whom you loved; it mattered *that* you loved. I don't know what made Dennis so wise at fourteen, but he always opened my mind to possibilities that I was quick to dismiss. Dennis never talked about the fact that we ourselves might be boys who liked boys. We always skirted the issue.

In the eighth grade we were handed a large and heavy handbook listing hundreds of job possibilities. It was called *Project You*. In the book we were asked which careers interested us most. I didn't have to think twice: it was journalism. I wanted to be the next Walter Cronkite. He was the most trusted man in America, and I wanted to be trusted too.

By fifteen I longed to be like the blond American surfer boys at Hialeah Junior High. They wore their hair in bangs that cascaded into their eyes (think Dennis Wilson of the Beach Boys). It was the era of "California Dreamin'," and they wanted to be cool. I coveted their desert Chukka boots and their swagger too. But I was a Cuban-American nerd with baby fat and thick glasses. And my hair was coarse and curly. I would watch the commercials for Curl Free and Uncurl and long to have straight, sleek and shiny hair. I begged Mami to buy me Curl Free, but she said it was too expensive. So, I had to opt for Dippity-Do. It was a clear gooey substance that was the precursor to modern-day hair gel. I couldn't get that catchy TV commercial out of my head: *"Dippity-Do—You! Dippity-Do—For setting your hair! Dippity-Do—No zip, no drip! Dippity-Do. Dippity-Do, Dippity-Do, you or you!"* But try as I might, I couldn't get the rows of ridges out of my hair. I was hopeless. I was a Dippity-Don't.

I started high school at the height of the Vietnam War. Lieutenant William Calley Jr. had just been charged with six counts of premeditated murder for the deaths of 109 Vietnamese civilians. My father and grandfather were late-blooming Republicans (they voted for JFK) but initially seemed to support Lyndon Johnson's decision to keep troops there. Communism was the enemy, and events in Cuba had affected their views and influenced mine. But by the time Richard Nixon ran for office and called for the withdrawal of American troops, Papi and Pipo were on the bandwagon. I think Papi and Pipo hoped I'd become a Republican too.

By 1969 Hialeah was well on its way to being Florida's fifth largest city. And the waves of Cuban exiles that started arriving in Miami (continuing through the Freedom Flights from 1965 to 1973) had changed Hialeah from a predominantly white working-class enclave to a Cuban mecca. That change was just beginning to appear at Hialeah High, but in 1967 it was still predominantly white. Still, this *Cubanito* was excited to finally be a high school student. That first day of school is still so vivid in my mind. Hialeah High's hedge-lined entrance led to a granite hall. There I stared at a large round seal emblazoned with the words *To seek, to find, to share.* That motto guides me to this day.

Dennis and I promptly signed up for a variety of school activities, from the National Honor Society and Yearbook to the Debate Team. The episode involving the boy who tried to pull down my pants was long past. I set about proving to myself that I was straight. I started dating a lovely girl with red bangs. She smelled of Jean Naté body lotion and Aqua Net Hair Spray. We would make out in her house when her parents weren't there. I remember thinking I didn't mind kissing girls. In fact, it was fun. As for Dennis, he had his own *novias* (girlfriends).

It was my sophomore year and I was now a Thoroughbred. Thoroughbreds were our school's mascots, a reference to the Hialeah Race Track. But I still felt like a hopeless kid trying to fit in. It was a world of cliques within cliques. There were the Yearbook geeks and the Debate Team geeks. There were the Drama Club outcasts and there was the Band. There were the beautiful girls in their long shiny hair parted down the middle. Cliques never mingled. And if you dared to infiltrate the chosen group, the ostracism was far more subtle. Turned-away faces. Silent sneers. The stink eye. The geeks would cast their eyes downward as the popular girls and guys walked by. We thought we weren't worthy. But every once in a while, one of the chosen girls would acknowledge one of the geeks. They were articulate and thoughtful and gentlemanly compared to the oafish quarterbacks. That's how I met Karen Evans.

I had a crush. She was tall and graceful with brown hair that cascaded to her shoulders. She had sparkling blue eyes. I was still slightly chubby with wavy coarse hair. The Dippity-Do still wasn't doing the trick. I was so in awe of Karen. She was an Anchor and I was still a Dippity-Don't. And what was Anchor? Well, it happened to be the most exclusive girls club at Hialeah High.

I tried to tell myself that my crush on Karen proved I couldn't be gay. Back in 1967, students who were gay never acknowledged it even to themselves. There was no coming out of the closet. The closet was for your clothes. Period! You may have recognized the feelings stirring inside, but there were few role models for gay kids to emulate.

Dennis and I saw gay sex depicted on the movie screen. I remember how deeply affected we were by the film *Women in Love*. In one scene the male leads (played by Oliver Reed and Alan Bates) strip and wrestle naked to the flickering flames of a nearby fireplace. Somehow watching this scene made me feel that perhaps it wasn't wrong to love another man. But you kept such thoughts to yourself.

In real life, Dennis and I were very much still in the back of the closet. The Stonewall riots wouldn't happen until the summer of our junior year. And the ripples of the emerging gay rights movement hadn't yet reached hopelessly conventional Hialeah High.

About a year or so after I met Karen, I remember that a local anchorman began an investigative report with the words "And now we take you into the sad, twilight world of the homosexual." The images that followed were grainy and shot at night. They showed men furtively going in and out of a bathroom on the beach. But this wasn't *Beach Blanket Bingo*. The shots flickering on the TV set reminded me of a horror movie, and the gays were depicted as monsters. Night cameras rendered the images a ghoulish green. It almost scared me into not wanting to be gay.

The same year that I entered Hialeah High, CBS News aired a documentary anchored by Mike Wallace called *The Homosexuals*. I was switching channels on our TV at home when I caught a somber-faced Wallace dressed in a black suit, sitting in front of a bookshelf. Was this display of literature meant to signify truth?

"Homosexuality is an enigma," Wallace stated. I remember thinking that I did not want to be what he was talking about. He reported that some medical experts still considered homosexuality to be a mental disorder. Could Dennis and I possibly be these homosexuals? Were we crazy too?

It wasn't until decades later that I learned what else Mike Wallace said in his report. What were the words that disturbed me so sitting in front of my TV as an impressionable fourteen-year-old?

"Americans consider homosexuality more harmful to society than adultery, abortion or prostitution," intoned Wallace. "Most Americans are repelled by the mere notion of homosexuality. The CBS News Survey shows that two out of three Americans look upon homosexuality with disgust, disbelief or fear." And the final words sliced through me like a machete. "One out of ten says hatred."

If America hated us so much, imagine what a kid struggling

with his or her identity was thinking. The message was clear; it was disgusting to be gay, so don't be.

It was against this backdrop of fear and shame that I met Karen. Every spring, the Anchor Club would choose their Sweethearts. The Sweethearts usually included the biggest jocks in the school. A night or two after the audition, the selected shipmates would be surprised by a gaggle of screeching Anchor girls. They hung large paper anchors around the guys' necks. I told Karen I was trying out for Anchor Sweetheart. She encouraged me but warned me not to be too upset if I wasn't chosen. I think she realized I was placing too much stake on a popularity contest.

I practiced the routine that would become my audition. Each prospective Anchor Sweetheart had to come up with a talent. For some of the guys it would be a skit, a dance or a song. I decided on singing even though I couldn't carry a tune. On the appointed evening my dad drove me to a house in Hialeah. As I walked to the front door I heard loud music and the chattering of teenage girls.

Enter the nerd. In the living room, the most popular guys at Hialeah High were gathered. They wore letter jackets and their bangs fell in their faces just like the surfer boys I tried so pathetically to emulate. Karen, dressed impeccably in a blazer and plaid skirt, emerged and reassured me. "Now, don't be nervous, Chuck. You're gonna nail this," she said. I sat on the sofa wearing my gold blazer and a ridiculously wide green tie, waiting to be called in for my audition.

Finally, the moment arrived. I surveyed the room and was overcome with a bad case of stage fright. The Anchors sat in judgment. They were the prettiest girls in school and they whispered conspiratorially as I gathered the courage to perform. It was now or never. "*Anchor, Anchor, I do hold to your colors green and gold. Anchor, Anchor, be my fate, please pick me as your shipmate,*" I warbled miserably. I gulped like a goldfish and continued the ridiculous song. "*And Anchor, Anchor, if you do, I do promise to be true. Anchor, Anchor, be my fate, please pick me as ship-pip-mate!*"

I finished with a grand flourish, arms outstretched, like a Cuban Al Jolson. At first there was silence. Deafening silence. Then it started.

First one girl began to laugh. Then another. Soon it seemed like they were all laughing hysterically and pointing at me. "I can't believe it," I heard one of them saying, flipping her long hair back over her shoulder like Cher. The popular girls had turned into the mean girls. I felt like Carrie after she was crowned prom queen. But instead of unleashing bloody fury, I ran. I ran out of the room. I ran out of the house. And I didn't stop until I ran all the way home. I had been humiliated. The king of the nerds cried himself to sleep that night. In his nightmares, he heard the Anchor girls laughing louder and louder.

The next day I bumped into Karen. "Don't pay attention to those dumb girls," she advised. "They were being jerks. I voted for you. That's all that matters." The next day the Anchors chose their shipmates. I wasn't among them. I learned later I had received only one vote: Karen's. With the disappointment still fresh in my mind, I decided to seek comfort in what I loved most: writing and reporting. Journalism would never let me down.

Soon I was named editor of *The Record*, the school newspaper, and launched several campaigns. In one of my reports, I detailed the growing number of accidents on the street in front of Hialeah High. The reports eventually led to turning the street one-way, making it safer for students arriving and leaving school. With the Debate Team I traveled to high schools around Dade County. One popular subject was "Should the Electoral College be abolished?" I had perfected my stentorian delivery and my dramatic masculine gestures in an attempt to ward off any suspicions that I might be attracted to the same sex. Was I? It was so confusing.

Later that year, Mart Crowley's groundbreaking play *The Boys in the Band* opened at Miami's Coconut Grove Playhouse. It was the first time homosexuality was shown so honestly on the stage, at least in Miami. Dennis insisted that we go. So once again Berta drove us to the theater. I can't begin to put into words how I felt watching this group of men engaging so honestly with their homosexuality. The play was funny and sad. It was also brutally honest. One line stuck with me: "If we . . . if we could just . . . learn not to hate ourselves so much." *The Boys in the Band* was hardly a positive portrayal of the gay lifestyle. I remained confused and conflicted.

As part of my responsibilities as senior class president, I took a bus to the Fontainebleau Hotel on Miami Beach and met with the banquet director. I had to make the final arrangements for the prom. When I was done, I stopped next door at the Eden Roc Hotel to use the bathroom in the lower lobby. As I was washing my hands in the sink, an older man (a clerk from one of the hotel shops) put his hand on my shoulder. I flinched but I didn't storm out. He asked me to return the next day at the same time. He said we would drive to a nearby park to get to know each other "a little better." That night I couldn't sleep thinking of the next day. I felt I was about to do something wrong again. Certainly what I was considering was in my mind a sin, but it didn't stop me from taking the bus back to Miami Beach the next day.

The man met me outside his shop and he drove me in his car to Greynolds Park. We got out and walked through an area of brush. When he began to fondle me, I froze.

"No, I can't," I said. "Drive me back to the bus stop?" I had experienced my first gay encounter. But because it was so unfulfilling, I convinced myself I wasn't gay. I was relieved. I wouldn't have to live the sordid life I saw portrayed in *The Boys in the Band*. When I got home, I told Dennis about my rendezvous. He asked me a lot of questions. He may have been surprised, but he didn't seem shocked. At the end of our conversation I thought I noticed a slight smile cross his face. Of the two best friends, look who had embarked on the first adventure of our true sexuality.

As my senior year ended, I found out that I had graduated twenty-third in a class of over 1,200 seniors. Dennis finished high on the list as well. We both set our sights on going to Miami Dade Community College and the University of Miami.

I decided to enter a prestigious countywide competition sponsored by the *Miami Herald* called the Silver Knights Awards. The Silver Knights were the Oscars of the Dade County scholastic world. Every senior across the county secretly coveted the gleaming statue. If you won one, you were treated like a local celebrity. I was Hialeah High's nominee for journalism. I had learned so much since that day I opened the *Project You* handbook and decided my dream and life's ambition was to be a journalist.

My teachers taught me that to be a good journalist, one must be an excellent storyteller. It wasn't enough to regurgitate facts. Little did I know then that these lessons would lead to a career that would take me all over the world to observe and report history.

A month later I sat in Dade County Auditorium with my fellow nominees and hundreds of friends and family members. I looked through the program and saw that Dr. Joyce Brothers was the keynote speaker. She was a noted TV psychologist. Boy, was I impressed.

I sat near the front row. My throat was dry and I kept swallowing awkwardly. A few rows back, Mami and Papi sat anxiously. When they got to the category of journalism, Mami squeezed Papi's hand tightly. She told me later, "I was praying to *la Virgencita* to help you." The master of ceremonies made his announcement like a news anchorman reporting on the moon landing: "And the winner in journalism [pause for dramatic effect] from Hialeah High School is [another pause] Charles Gomez."

In that instant, as the cheers and the applause thundered in my ears, any feelings of inadequacy and inferiority seemed to fade. The boy my father said would never amount to anything because he couldn't screw on a garden hose no longer existed. I wasn't a sissy anymore; I was a Silver Knight! But I still had my doubts. I had no role models to reassure me that I could be both gay *and* a successful reporter. As the applause wound down, I wondered where journalism would take me. What stories would I tell? What new places would I visit? And what dangers would I encounter along the way?

You are free to go. Nonetheless you will go ahead and Eurydice
will walk behind you and you will never look back. Otherwise
you will lose her forever.
—Hades, from the Greek myth *Orpheus and Eurydice*

So, like Orpheus, I would "go ahead" on this new journey and
begin with the smallest of steps. This wasn't the Yellow Brick Road
of my childhood games in Allapattah. Wars, revolutions, addiction
and AIDS lay ahead. But I couldn't see them now. The path beyond
Hialeah had too many twists and turns. Suddenly the image of the
Hialeah High seal flashed before me like a neon-lit road sign on a
highway. The words of our motto were all capitalized and flashing:
TO SEEK, TO FIND, TO SHARE. I took a bigger step this time.
Unlike Orpheus, I never looked back.

THE IMMIGRANTS: In this remarkable group photo taken around 1944, members of the Gomez, Gonzalez and Alvarez family gather at a resort outside Havana. These are the original "Cuban sons and daughters" most of whom left Cuba for the United Stares to pursue their American dreams. That's my dad in the foreground about a year before he left Cuba headed to New York to work at a factory in the middle of the garment district.

MIAMI 1950: One year before marrying my mother in Havana and bringing her to the U.S., my father (on the right) posed with his stepfather at their first home. That's "pipo's" sons, Peter on the left and Eddie on the right.

HAVANA: It was 1959 and my brother Willie and I were taken by a cousin to an amusement park in Havana. In 2016 when I found the same park (Monaco) but it was abandoned. I spotted the kiddie cars on a broken track. By now they were rusted.

INTERVIEWING CASTRO: As a young reporter for WBBM-TV, I traveled to Havana with U.S. businessmen. I asked Castro about food shortages in Cuba. He changed the subject staring at my name tag. "What kind of Cuban name is Chuck?" he asked.

In El Salvador covering the civil war as Latin American correspondent for CBS News in 1979. I was unprepared for the bloodshed I witnessed. Many of my colleagues were caught in the crossfire and did not survive.

EMMY AWARD: I won an Emmy Award in 1993 as an Investigative Reporter for WWOR-TV. My parents traveled to New York City from Miami to be at my side. I wore a red AIDS awareness ribbon on my tux but I couldn't bring myself to tell my parents my secret: I had been diagnosed with HIV/AIDS.

SEEKING PAPI'S ACCEPTANCE. I traveled with my father to his beloved Cuban homeland for the first time in six decades. I was hoping the trip would lead to a reconciliation between us. But would the stigma and shame of AIDS cause my father to reject me?

CHAPTER 5
MOON OVER MIAMI

Moon over Miami
You know we're waiting for
A little love
A little kiss
On Miami shore
—Ray Charles

SO, YOU'RE IN MIAMI on a sweltering Sunday in the summer of 1976 and you turn on your old-fashioned T V set (you know, the one with the rabbit-ear antennas) to Channel 10, WPLG. It's just before noon. This is what you see. Commercial: A blonde bouffant-haired woman in a pink bow blouse, pencil skirt (below the knee) and sensible brown shoes sashays in front of huge pink prop boxes emblazoned with the words *Weight Watchers*. She could be a housewife from a sixties sitcom. But there's a come-hither quality to our seventies homemaker. And then she speaks in a lilting voice with the slightest of Southern accents, smiling suggestively into the cameras. "I've got what it takes to keep you in the pink: Weight Watcher lunches and dinners in huge pink packages, the ones with the nutritional information on the front of the packages!" She bounces her head to the left and gives us a backward kick. You can't help but chuckle.

It was a different time. Miami was growing. Cubans were moving into all parts of the city. Some began to run for political office. We were still years away from the "cocaine cowboys" that infiltrated this tropical paradise. And it was at least a decade before the TV cop show *Miami Vice* glamorized the city (in pulsating neon and pastel shades of pink and blue) to a disco soundtrack. Keep in mind that disco as we knew it, with its upbeat vocals over a steady four-on-the-floor beat, was just hitting Miami in 1975 and 1976. In clubs from Hialeah to Hallandale you could hear catchy ditties like "Rock the Boat" by the Hues Corporation and the ubiquitous "Do the Hustle" by Van McCoy and the Soul City Symphony. Donna Summer was our queen and Gerald Ford was our president. Watergate was over, but we were still feeling its effects. Nixon's appointments director, Dwight Chapin, was finishing up seven months in jail for his role in the scandal. But TV commercials and TV news were still hopelessly backward. Videotape was still in its infancy. And the first news stories I covered were still shot with film cameras. Yes, film cameras. Like the silent era in cinema, it was the film era in television news.

Back on TV, the Weight Watcher lady continues her spiel: "On my left, ziti macaroni and veal parmigiana and now turkey with stuffing! We're in the pink. What about you? Stay in the pink." She puts her hands on her hips and accentuates her tiny waist. She all but gives us a wink: "You just might be seen [cinching her waist with her fingertips] in all the right places." So clever.

Then, without missing a beat, a pounding musical interlude starts and the voice of a male announcer interrupts the music with all the authority of Charlton Heston as Moses in *The Ten Commandments*: "Newswatch is next on WPLG 10, Miami." As the music plays, the names of cities in the South Florida television news firmament pop on screen in bright-yellow lettering: *Miami, Ft Lauderdale, Miami Beach, Coral Gables, Dania, Hallandale, Kendall, Plantation,*

Florida City. And then viewers are hit with the image of a twenty-one-year-old Cuban-American against a backdrop of swaying palm trees and a brilliant blue sky. "Hello, everybody, I'm Chuck Gomez."

He's wearing a baby blue–colored jacket with a tie as wide as a bib. It's emblazoned with diamond-shaped squares. The hair is a helmet of black, with bangs sweeping the forehead. The hair on the sides is completely covering the ears. His thick black Groucho-like eyebrows shade deep-set dark eyes. He flashes a smile. And then he speaks with a perfectly pitched voice enunciating his words as carefully as Henry Higgins getting Eliza ready for the ball: "A scuffle last night in Little Havana between a Miami police officer and a man he stopped for driving without a license erupted in violence. Thirty-two-year-old Osvaldo Espinosa was shot in the arm. Police say he grabbed Officer Puig's flashlight and hit him in the head with it." And so begins my first stint (and one of my few) as a Sunday anchorman in Miami.

In the summer of 1975, a precocious twenty-one-year-old armed with a misplaced confidence and a shot of entitlement returned to the city where he was born and raised. He was hoping to be the Cuban Walter Cronkite. He was living in a world of unlimited possibilities. Youth and naiveté were his armor. It wasn't that he was delusional. He truly believed he could climb to the top of the TV news mountain. He was convinced (and his mother fueled his ambition) that he was God's gift to modern-day journalism. He had already worked as an intern reporter for the *Miami Herald* and the *New York Post.* And now *la televisión,* as his mami put it. *"Estás en la televisión!"* she'd say proudly. (You're on television!)

He had no experience in front of the camera, but what he did have was sheer gall and an unstoppable drive to succeed at whatever cost. Now, if he could only hide his jitters from others and excel in this strange world of television news. He had taken WPLG general manager Gregory Favre up on his offer to work at the local ABC affiliate in the fifteenth largest market in the US. Goodbye newspapers. *Adios, Miami Herald. Hola,* Newswatch 10.

Each of the young reporters at WPLG-TV was given a stab at trying out for the anchor chair on the weekends. Eventually the job would go to a Tom Selleck look-alike by the name of Art Carlson, a former radio reporter for WIOD. But for now, I was being given a shot. At home (where I was still living with Mami and Papi) I spent an hour artfully blow-drying my mane of hair in the style of moment. Once in the newsroom, I applied Max Factor Pancake, Deep Egyptian #2 makeup to my face in every nook and cranny. I had copied this technique from one of our suave anchormen, Ron Hunter, the original Ron Burgundy as far as I was concerned. "This makes you look good, poppa," he would say as I studied him applying it one day in front of a large Hollywood-type mirror outfitted with globe-like lights.

I walked down a winding staircase to the harshly lit news set. I was followed by an impossibly tall and nerdy news intern with an obvious overbite and a winning attitude. "Here's your hand script," he said. The script would supplement what I'd be reading off the teleprompter. I sat behind a desk and took out a small compact mirror, smoothing my eyebrows with a dab of saliva applied artfully with my right index finger. I carefully read and reread my copy. I had yet to master the art of reading a teleprompter. It was tricky, and sometimes the words would move faster than you were ready to read them. It required a knack, one that could only be learned from practice. I braced myself, and when the little red light blinked on top of the camera, I went into action.

No one in 1976 could have possibly predicted the advance of the technological age or that one day we'd all be watching seventy-inch high-definition screens. Our pregnant TV sets would be tossed to the curb. It was a time when local banks in South Florida offered eight-piece china sets just for opening a checking account. And if you opened a savings account with twenty-five bucks, they'd throw in a casserole pot as well. A perfectly coiffed Farrah Fawcett look-alike pointed proudly to a mahogany dining table and showed off the fancy place setting. "Why not open an account when you can get all this?" Why not indeed?

As I anchored my first newscast, I daydreamed that it would propel me onto the national stage. I would interview presidents and cover wars. By the time I was thirty, I thought, I'd be doing stories introduced by the most trusted man in America himself, Walter Cronkite. Back in Hialeah, as my image flickered on our faulty set, Mami told Papi to remind me to get a haircut. "He looks like one of those Beatles," she said. In a Cuban household, image was everything. And the image I was expected to project was of respectability, an image that would make my parents proud. Looking like a Beatle wouldn't do.

But being gay wasn't part of that carefully crafted image, nor was it part of the plan my parents imagined for my future. I would marry. I would have children. I would buy a house. I would live the straight American dream, not the gay American nightmare. I wasn't comfortable with being gay myself, let alone confiding in my family (or, for that matter, in my colleagues). I think if I had met a genie who asked me to make a wish, I would have wished I was straight. I was living a double life. As successful as I seemed to be, I was conflicted. I felt I had to live secretively. And on camera I had to project a certain image.

WPLG-TV Newswatch 10 was housed in a two-level concrete structure with a huge parking lot on Biscayne Boulevard and Thirty-Ninth Street. It was located in somewhat of a no man's land in Miami. The station was a few blocks away from the entrance to the I-95 expressway. Today the neighborhood is part of the bustling Design District. The newsroom was cluttered with a beehive of hospital-green desks under harsh fluorescent lighting that was hardly flattering. I co-hosted *Job Line*, a show with a darling little old lady and a fake owl made out of coconut bark we named "Joe the Job Line Owl." She announced the jobs in English and I translated them into mangled Spanish. Viewers would tune in to see what travesty of language I would come up with next. Instead of public affairs, we accidentally became a comedy show. I wasn't playing it for laughs, but to many viewers *Job Line* was so entertaining that it became an unintentional hit.

In the back of the newsroom, there were tiny rooms where cameramen sometimes did double duty splicing the film they had shot on their news cameras. When I tell young reporters that I started in television in the days of film, they look at me like I am an old-timer.

It was here that I met my first cameramen, a caring coterie of men in their late twenties and thirties who would become my first television family. I was so happy that many of my new colleagues were fellow Cubans. They had names like Al Rodriguez and Emilio Rangel and Abdiel Vivancos, and they treated me like a little brother. There were also *los Americanos* like Andy Kay, Lenny Yeoman and Randy Fairbairn. At that time, I was the only Cuban-American reporter on the staff.

The newsroom was filled with young reporters. At twenty-one, I was by far the youngest. There was Tom Sanders (a Bradley Cooper type) and Rick Edlund (a Rob Lowe look-alike). My desk was right next to the desk of a brilliant African-American reporter by the name of Maynard Eaton. I still have a funny picture of the both of us in the newsroom in which I am smiling and he is gesturing at the camera with his middle finger extended (flipping the bird). And, of course, there was Art Carlson, who took over the Sunday newscasts. But my favorite fellow reporter was Sheila Stainback, a African-American woman and trailblazer in TV news. To me Sheila was a goddess, supremely intelligent, with a glowing Afro and a gleaming smile. Everyone loved Sheila. She was one of our top reporters and also one of the first to do a live shot. We would come to be inseparable. With Sheila, I felt I could be myself. And, indeed, she was the only reporter (except for a legendary anchorwoman I'll get to later) I dared to confide in that I was gay.

For my first few months at WPLG-TV, it was the honeymoon phase. I proposed doing stories about the often-neglected Cuban community. One of my first reports was about a hunger strike outside the *Miami Herald* carried out by former Cuban political prisoners attempting to call attention to the plight of prisoners in Cuba:

> *Cuban flags fluttered outside the Miami Herald building, casting shadows on the faces of four Cuban men. Since Friday they have camped outside the building. They will drink only water. The men, two who have served time in Castro's jails, say they hope the hunger strike will call media attention to the plight of Cuban political prisoners. Their ordeals—corroborated by hundreds of letters smuggled out of prisons—tell of midnight massacres by firing squads. In September there were reports of a massacre of eight persons at the Boniato Jail. That event sparked the first of the protests. Many Miami Cubans have visited the strikers, listening to the tales of alleged horrors in Cuban jails.*

Despite my honeymoon phase, there were rumblings that didn't bode well. One of my news producers locked horns with me at every turn. He criticized my writing. He nit-picked my on-camera appearance. He talked about me behind my back. Months later when he was asked to write an evaluation of all the reporters, mine was scathing. A colleague saw the evaluation on his desk. Under each of the reporters' names, a paragraph detailed their strengths and weaknesses. The last on the list was mine. Under it was just one sentence: "Gomez: He's our weak link. Get rid of him!" Talk about writing on the wall. To be fair, I wasn't entirely blameless for the events that led to my bad review. But there was more to the story than just an evaluation report.

At twenty-one, I was beginning to feel more at ease in the gay world. My friend Dennis and I would hit the bars on Saturday nights: Warehouse 8 in Miami and Ambassador's on Miami Beach. But I was always looking over my shoulder, it seemed. I was afraid that if my homosexuality became known, it would lead to ridicule, the loss of my job and even worse.

One day I decided to tell Sheila the truth. We were both children of working-class parents who believed in the American dream. Her father was African-American. Her mother was from Guyana. My parents were from Cuba. Our moms and dads worked tirelessly to give us a better life than they had known. And now here we were, both reporters at a Miami television station. Sheila and I had met in the *Miami Herald* newsroom about three years earlier when I was an intern and she was already working at the Miami radio station WIOD. By the time we met at Channel 10, we knew and liked each other in a special way. Little did I know then that we would remain best of friends for more than four decades. We'd end up working in television in the same cities. It was as if fate brought us together time and time again. It wasn't just a coincidence; it was kismet. We laughed at the same jokes and I loved when Sheila threw back her head and let out a Stainback guffaw.

We also both loved the same things, especially old movie musicals. One day when everyone was gone from the newsroom, Sheila and I found ourselves in an empty studio with a large green screen. We found two huge umbrellas in the corner. And at the very same moment we grabbed the umbrellas, and, as if we had rehearsed it, we burst into "Singing in the Rain." We opened and closed the umbrellas laughing and dancing badly. Gene Kelly we weren't. By the time we finished, we collapsed in glee on the floor. Sheila laughed theatrically, and it made me laugh just to hear her distinctive cackle. Little did we know that a cameraman was still in the building and secretly filming our Gene Kelly moment. Where the clip is now is anybody's guess.

There would be a chance to revel again in the sound of Sheila's laughter when we attended the Channel 10 Christmas party. We arrived in matching sweater ensembles, looking like twins. Sheila wore a blue top and fitted cream-colored slacks. I wore a blue harlequin-pattern sweater and tight white jeans. We looked like a pair of ice skaters ready to perform figure eights at the Olympics. When the elevator doors opened, we were in for a shock.

Years later, when we reminisced about that evening, Sheila said to me, "We were seriously underdressed, weren't we? The women were wearing sequined evening gowns and the men were in dark suits." I recalled that as we sauntered to the bar, we started getting the stares. We were given the stink eye and made to feel like the poor relations crashing a swanky affair. I was mortified, but Sheila had a different reaction. She began to laugh and wouldn't stop. The laughter got louder. The more Sheila guffawed, the more dirty looks we got.

"I didn't care," Sheila said. "I just pounded the alcohol." We stumbled out of the soiree doubled over in laughter. I drove Sheila back to her place. Her apartment building was on Biscayne Bay, and a tropical breeze blew gently. I looked up in the evening sky and noticed an almost full moon. Moon over Miami. Suddenly a song I heard on a radio station dedicated to the oldies played in my head. It was sung by Ray Charles:

Moon over Miami,
Shine on my love and me,
So we can stroll beside the roll,
Of the rolling sea.

If there were ever a moment when I should have kissed Sheila, this was it. When we recently spoke about the night, Sheila said, "When you walked me to the door, I wondered if you were going to kiss me, but you turned on your heels and walked away. It was then that I thought you might be gay." I was torn by the conflict between what others expected of me and the truth that I couldn't escape about myself. Sheila never mentioned the abrupt end of the evening until recently.

One day we decided to have lunch and drove to a nearby fast-food joint, and over a hamburger I laid it on the line.

"Sheila," I said ominously. "I don't know how to tell you this, and maybe you've put it together yourself, but . . . but . . . [pause for dramatic effect] I'm gay!" Sheila broke into a big smile followed by a hearty laugh. "Of course, I knew," she said. We never overanalyzed the disclosure. For now, it was enough that we respected and loved each other.

Around this time, I befriended the station's anchorwoman. She was a legend in Miami television who I'll refer to as D. She had an authoritative presence. She wore her hair in a platinum bob and favored brightly hued polyester pantsuits. She was a powerhouse of a reporter and an even stronger anchorwoman. D. had the ability to be intensely serious and friendly at the same time. From stern to effusive, she could switch personalities just like that. And there was something else that drew me to her. She was gay. The reason I won't identify her is because I don't believe one should out someone without their consent, even after they've passed away. The late seventies were not a time when gays in the newsroom would proclaim their homosexuality. We kept it to ourselves. I don't know how D. knew that I was gay as well, but there was an understanding between us. Much has been written about *gaydar* (the ability to sense if someone is gay). Gaydar, per se, wasn't articulated as such in 1976. But it was clear to me, if not to others, that D. was a member of my team. We rode the same bus.

In time we developed a rapport and would joke using double entendres or raising an eyebrow. It's a way gay people communicate, especially in settings where heterosexuals outnumber us. I constantly fought with myself, trying to reconcile two distinct personas. One was a reporter projecting a macho image on the air, the other a gay man afraid of being unmasked. As a newspaper reporter, my gay self wasn't important. My stories had bylines. No one saw me. But on television I felt the camera could see right through me. It was like an X-ray. I imagined my news director calling me into his office and saying, "You're gay; you're fired."

Fast-Forward, October 8, 2019

Job discrimination against gay and transgender workers is legal in much of the nation, and the wide ranging arguments [before the Supreme Court] underscored the significance of what could be a momentous ruling. If the court decides that the law, Title VII of the Civil Rights Act, applies to many millions of lesbian, gay, bisexual and transgender employees across the nation, they would gain basic protections that other groups have long taken for granted.
—*The New York Times*

Rewind, 1975, Miami

I was at war with myself. I mention this because it might be easier to understand the events that almost led to my dismissal. Was I subconsciously trying to punish myself for being gay?

Not too long after these bouts of self-doubt, I found myself being reprimanded for doing a stand-up with a corpse lying on the street behind me. How was I to know that it was an unspoken rule never to show a body in TV news? The story was about a bizarre struggle involving a man who confronted a cop at Miami International Airport. The man jumped the officer from behind, demanding his gun. After a scuffle, six shots rang out while the gun was still in the officer's holster. When a customs officer showed up to assist the cop, the perp fought him as well, demanding his gun. The officer handed it over. Then the bad guy commandeered a yellow cab and tried to make a getaway. But instead the cab hit a concrete embankment. At this point shots were heard, and it was unclear whether the suspect somehow shot himself or whether he was killed when cops fired at him.

In my report, the camera zoomed in on the smashed taxicab,

slowly opening up to reveal me standing in front of a body laid out on the street. A tarp covered most of the body. But part of the man's upper feet could be clearly seen sticking out from under the tarp. There I was in a wide-lapelled tan sport jacket, one hand on hip like a fashion model, the other clutching a microphone as I began to speak:

> *Homicide detectives are still investigating another theory. The man may have put a gun to his head and committed suicide before the car crashed on the concrete embankment. Police say the exact cause of death may not be known until later today. Chuck Gomez, NewsWatch 10.*

When I got back to the station, I got hauled into the news director's office. He told me to never do a stand-up in front of a corpse again. It seemed like the harder I tried to be the perfect reporter, the more I made mistakes. Things weren't going to get any better.

One weekend as I made the rounds of Miami gay bars, I met an attorney. He was in his early thirties. We had a few drinks and I went back to his place. His apartment overlooked downtown Miami. From his floor-to-ceiling windows, the Miami skyline twinkled like a diamond necklace, and I could even make out a crescent moon disappearing behind a gray cloud in the Miami night sky.

"Do you want to try something new?" he asked.

"What do you mean something new?" I asked.

"It's THC. I have a little oil and I'll just put it in a joint and you'll love it."

Now, until this point I had experimented with marijuana but never heavily. THC was something I hadn't heard of. I would later learn that THC was tetrahydrocannabinol, the main mind-altering ingredient found in the cannabis plant. At high doses THC can induce hallucinations, change thinking and even cause delusions. I smoked the joint laced with THC oil and immediately felt a sense of elation. But within an hour I began to feel a terrible sense of anxiety. For what seemed like hours I felt dizzy and off-balance. Somehow, I fell asleep in the attorney's home, and when I woke up it was about 5 a.m. By then I felt sober enough to drive to my parents' home in Hialeah.

When I walked in my mother asked me if there was anything wrong. "No," I replied. I quickly got dressed and headed out to work. I thought everything was fine, but soon I would learn that the THC was still very much in my body. That morning I was assigned to the courthouse to babysit a story that involved prosecutors calling for the exhumation of a body. I don't remember the particulars of the case, but prosecutors apparently had reason to believe the victim might have died under mysterious circumstances. I remember going into the elevator with one of the prosecutors. We were alone. Suddenly the elevator stopped on a floor. I remember the prosecutor, a tall imposing man, looked at me and said, "You want to know what's on this floor? It's the morgue. You wouldn't want to end up like our victim." Somehow those words (Did I misinterpret them? Did he really say them?) triggered something in me. I began to sweat profusely. My breathing became labored. "Mr. Gomez, Mr. Gomez," I heard. But it seemed as if the voice were coming from a million miles away. By this time the elevator had gone down to the lobby, and when the doors opened, I ran.

I ran through the double glass doors of the courthouse, down steps until I reached the street. I turned around convinced I was being pursued. No one was behind me. I started running some more. I decided I had to run straight to the Channel 10 building from downtown. I had to run to the station and report what the prosecutor had told me. I would later come to recognize that I was having a THC-induced breakdown. But how could this be? I had taken the THC the night before. There was no sensible explanation, but it was clear that the THC was still affecting my system.

I must have run for twenty minutes or more, through streets congested with traffic, through lights, past office buildings and banks. I just kept running. I felt like I was the character played by

Dustin Hoffman in the film *Marathon Man*. I was convinced I had a story to tell and that it had to be told on the news. I finally arrived at Channel 10. I took the elevator to the newsroom. There I noticed everyone was looking at me like I was crazy.

"I have to report a story, I have to report a story," I kept repeating. I remember seeing Sheila's face.

"What is it, Chuck? What is it?"

I couldn't tell her. The newscast was about to start. Ron Hunter, the anchorman, walked past me.

"I have a story. I got to go on set," I told him.

"Hmm, poppa," he said. "I don't see you in my script." I started walking toward the winding staircase that went down into the news studio. The lights were glaring. In my mind I thought they were searchlights. They were crisscrossing and now they found me. There was a heightened sense of urgency. My breathing became increasingly shallow.

"Chuck, Chuck, what's wrong?" Sheila asked. The newscast was moments from beginning.

Then I heard the anchorwoman's voice, stern and mean: "Get him outta here!" she screamed. "Get him out of here!"

I was quickly led into the news director's office. Sitting on a couch was a man I didn't recognize. As soon as I walked in, he began peppering me with questions. "What is it you're feeling?" he asked. "Don't worry; you're in a safe place." Was he a shrink? How had he known I was here? I found out later that the man asking me questions was a doctor who had been brought into the newsroom. He was being interviewed for a position as a medical reporter. It was all so surreal.

"Did you feel threatened?" the man asked. I remember the questions, but I don't remember my answers. It was a professional nightmare. I was sent home and placed on suspension. My mother doted on me, cooking me my favorite Cuban dishes: *arroz con pollo* (chicken with rice) and flan (sweetened egg custard with a caramel topping). But Papi seemed strangely distant, and I could tell that he disapproved of my "breakdown." What was wrong with me wasn't just "an attack of nerves." I sensed Papi knew that I was struggling with something else. But he didn't ask any questions. Maybe he was afraid of the answers I might give.

But he grabbed my arm and said, *"Hijo, tiene que controlárte!"* (Son, you need to get ahold of yourself.) He told me that I wasn't just representing myself. He said that I was representing our family. "You have a master's degree from Columbia University. That is something that no one in our family has achieved."

He urged me to stay away from "influencias negativas" (negative influences). Then he looked at me sternly and said in Spanish, "Only you can change the direction you're going in. We can't do it for you. We have faith in you, and we love you very much."

Although Papi could sometimes be gruff and menacing, at this moment care and compassion flowed from him like a cool cascade. His words were less admonition than sage advice for a son he felt had lost his way.

I returned to work at the end of the week fearing I was going to be fired. But it didn't happen. My news director and colleagues seemed supportive. It was clear that I had some sort of mental breakdown. I assured my bosses I was getting help. And indeed, I called a psychologist someone recommended and began seeing her. The only person I told about the THC was Sheila. She didn't judge me. I remember her saying simply, "I just want to make sure you're okay." I assured her I was fine. But was I?

In the next few months, I became mentally stronger. But there were some bosses who determined that I wasn't an asset to the newsroom. I began getting my story tapes together. I sent them to news directors around the country and hoped for the best. I knew I was a good reporter. I just needed to get out of my own way. I had to learn that being gay wasn't something to hide or to be ashamed of; it was an important part of me I didn't need to hide.

One day I received a call from a New York agent by the name of

Bill Cooper. "I saw your work on the air. You're good. I can get you a better job," he said. I wasn't sure I was hearing right. "Can you send me some tapes of your reporting?"

I sure could. Within weeks he got me an interview with WBBM-TV in Chicago. Chicago was the number three television market in the US. I walked like a toy soldier into the bustling fluorescent-lit newsroom that day. Suddenly I just knew this would be my new home. In less than a week I received the news that WBBM-TV wanted me as an on-air reporter. I had just turned twenty-three. Suddenly, my breakdown, my producer's nasty evaluation, my stand-up in front of a corpse, all of it evaporated.

"Chicago is cold, son," my father said out of nowhere one day. He then walked me to his closet and pulled out a long gray and somewhat tattered coat. "This is the coat I wore in New York when I first came from Cuba. I want you to have it," he said. He gently put it in my arms. It was such a kind and simple gesture. But to me it meant the world. I wanted to tell him I was gay right then and there, but I didn't have the guts. Instead, I hugged Papi as hard as I could.

In the days before I left for Chicago, the anchorwoman who screamed "Get him outta here!" came up to me. D. put her arm around me and we walked slowly down a long hallway. "Whatever happened in the past is past. Be careful, my friend. Now get out there and make me proud."

I would miss Miami, but I would miss my parents more. And, of course, Sheila.

"I'll be seeing you soon, I'm sure," she said. And little did I know that months after I began working at WBBM-TV, my best friend would get a job at WLS-TV and we'd be gossiping in a new and different city. Frank Sinatra's song "My Kind of Town" played in my head: "This is my kind of town, Chicago is." I drove to Chi-Town in my beat-up white Dodge 300 convertible. It was already November, so I couldn't ride with the top down. My old and worn cloth suitcases were in the back seat. And in the front seat right next to me lay my father's coat. I smiled as I stroked the sleeve. I was sure to need Papi's coat as the winds whipped off Lake Shore Drive on a bitter-cold December morning.

As the highways brought me closer to Chicago, I found myself reflecting on my life in Miami and in my mind replaying that old Ray Charles classic that I loved so much:

Moon over Miami,
Shine on my love and me,
So we can stroll beside the roll,
Of the rolling sea.
Moon over Miami,
Shine on as we begin,
A dream or two that may come true,
When the tide comes in.

CHAPTER 6
REMINDERS OF REVOLUTION

Men more frequently require to be reminded than informed.
—Samuel Johnson, Author of *The Rambler*

HE'S ONLY A CHILD. Three fingers of his left hand wrap tightly around the barbed wire fence. The boy waits for the men with the guns. They are the youngest guerrillas. Their enemy: Nicaragua's National Guard. The boy wears a burlap mask. It's a traditional dance mask from the town of Monimbo. He and the other boys who've joined Frente Sandinista Liberación Nacional (FSLN) wear the masks to hide their faces. They hide them in the fight against what they consider the face of evil. That face belongs to Anastasio Somoza Debayle. He is the president of Nicaragua. It is 1979. A sparrow perches precariously now on the barbed wire. The expression on the child's mask is benevolent, watchful. Two large brown eyes have been painted on the burlap, framed by delicate arches meant to signify eyebrows. Beneath a delicately painted nose, a reed-thin mustache (like Errol Flynn's) has been drawn in ink. And below that, a small mouth in red. The mouth is shaped like two small Vs.

In her beautiful book of photographs *Nicaragua June 1978–July 1979*, photographer Susan Meiseles includes a letter written by a young rebel to his parents. And as I read it, I think of the boy in the burlap mask clutching the gray barbed wire. The letter is from Edward Lang Sacasa. His father, Frederico Lang, was a wealthy businessman and Somoza supporter:

> *I am a revolutionary, which is highest rank to which a human being can aspire. I had hoped our parting would not be painful but circumstances have so determined it. I, like Sandino, would like a free country or death and that is why I am going. Embraces and kisses from your son who loves you more than ever. Until soon, that is, until victory.*

He was killed by Somoza's US-trained National Guard on April 16, 1979, just two months before I was dispatched to Nicaragua by CBS News to cover the final days of the Somoza regime. I was twenty-five, just a few years younger than the revolutionary.

I find Susan's mesmerizing book stacked at the bottom of a dusty box in my storage unit. I haven't opened it for decades. As I leaf through its loosening and crumbling pages, memories of my days in Managua come flooding back, some lovely, others too disturbing. They were locked deep in the vault of my subconscious. And now here they are again. On the title page, a dedication by the gentle CBS News producer who accompanied me on many of my turbulent stories in Central America. The way the words are scrawled remind me of crows flying hurriedly across an early winter sky: "To Charles, my best and dearest friend in the world. Despite all the wolves and *mercenarios.*"

As I look through the book for the first time in thirty-six years, Susan's startling images bring up events too painful to remember. It was a life-changing year. As Susan herself writes, "Nicaragua. A year of news, as if the roots were not there and the victory not earned.

The book was made so that we remember." And so, my *recuerdos* (memories) come flooding back. The photographs bring back the sights and smells, reminders of revolution. A woman washes laundry in a sewer of downtown Managua. Her face is resolute, unflinching. Hers is the face of a refugee forced to flee the familiar. Her brown patterned skirt billows in the breeze. Behind her, the sky is filled with fluffy cotton-candy clouds set against an azure-blue sky. *El cielo azul. Tan azul.* (The blue sky. So blue.) We see old dilapidated buildings in the distance, church steeples too. As the woman wrings out a piece of clothing, our eyes are drawn to the clothes on the ground. They are drying just inches away from the filthy water. The woman has left an orange sandal in the muddy waters. Nicaragua, a country embroiled in a civil war. Her face reflects a resigned acceptance to her fate.

To put Susan's photos in context, one must understand the events that led up to the uprising against Somoza. The civil war pitted supporters of the Sandinista Liberation Front against those who backed Somoza's militaristic government. The Sandinistas' ideology was rooted in Marxism and named after Augusto César Sandino. Sandino led a peasant army against US-backed governments in the late 1920s and early 1930s. The FSLN sought to unite Nicaraguan workers and peasants to bring down what they called "capitalist exploitation" at the hands of Somoza. The Sandinistas were victorious against the National Guard in 1979. They forced Somoza to flee into exile. During the revolution the Sandinistas received support from Cuba's Fidel Castro, who wanted to see a socialist revolution in Nicaragua. By 1980 the Sandinistas were receiving Soviet weapons from Cuba.

I flipped the pages to another of Susan's photos. I see an indigenous woman dressed in a maid's uniform of red and white. She is tending to two well-dressed kids, children of the elite. A young girl is wearing a pressed pink party dress while holding an inflatable toy. She's trying to wear it like a hat. On another page, an unsettling image (the complete opposite of the woman washing clothes). It's a photo of Somoza opening a new session of the National Congress of

1978. Susan's photograph captures Somoza dressed in a white suit and formal black bowtie surrounded by an entourage of similarly dressed men—an image meant to convey normalcy to the world even as Nicaragua was crumbling.

Yes, I was twenty-five years old when CBS News sent me to Nicaragua to cover the civil war. I was naïve and I was scared. I couldn't begin to comprehend. Indelible images of that time have stayed with me: the body of a young woman in a red dress barely out of her twenties left lying in a ditch; camera crews ducking for cover in dark alleys as bullets ricocheted past them. And as I look at this photo of Somoza, I remember an interview with him in his well-fortified "bunker" headquarters two weeks earlier. He predicted victory against the Sandinistas. But it was not to be.

In Susan's other photographs, I begin reliving a Nicaragua I had put away in the recesses of my mind: children harassing guards in Matagalpa, their tiny hands cupped around their mouths; the Cuesto de Plomo, the hillside outside Managua where people searched for the bodies of loved ones. I wince as I scrutinize one of Susan's photographs showing the remains of a man. One can see a spinal column attached to a charred torso still wearing faded jeans. The National Guard's gruesome way of handling suspected guerrillas and their sympathizers was merciless.

The photographs remind me of graffiti scrawled on boarded-up homes in outlying towns: "*Dónde está?*" (Where is it?) Sometimes the graffiti would finish the sentence with a missing loved one's name. I remember the cars left burning on their sides in ditches, the smoke billowing into the Managua sky. I kneel in the hallway outside my storage unit in the August heat and I sweat profusely. But I can't turn away from the images. How could I ever forget the funeral processions for assassinated student leaders? Susan shows demonstrators hoisting a photo of Arlen Sin, an FSLN guerilla leader. They hold it as if they are carrying a precious religious relic. I flip back to the first photo of the boy in the burlap mask. Susan has captured the innocence of a moment. How often would we be sent into town where the fighters were just children and teenagers with scarves tied tightly around their faces to conceal who they were? I slowly turn the pages. Time slips away.

It is June 8, 1979. Walter Cronkite introduces a report on the CBS Evening News:

> *Sandinista guerrillas have taken the offensive in at least five Nicaraguan cities in their battle to overthrow the government of President Somoza, and the capital of Managua is suffering a guerilla-called strike. Charles Gomez reports.*

Gomez Voice-Over

Although not quite a ghost town, Managua at the end of a general strike is a city drained of its energy. The strike, called for by the Sandinista guerrillas, has taken an economic toll. But the rebels are using it more for psychological reasons, hoping to show the Somoza government the people are unified behind them. But the fighting has intensified elsewhere. In Masaya, just seventeen miles south of the capital, the Sandinistas are firmly entrenched. Here the guerrillas have been firmly entrenched for three days—their rag-tag assortment of arms ranging from modern automatic weapons to hunting rifles and pistols, facing superior government firepower trying to force them out.

Often this is a war fought by los niños [the children], young teenagers, on both sides, and this veteran of last year's unsuccessful insurrection—a seventeen-year-old Sandinista patrol leader. He says: "Here we either die or triumph. We are a free country to the death. It is better to live as a rebel than as a slave."

Despite the upheaval caused in their city when the guerillas moved in, the people are clearly siding with the Sandinistas. They express fear and resentment toward the government forces. He says, "They don't consider anyone—not children, not old people. They kill everyone. They enter a house firing and just shoot."

Gomez Stand-Up

In Masaya, as in other countryside villages in Nicaragua, the Sandinista guerrillas continue to mount sufficient strength to quash the mounting offensive by Somoza's National Guard. And it is in the countryside that the Sandinistas believe the battle will finally be won. As one guerrilla told me, "Make no mistake about it. We are launching our final drive." Charles Gomez, CBS News, Managua, Nicaragua.

Cronkite was the man I had watched as a ten-year-old *Cubanito* in Miami telling America that President Kennedy had been assassinated. How I idolized him. He was the newsman I always longed to be.

In another photo by Susan, a National Guard tank rolls into Esteli as a soldier accompanies it brandishing a machine gun. It reminds me of the day the National Guard entered Masaya.

We had spent the day covering skirmishes in that city and were headed back to the Intercontinental Hotel in Managua. Our tiny car, driven by a Nicaraguan, featured a sign reading *PRENSA, NO DISPARA!* taped on the windshield. (PRESS, DON'T FIRE!) As we traveled on a highway approaching a small hill, the camera crew and I froze. A National Guard tank appeared on the horizon about a mile in front of us. This was it, I thought. We were goners! I thought that at any second, the tank's guns aimed in our direction would start firing. The color left my face and I gripped the torn red vinyl of the back seat and shut my eyes. I held my breath. Our driver drove by the tank ever so slowly. We were so close I felt that I could reach out and touch the armored vehicle. The shots we anticipated were never fired.

I continue flipping through the pages of Susan's book. The binding is pulling apart at the seams. The corners are yellowed. A page comes apart in my hands. It is a photograph of a woman in a red dress. Her head is turned away from the camera. Her mouth is half-opened. Her tiny hands grip a wheelbarrow. In it is a figure wrapped in cloth and tied with rope. Anguish. She is a woman from Monimbo. She is carrying her dead husband home. Susan writes that she is transporting him to be buried in their backyard.

On another page Susan interviews Irma, a housewife from Matagalpa. Irma says, "The first time we saw the planes in the sky was that September. They were firing rockets and we thought we were going to die. We heard this *pra-pra-pra* sound. We crouched down looking for somewhere to hide and my stomach churned, my whole body shook, just looking at the beast flying over us."

I remember scurrying with a crew through alleys, hiding in a *casa* (home) as planes fly overhead. I can still see the faces of the villagers, faces frozen in fear. Children huddle in doorways. A mother of two little girls raises a finger to her lips: "*Calladitas*" (Stay silent). In the distance, we hear an explosion. Is it from the government planes dropping their bombs indiscriminately? Do they care that civilians might be killed? A little girl begins to cry. Her eyes well up with tears. She opens her mouth to wail but stops herself.

In Susan's book, Fernando, a twenty-year-old civilian, says,

The smell of gunpowder was in the air, the smell of war. The people were expecting us. So was the Guard. We fought inch by inch and street by street to take Esteli again. The Guard set up fortified stations on practically every block, in schools and stores, pharmacies, even churches with up to thirty men at each one. We began our advance at one house where, I remember, the owners had run out so fast they left a pot of beans soaking on the patio. We crossed the backyard, dragging ourselves on our bellies and running from tree to tree. After we broke a hole through the back wall, we were right next to the Guards' position. It seemed like the entire world had gone silent.

Bang bang news had come to Managua. "Bang bang" was a term popularized by camera crews who covered the civil war from the beginning. Soon everyone was saying it. *Bang bang!* It was a kind of shorthand for the shootings and the bombings and the bloodshed.

I was at the hotel when I learned the news that Bill Stewart, a courageous ABC newsman, was executed by a National Guard soldier. Like all the journalists who were there, I couldn't believe that one of our own had become a casualty of this war.

Stewart's execution was shown on network newscasts that evening as anchormen sternly issued warnings to viewers. We were told that scenes were graphic. "View at your own discretion." We could choose to turn away. We could turn off our sets. But did we?

Stewart was traveling in a press van in the slums of Managua, Nicaragua. With him were his camera and sound crew. The van rolled up to a dusty roadblock manned by the National Guard. Stewart and his Nicaraguan interpreter got out of the van. They slowly walked up to a barricade. Stewart showed his press pass. How many times had I and other journalists shouted out to soldiers in a war zone *"Periodista, no dispara"* (Journalist, don't shoot)? Inside the van ABC News cameraman Jack Clark began filming. No one could predict the savagery that would follow. Stewart was ordered to his knees. The camera captured the tense standoff. Suddenly Stewart was told to lie facedown. A soldier kicked him once. A moment later Stewart was shot behind the ear. He was killed instantly, a moment of barbarity captured on tape for posterity.

The video of the execution went out on the live feed that afternoon from Managua's Channel 6, according to newsman Ike Seamans.

Seamans, the correspondent covering the civil war for NBC News, remembered that day vividly. "The day he was shot, I was covering the fighting between the Gs [the guerrillas] and the army," he told me. "We were pinned down for hours and didn't get back to the TV station in Managua until mid-afternoon. At Channel 6, Randy Fairbairn and Ellen McKeefe came running up to us screaming, 'Where have you been? Bill Stewart has been killed. We thought you were dead too,'" Seamans recalled.

Inside Channel 6, they had just finished feeding the video shot by cameraman Jack Clark. The incident had occurred around 10 or 11 a.m. By noon at the Intercontinental Hotel in Managua the video was being distributed to all the TV networks. That night (June 20, 1979) CBS News anchorman Walter Cronkite reported the horrific shooting on the CBS Evening News: "The ABC cameraman with Stewart recorded the murder. Because it is an important documentation of the savagery of the Nicaraguan War, we will show this NBC News videotape with a warning: that parents may not want their children to view it. Colleagues of the thirty-seven-year-old Stewart called the killings executions. ABC News soundman Jim Cefalo witnessed the incident, and here's his telephone description along with the videotape."

Then we hear Cefalo's voice over the grainy video:

We got to the area where the guard motioned for him to get down. Bill got on his knees and was talking to the guard. A guard comes over to him and motions him to get down, facedown on the ground, which Bill did. He kicked Bill and we realized there was a problem. Uh, he motioned back, motioned like he wanted Bill to put his hands on his head. Bill started to do so, and as he did, the Guard took one step forward, as I recall, and shot Bill once in the head.

As we watch we hear the explosive shot and see Stewart's body jerk. The camera lurches toward the sky. We hear a shaky voice saying in stunned disbelief, "Killed him."

As the world reacted with horror, according to published reports, ABC News told its news staff to leave the country. NBC News and CBS News reportedly gave their news people the option to go or stay. But Seamans remembered NBC was adamant that they leave. "We objected strenuously, to no avail," Seamans said. "We had been sent to cover a story." About a third of the newspeople in Managua, Seamans included, were airlifted by a C-130 military plane out of the country.

All but one of the network's twenty-four representatives were flown out. I made the decision to stay. Of course I was scared. But my rationale was that if we all left, it would give the Somoza government the impression we were afraid to cover the brutality of the regime. That night I called home from the hotel. Papi answered the phone in his gruff voice.

"Hello," he bellowed into the phone. I tried to say something, but no words would come.

"Papi, they killed a journalist here," I finally said.

"Yes, your mami and I saw it on the news. Are you OK?" he asked. I explained that I was fine but that the other journalists were getting out. "But, Papi, I'm staying."

At that moment, I wanted my father to tell me how much he loved me. I wanted him to tell me that I was being brave. But he said none of those things.

"Here's your mami," he said, handing the phone to her. I felt that we had missed a moment to talk father to son, man to man. I was still the weak son who couldn't please him.

A week later the news personnel, including Ike Seamans, returned to Managua. In September 2018 I learned that my friend Ike passed away from cancer. I had looked up to him. He was the reporter I wanted to be.

Somoza's days appeared numbered now. In the midst of all the chaos, I learned that I was an uncle. On July 11 Summer Brooke

Gomez came into the world. It would be many weeks before I'd get to hold her in my arms. Stewart's execution and its savagery sparked a public outcry for the end of the Somoza dictatorship. Somoza fled Nicaragua on July 16, 1979.

That night Roger Mudd introduced my story for the CBS Evening News:

Gomez Voice-Over
Throughout the day there was every indication the president was preparing to depart. His limousine was left parked outside the "bunker"—his command post—with the engine running. Suitcases were left just inside a garage. Boxes were carried out of the bunker, and Guardsmen sifted through documents in the limousine's trunk. But when the president finally appeared, it was not to say goodbye but to talk about captured arms and ammunition.

Somoza On Camera
This is a recoilless 75 millimeter round made in mainland China that most probably comes from Cuba—so we have Cuban ammunition killing Nicaraguans. Thank you so much for your attention.

Gomez Voice-Over
Following the exchange, the president rushed into the bunker. Asked if he was resigning, he said, "Not yet! I'll let you know." Later in the day his limousine pulled out of the bunker with Somoza seen waving goodbye. Charles Gomez, CBS News, Managua, Nicaragua.

I turn back to the book. Hours before Somoza left, a stunning photograph in Susan's book captures the Sandinistas' final assault on a National Guard headquarters in Esteli. We see four guerillas firing through holes in a wall of bricks. In another riveting image, an official portrait of Somoza is burned alongside the body of a National Guardsman. For Somoza, a bitter defeat: 40,000 dead (1.5 percent of the population), 40,000 children orphaned, 200,000 people homeless. Four days later, the Sandinistas poured triumphantly into the Plaza de la Revolución.

And now Susan's photographs begin to fade in my mind. I hear my voice recalling that momentous day for CBS News:

A new day in Managua and overnight a new way of life. They celebrate the birth of a new Nicaragua. It is a bittersweet victory. Too much death. Too much devastation. The people still remember the planes flying low, the bombs unleashed. Some places do not survive. Masaya for one. But the people say it is not dead, just taking a nap. For the Nicaraguans, victory comes at the price of being forced to flee their homes, of packing belongings in makeshift carts. Before victories, there were refugee centers—long waits in line for a few sacks of rice. For other Nicaraguans, the new days means defeat—a once proud army, disappearing with the dawn. But for another army, there is elation; the Sandinistas—well-organized rebel forces. They went days without eating. They lived in the hills. They plotted the shortages that would take them on the road to Managua. On the border, the southern forces rally. Theirs is a revolution of discipline—a discipline they say paid off. The jeeps move on roads no longer patrolled by La Guardia. The people wave and cheer as they pass. "Our victory cannot be detained," chant the troops. As they head to the capital there is barely enough room in the trucks. They arrive in Masaya and they receive a hero's welcome. From Masaya it is only forty minutes into the capital, and they hear the celebration miles away. They arrive in the Plaza, the Plaza many have not seen for months. After the long days and nights of endless fighting, victory is theirs.

I still remember the celebrations in Managua on that day. Today I look at Susan's book and smile. For thirty-six years it was forgotten, discarded at the bottom of a torn box in a storage unit. But now it's back in my hands, a vivid reminder of a revolution that will never leave me, a revolution that is now a part of me.

CHAPTER 7
BANG BANG BLUES

I got the bang bang blues
Wearing out my shoes
Hitting dusty highways
For the network news
I got the bang bang blues
I'm paying my dues
Taking big chances
And I hope I don't lose
—From the play *Bang Bang Blues*

THE BODY COUNT WAS rising in El Salvador. Already thousands had been slaughtered. *Los Guerrillero*s (the Rebels) had launched attacks in the capital of San Salvador and had begun to mobilize throughout the countryside. A newly installed civilian-military *junta* (cobbled together after a military coup) was on shaky ground. Anti-government demonstrators took to the streets. At the same time, bodies were being dumped in a lava pit called El Playon as vultures flew ominously overhead. These were dark days.

On February 14, 1980, I was dispatched to San Salvador from the CBS News Bureau in Washington DC. Just a year earlier I'd been hired from WBBM-TV in Chicago to become the network's first Cuban-American on-air correspondent. On this day I witnessed mothers and wives throwing themselves over the open coffins of their loved ones. How had they died? They were reportedly gunned down by the military or *escuadrons de la muerte* (death squads). They were suspected of being rebel sympathizers, or even guerillas themselves.

A year earlier, I had dodged a barrage of bullets with my camera crew as thousands of anti-government protestors took to the streets on Salvadoran Independence Day. Shots were being fired into the crowd. *Rat-tat-tat-pa-pa!* the gunfire sounded. "Get down!" I remember cameraman Bernie Nudelman screaming. Another volley of bullets followed, but no one could tell for sure where the gunfire was coming from. We took cover behind cars and the shooting continued. Bernie looked through the lens and recorded the mayhem as Steve Von Born got the sound. When it was over, two were killed and dozens were wounded. The wounded included my good friend and colleague, Kathy Hersh of ABC News. The Salvadoran Civil War was underway. What a bloody conflict it would turn out to be.

Before it was over in 1992, over 75,000 civilians would die at the hands of government forces. Three well-known atrocities stood out in the twelve years of violence and bloodshed. The assassination of Archbishop Oscar Romero, the rape and murder of four American church women, and the 1989 Jesuits Massacre.

Throughout the 1960s and 1970s, left-wing guerillas and right-wing death squads engaged in political violence. In 1980 right-wing factions battled the Revolutionary Government Junta (JAG), and death squads intensified. They were backed by a Salvadoran army officer named Roberto D'Aubuisson. He founded the right-wing Nationalist Republican Alliance Party (ARENA) and remained a leader of the death squads throughout the war. Meanwhile, the five major leftist revolutionary groups formed the Farabundo Martí National Liberation Front (FMLN).

As a young correspondent thrown into the middle of the Salvadoran conflict, everything made an impression on me. I was repulsed by the slaughter of innocent civilians by the death squads. In my journal, I wrote of a funeral that touched me.

San Salvador, February 14, 1980

The open coffins in the Cathedral were a grizzly sight. Many of the leftists had been shot in the face. These people were poor. There are no fancy funeral parlor people to make the dead look cosmetically acceptable. Their faces looked like monster masks—melted looking, swollen (dark purple to black in color). Their mouths were half open. The caskets were adorned with plastic wreaths. The people couldn't afford real flowers. The funeral march was touching. At the cemetery, the poor carried the crude wooden caskets past the elaborate monuments to the rich. They screamed: "El color de la sangre no se olvida." (The color of blood can never be forgotten.)

Leaving El Salvador, I returned to Washington DC, packed my bags and headed to the newly formed CBS News Miami Bureau. In the four years I was Latin-American correspondent for CBS News I'd witness revolutions and upheaval. I'd cover the last days of dictators ousted by the winds of revolution. I'd watch as sleepless soldiers hunted down indomitable guerrilla warriors. And then there was the "bang bang." Always the "bang bang": the gunfire and firefights, the mortars and the grenades, the planes buzzing overhead unleashing their bombs through gray clouds, the rumbling tanks rolling up hills, the hiding and the ducking and the scurrying, the fearless cameramen and photographers rushing into danger to get the story. I'd witness mothers crying for their *hijos* and *hijas* (sons and daughters), faces of war etched in grief. I saw all this and more. But barely out of my twenties, I'd also plunge into a deep depression and suffer an emotional breakdown. I'd get sick time and again. I got hepatitis from the water. I came down with a raging and debilitating fever covering the Miskito Indians in the jungles of Nicaragua. And for years after I left CBS News, I would wake up from nightmares and panic attacks to the sounds of gunfire, to the images of decomposing bodies in cardboard coffins, of remains left on rainy roadsides. I would leave "bang bang," but "bang bang" would never leave me.

President Ronald Reagan rose to power in 1980, with the Salvadoran government receiving US aid that bolstered the military and increased the number of advisors sent to El Salvador. Still, many US officials denounced the atrocities committed while fighting the guerillas.

Many years later, when I would lose so many friends to HIV/ AIDS, the memories of Central America (particularly Nicaragua and El Salvador) would come flooding back to me. In the faces of my friends I remembered the journalists who risked their lives to report the truth of the Salvadoran Civil War. They included Dial Torgensen of the *Los Angeles Times* and John Hoagland, a courageous photographer for *Newsweek*.

El Salvador was a different kind of struggle. In Nicaragua, even the rich seemed to want the end of the Somoza regime. But in El Salvador, the war seemed to be about class. The ruling class and the right wing believed a guerrilla war had to be crushed before it could take hold. From the pulpit of the Metropolitan Cathedral, Archbishop Oscar Romero preached "liberation theology." Romero believed the ruling class and wealthy businessmen were supporting the military government at the expense of the poor. "The people must be heard," he said in his sermons. To the ruling elite, that meant only one thing: a "people's revolution" led by leftist insurgents. The extreme right factions in the government and military were furious. They wouldn't stand for it. The killings escalated.

As Hugh Byrne wrote in his book *The Origins of El Salvador's Crisis,*

> *Leaflets appeared reading "Be a patriot, Kill a priest." Between 1977 and 1980, eleven priests were beaten and many more beaten, tortured and exiled. Archbishop Romero called for an end to the repression, supported the rights of peasants and others to build popular organizations, criticized*

the institutional violence of the state as fundamentally responsible for the society's crisis, and accepted, in extreme circumstances, the legitimacy of counterviolence.

The US believed El Salvador presented a serious communist threat in the region. The Soviet Union and Cuba were already assisting the newly formed Sandinista government in Nicaragua. Reagan was fearful El Salvador would be a "domino" that could result in all of Central America falling to the communists. The guerillas capitalized on anti-US sentiment, engaging the military in a conflict that lasted twelve years. By 1984 the US-backed government of President José Napoleón Duarte brought some stability to El Salvador. But the cost in lives was staggering.

The El Salvador that Kathy and I were sent to in 1979 was already turning into the carnage capital of Latin America. Kathy remembered fighting cynicism and being imbued with a sense of obligation to "get the story." I just wanted to impress the bosses in New York. We weren't ready for what we faced. El Salvador was a place where a dusty road from the airport could become a grotesque killing ground. Right-wing death squads roamed under the cloak of darkness. This tiny country was gripped by fear. Men and women (and sometimes children) were dragged out of their homes, summarily executed and transported to the airport road to be thrown out like trash. Killed at night. Found by day. Their corpses littered roadsides. You'd see their faces still frozen in terror. You'd find bodies still clinging to each other. Sometimes you'd notice hands or feet were missing.

It was these nightmarish images that made me return to my hotel room after a day of covering "bang bang" and hastily draw pastels of the bloodshed I'd witnessed. It was my way of coping. I called one drawing of the dumped bodies of a mother and her young daughter *Death Dance In El Salvador.* Kathy Hersh owns it today. Others coped by turning to alcohol or drugs in hazy bacchanals that stretched into the night with young women who accepted payment for their services. The sex workers and local "facilitators" were suspected of stealing hundreds of dollars in cash advances. They were earmarked for reporters and crews. But in the hands of one network producer in particular, the money seemed to disappear.

While sober, this producer (who I won't name) was a top-notch newsman, but after a night of nonstop drinking, he was a wreck. He'd stumble through the hotel hallways, slurring his words. I couldn't let him speak to New York in that state. I covered for him and took the calls myself. I'd spot him carelessly leaving one-hundred-dollar bills (stacked like pancakes on his night table) for anyone to steal. The next day the money was gone and so was the producer's memory. War-induced amnesia. The horror of the Salvadoran War did that to people, the sheer relentlessness of the "bang bang" and the gruesomeness of the carnage. It was something we tried to erase from our minds any way we could. The war turned normalcy on its head.

Imagine reporters with their crews coming across the bodies of men, women and children piled up in garbage dumps. Carl Hersh (Kathy's husband and cameraman) remembered taking his camera to the pit known as El Playon. "I remember all the buzzards flying overhead and seeing a body with its upper torso missing and only a spinal column in view." Carl also remembered family members picking through the rubble to see if they could find a relative. Raymond Bonner, writing in the *New York Times* on November 17, 1981, said this of El Playon: "A walk across the hardened lava reveals pockets of jumbled skulls, jaws, pelvic bones and thighbones sometimes protruding from the porous rock as if someone sought to save them a burial." Also in 1981, hundreds of villagers were massacred in the town of El Mozote. The killers reportedly belonged to the Atlacatl Battalion of the Salvadoran Army, trained by the United States.

The grizzly morning ritual at the Camino Real Hotel where the journalists stayed was always the same. Wake up at dawn and patrol the streets for the body count. On any given morning, we spotted as many as a dozen bodies, including women and children, their hands crudely tied behind their backs, dumped and forgotten. Sometimes one could still see the puddles of blood spreading out on the mud beneath them. The red would mix with the gray of the dirt and turn into a garish shade of brown. *El color de la sangre no se olvida.* (The color of blood can never be forgotten.) The body count tallied, it was time to head back to the Camino for *desayuno* (breakfast time).

CBS News cameraman Mario R. de Carvahlo remembered El Salvador then as bestial.

"El Salvador was something else," he said. "It got under your skin." He recalled "the bodies dumped in the parking lot of the Camino Real Hotel." One morning after shooting video of bodies in ravines as part of the body count, de Carvahlo returned to the Camino Real for a hearty breakfast of *huevos rancheros*. As he put it, "If you could eat [their] *huevos rancheros* for three days in a row and not get Montezuma's revenge, you were ready for the street vendors' *pupusas*" (thick corn tortilla stuffed with a savory filling). De Carvahlo remembered, "A man strolled over to our table and reaches for a pistol tucked into his pants. He looks at us and says, 'You know, we really don't like you journalists in our country.' They always thought it was all our fault."

He shuddered when he remembered the four Dutch journalists he befriended. They were gunned down by a right-wing death squad. They thought they were meeting guerrilla leaders. "You hope you don't get shot, but it's always a possibility." He remembered mortar attacks on the road to Suchitoto "where kids got killed." He said, "You have to keep going, but it drained me. It really did."

As he spoke I thought back to my own meeting with two rebel commanders in a small house in San Salvador. I was afraid. What if a death squad had been alerted and ambushed us in the middle of the interview? Thankfully there was no incident. Another CBS News cameraman, Manny Alvarez (I called him my little brother), told me about the time he went to the morgue only to find "six, seven, eight, maybe ten bodies piled on the floor like they were just garbage." As I spoke to Manny my own crippling fear returned. I could see the scenes of the men with the guns, and I could hear the same deafening sounds of gunfire. They never left me. In my dreams, I saw that mother's body lying facedown on a road and thought of my own mother. I could hear the *pa-pa-pa* sound of the gunfire. I heard the piercing scream of a woman wailing for a husband gunned down in the middle of the night. And now as I listened to Manny's voice I recalled that first visit to San Salvador so many years before.

It was September 14, 1979. I could see police crouched in the parking lot of the military hospital, their weapons poised. To my left I noticed a young officer gripping his gun still in its holster. Government officials had insisted they wouldn't be provoked into violent clashes on this Independence Day weekend. But in El Salvador, I'd come to learn, *"Promesas hechas son promesas rotas."* (Promises made were promises broken.)

In my story for the CBS Evening News I reported,

> *But suddenly the calm was shattered by the sound of automatic gunfire coming from the hospital. The demonstrators scattered for cover, but many were wounded and had to be carried from the street to nearby buildings.*

As I hid behind a car with Bernie and Steve and the gunfire continued, I had one thought: *Please let me live long enough to hold my niece in my arms.*

"A government spokesman later said they were responding to shots being fired by the leftists," my report continued. "But witnesses said police opened fire after someone set off a string of firecrackers." The shootings touched off the burning of cars and buses on the street. A van rented by CBS was also burned. I watched as demonstrators uprooted trees, blocking police access.

I didn't know then that my friend Kathy was one of the almost three dozen wounded. "Carl got the shot when a member of the treasury police fired," she told me. "They stood behind parked cars and opened fire. So many bullets were flying through the air, it was cutting the leaves in the trees above. The leaves were falling like rain on top of us." Kathy was pinned down for a good half hour. She lost Carl in the melee. She didn't realize she had been hit in the arm by a bullet fragment, becoming the first correspondent to be wounded in El Salvador. "I kept saying to myself, I'm not going to die because I'm supposed to have children," she said. "I always saw myself being a mother. It was strangely comforting."

Kathy managed to get to the next street and eventually back to the Camino Real Hotel. "I needed to have a doctor and I needed a telephone line as soon as possible." Kathy realized that on tape she had the evidence military police had fired on civilians. She had to call the network. "All the journalists' rooms were bugged. Finally, I said, 'I think I've been hit by a bullet fragment.'"

Kathy was transported to the embassy. An armored car took her part of the way to the airport. A cab took her the rest of the way. ABC News sent a Learjet that whisked her to Miami. She turned over her tape to ABC News "fixer" Bill Blanco. She was then whisked to a hospital for X-rays and eventually managed to file her story from a hotel. Just four months after Kathy was shot, a military coup led to the killing of anti-coup protestors while the rebels called for "mass disorder." It was the tipping point that would spark the full-blown civil war.

"War breaks down mores," Kathy remembered. "It breaks down everything. You get down to survival on a gut level. It causes soldiers to do atrocious things." She added, "It brings out the worst in people and also the best in people. El Salvador was something else altogether." When Kathy returned to Mexico where she was based, she said she had a hard time compartmentalizing. "I saw a shrink, and when I talked about the war, I saw tears rolling down his face," she remembered. "War never solves anything. It perpetuates itself and it never leaves those who live through it."

In the meantime, death squads were targeting not only rebels but religious leaders believed to be backing the insurgents. In March 1980, I reported on a sermon given by Archbishop Oscar Romero. He criticized Christian Democrats who had accepted an offer from El Salvador to join the civilian military junta:

"Archbishop Romero says the government has been unable to control the armed forces, which he blames for killing leftist students." In my same report I showed the bloody bodies of two Salvadoran treasury officials. Slumped in the front seat of their car, they had been shot in the head. Guerrillas were blamed for the assassinations. On March 24, just weeks later, Archbishop Romero was shot as he stood at the altar. The gunman got away. No one was brought to justice for the execution, but many believed it had all the earmarks of the death squads. In fact, the United Nations Truth Commission concluded it was D'Aubuisson himself who ordered the assassination.

Back at the Camino Real Hotel, journalists buzzed about the execution. We worried that our names were on a death list and that we'd be killed too. "It targeted mainly American journalists," Kathy remembered. "They felt we were biased." As the war intensified, bodies were dumped with more frequency near the entrance to the hotel. "It was a message," Kathy said. "They were saying we [the journalists] were just as vulnerable as anyone else." NBC News producer Don Critchfield was number six on the hit list, one he believes was made after a news conference by the brass of the Salvadoran Treasury Police. The journalists were ordered to list their names before taking their seats.

"My name on the list was spelled something like 'Crutch,'" he said, laughing. "I thought it was funny. I've never been on the varsity of anything." But other journalists clearly weren't laughing.

In the middle of all this mayhem, I interviewed José Napoleón Duarte, the president of the civilian military junta. He was a barrel-chested man with sad, dark, downcast eyes. He told me, "This is not a one-day battle. We've been under dictatorship for fifty years. It's not going to be solved in one day. It will mean years and years of hard work."

I'd return to my hotel room trying to process the raging war. I'd call my mother in Hialeah just to hear news about my niece, Summer Brooke.

"She calls me How-How," Mami said in broken English. "It's because I get on my hands and knees and make sounds like a dog: *how, how.*" We'd share a laugh and it would help me to cope. During my phone calls with Mami, she'd sometimes ask me about the war, but I didn't want to scare her by telling her all that I'd seen. I never asked to speak to Papi. When I had called him from Nicaragua after the execution of newsman Bill Stuart he didn't seem to want to talk on the phone. Now I didn't want Mami to get him because I didn't want him to sense how scared I was. I didn't want him to think I was a coward.

Another journal entry from August 17, 1980:

And so here I am writing this after four days of covering a general strike and assorted firefights in the city. El Salvador is on the brink of a terrible civil war and we've done our best to show the junta is really trying, but the violence goes on. I hear gunfire now outside the hotel room. Geez, after Nicaragua, how can I really deal with this nightmare?

It wasn't only the war I worried about dealing with in El Salvador. I was a gay man in the closet, and I didn't want to be perceived as too weak to cover the war. How one was perceived could be a factor in getting an interview with a tough general or gaining the confidence of a guerilla leader. I kept my sexuality from my colleagues. I kept it from the network. I had already heard the gay jokes that circulated in the field. I worried that if the news got back to my CBS bosses in New York, I might even be fired. Perhaps it was a groundless fear, but I felt it nonetheless. And some of my colleagues sensed my reticence.

"You looked like you were thinking, 'I'm not ready for this,'" said Steve von Born, one of the CBS News cameramen who worked closely with me. "I thought here's this young guy in something he's not ready for."

I may not have been entirely ready for the network. But between 1980 and 1982 I was jumping on and off flights covering a dizzying array of stories. There was the Dominican Republic Embassy siege from February to April of 1980. M-19 guerrillas in Bogotá, Colombia, held nearly sixty people (including fourteen ambassadors) for sixty-one days. From there I was dispatched to cover the Mariel boatlift in Cuba, which brought 125,000 Cuban refugees to the United States. I covered the story from Havana as well as Key West. As a Cuban-American I was touched to see so many Cubans arriving on our shores for a better life. The Mariel boatlift took me back to 1978 when I was a reporter for WBBM-TV. I covered the first visit of US businessmen to Havana. Fidel Castro himself made a surprise appearance and I got to speak with him:

A golden-lit hall sitting on a grassy knoll—the House of Receptions built two years ago in the shadow of Havana's Malecón Drive to entertain and impress visiting heads of state. But it was the first night a large group of Americans were in a receiving line to meet el Presidente Fidel. Dressed in formal military wear, Castro laughed wholeheartedly with the midwestern businessmen and their wives. He appeared genuinely concerned, his eyes registering sincerity, a flick of his beard signaling an apparent pang of thoughtfulness. He would comment on the vibrancy of a particular dress, on the seemingly strange-sounding name on a businessman's identification tag. Fidel was joined in the reception line by his sister-in-law, Vilma Espin, wife of Castro's brother, Raul. She is president of the Cuban Federation of Women. While some Americans seemed mesmerized by the Comandante, as he is often referred to here, others were entertained by his effusive graciousness. They gestured to make points clear to him. Others laughed heartily at the Fidel-styled wit. The reception line filtered into a marble-laden lobby. There Fidel's brother, Raul, Cuban minister of the Ministry of Defense and member of the Communist Central Committee, joked with businessmen. Journalists were caught by surprise when Fidel himself appeared to wave us inside the hall.

At this point we hear a female functionary say, "Please go inside with all your apparatus and cameras." Here we see Castro waving a cigar and gesturing. We hear him say in Spanish "Because you know" as he answers my questions. I'm surrounded by other reporters and cameramen.

When the press got its turn, I waded through a throng around Castro and was introduced as a first-generation Cuban-American, the son of Cuban parents. Castro asked me when my parents left Cuba. I answered 1945. He sighed and smiled saying that my pin-striped suit reminded him of his striped prison uniform when he was jailed on charges of conspiring to topple the Batista regime. After conversation, I asked him if Cubans in the United States would find it just as easy as Americans to go to Cuba to visit relatives.

Here we see Fidel use his hands expressively as he answers my question:

It is possible that could be accomplished. With proper relations between our countries, I think we could allow Cubans to return to their homeland. But we shall see.

As time went by, I became overwhelmed with the responsibilities of being a Latin-American correspondent. As the year ended in 1980, I wrote in my journal, "I feel at this moment a large lack of enthusiasm for the job of running around chasing stories and acting neurotic." I wondered if I was losing myself.

But there was no time to second-guess myself. I threw myself into my role. In El Salvador, I tried to embrace "bang bang" by acting fearless. One such example was my report for CBS Evening News on March 9, 1982:

Along the coastal highway guerrillas have left their calling card. A tire truck lies jackknifed on the road . . . a bus is left smoldering. For hours, the highway is left blocked. But our enterprising driver finds a way around the obstacles. Government troops fan out. They know the enemy is nearby, hiding and ready to strike. [Sound of gunfire]

They move cautiously along the roadside and finally into the brush as the soldiers engage the guerillas in a firefight. For several minutes there is an exchange of gunfire. [More sounds of gunfire] The guerrillas flee into the mountains, but the soldiers continue their search. Peasants who live nearby say the guerillas came at dawn. They report that government troops have threatened to kill them because they suspect the villagers are providing refuge for the rebels. Troops begin to burn the brush on both sides of the highway to destroy guerrilla hiding places. Tired and overextended, the Salvadoran Army is growing tired of the rebels' hit-and-run tactics. The best they can do is keep the guerrillas off the road by day . . . for they know that after sundown, the rebels are likely to be back again. Charles Gomez, CBS News, Usulután, El Salvador.

For every story involving gunfire, I'd propose pieces on refugee camps or the junta's program to distribute land to landless peasants (agrarian reform). But the New York show producers always seemed partial to "bang bang." When leftist leaders demanded that the US not send aid to the Salvadoran military and I proposed a story, there wasn't too much enthusiasm. But when guerilla leaders themselves proposed a clandestine interview to talk about a new "offensive," New York bit.

In my report from San Francisco Gotera:

CBS News was led to a secret location to meet with two top rebel leaders. They say they are preparing for another offensive and that now 75 percent of their weapons are coming from sympathizers in the army. There was no way of verifying that figure.

By 1982, after spending several days in El Salvador, I returned to Miami for rest, but the horrific scenes from the war zone kept running through my head. I thought I was losing it. Without warning, I'd feel myself unable to breathe. It was only later that I'd learn that I was experiencing panic attacks. At first, they were isolated episodes, but soon they grew more frequent. Was I losing it? The New York CBS bosses expressed concern.

The heading of the page in my journal for February 8, 1982, was "Black Wednesday."

The perception is that you dialed out six months ago. You're viewed as immature. The producers don't have confidence in you. Here's what I'm telling you. You have three months to show us what you can do to turn it around. You will get a notice that says we have no intention of picking up your [contract] option. Ignore the notice. What's important is the three months. I think you can turn it around.

That assessment came from the CBS News vice president. He

had flown down to Miami to take a look at the Miami Bureau when he pulled me aside and delivered the ultimatum. Everything I feared had happened. I beat myself up. This had come about because I was too sensitive, because I was drawing pastels in my room to blot out the bloodshed, because I was gay. My personal demons were dancing a mambo.

I set about proving to my bosses that I was the correspondent they hired me to be. In my mind I was the problem, not them. Two events were to change their perception of me, at least temporarily. One of them was a ten-minute story on a tribe of Nicaraguan Indians under siege by the Sandinista government. They were called the Miskitos. For five centuries they lived in peace along the Nicaraguan/ Honduran border until, without warning, their settlements were uprooted and their people beaten and shot to death. Flying in single-engine planes through the mountains that divided Nicaragua and Honduras, I interviewed Miskitos on both sides of the border. On the Honduran side, they told stories of being hunted down and killed. On the Nicaraguan side, they sang songs and clapped their hands in orchestrated displays for the camera.

The contrast between wailing mothers on one side and happy Indians on the other was stark. Behind it all was the fear of Sandinista leaders that the Miskitos were being recruited by counterrevolutionary forces supported by the United States (the Contras) to participate in military raids into Nicaragua. I'll never forget the words of one Miskito (whose arm had to be amputated): "They took me and four friends from a room where they were keeping us. They made us bury seven other Miskitos . . . and then took us by the river and began shooting us one by one. They killed three as they tried to escape. That's when they shot me." The story was well-received in New York (wasn't that all that mattered?) and I received congratulatory calls from producers. I felt I was on my way to redemption.

Despite receiving kudos for my reporting, I still was unsure about my future at CBS News. The panic attacks were intensifying.

Clearly, I was depressed. I kept having flashbacks to the firefights in El Salvador. Why was I alive when some of my colleagues had been killed? I was a mess.

I continued covering stories by rote in Nicaragua and El Salvador. By now the so-called Contra War was in full swing as the Nicaraguan army remained on full alert. As I reported for the *Morning News* with Charles Kurault and Diane Sawyer,

> *These troops are members of an elite border-patrol unit in the mountains of Nicaragua—part of the professional 25,000-man army. They are supported by as many as 60,000 militiamen. The Sandinistas claim they are merely defending their country from counter-revolutionaries trained in the camps in the US and based in the mountains of Honduras.*

The fear was a real one. The US was planning Operation Big Pine, war games designed to demonstrate the muscle of military forces in Central America. It was meant to scare the Nicaraguan government into stopping its support of communist insurrection in the area. Operation Big Pine was to be a joint US/Honduran military exercise, the largest of its kind ever held in the region. In other words, it was a big deal! I was dispatched from Miami.

All the networks were staying at the same hotel. No one knew exactly where or when the exercises would begin. Everyone was scrambling to get military personnel arriving at an airport. We were informed by officials that access was off limits. One day passed, then another. Suddenly at the end of the second day I got a call from a distressed desk person in New York.

"NBC got it. Where in the hell were you?" yelled the voice on the other line. I came to learn that other network crews and reporters got shots of the first soldiers arriving for Operation Big Pine. I had not. Why? I can't tell you. I wasn't prepared. I didn't send my crew to camp out at the airport overnight. I tuned out. I'd screwed up. My bureau chief read me the riot act, and soon New York was sending reporters to replace me. My career at CBS News was over.

I learned when I returned to Miami that my contract wouldn't be renewed. I had been axed. I had six months left on it. CBS News told me to use the time to look for another job. In the coming weeks, I descended into my own hell of blaming myself. In the mirror staring back at me was this colossal disappointment. In the mirror, too, I thought I saw Papi shaking his head in disgust. I had spent the last years in a feverish drive to succeed. Such a positive trajectory, so many might think. Until this moment, I had surpassed every hurdle put in my way. But growing up, I felt so inadequate, especially in my father's eyes. My brother was the favored *hijo* (son). I was the son who had no common sense. I was the weak son. I was the soft son. I was the son who couldn't play sports. I was the asthmatic son. I was the sensitive son. I was the gay son. And now I was the son who failed. Maybe I really wasn't good enough. Maybe Papi was right: I wasn't a man either.

It was my fault. I threw pity party after pity party. I stopped eating. I'd lie in bed for hours and stare at the ceiling. Then I'd swing into manic mode. I screamed at myself. I wailed like a lunatic. I paced around my bedroom in circles. I thought how easy it would be to gulp down a bottle of sleeping pills. My mother told me not to worry. But Papi didn't say too much about my firing. I knew he wasn't pleased. Before, he could boast to his friends about his son being on TV. Now I was unemployed. In Papi's silence, I substituted my own self-hate. Instead of one panic attack a month, I was having several a day. My asthma, which I had struggled with since I was three, got worse. The inhalers didn't seem to work anymore. At night, I would have nightmares involving firefights and grenades landing at my feet. I'd wake up in a cold sweat.

Finally, I got the courage to see a therapist. She told me that it appeared I had suffered some sort of emotional breakdown. She sent me to a psychiatrist who prescribed anti-anxiety medication. For six months I visited her twice weekly, and slowly I came to accept what happened but, more importantly, forgive myself for it. She explained that four years of covering civil wars and non-stop travel had affected my judgment and my performance. She said I was to some degree like those soldiers who experienced what psychologists call "shell shock." With time, I learned that leaving CBS was not the end of the world. I started applying for news positions. Six months later I was hired by WOR-TV (Channel 9). I'd be moving to New York to begin a new adventure.

While I was at WOR-TV I began the first critical steps toward reconciling my stint at CBS News. My new bosses welcomed my experience as a network newsman. They encouraged me and I thrived. I won the Edward R. Murrow Award for a news series in which I went undercover as a homeless person. And besides newfound confidence in my reporting, I found a way to work through my tough times as a war correspondent. I wrote a play. It was about a young Cuban-American network correspondent and a crew based in Managua, Nicaragua, during an invasion by the Contras. The reporter wanted to cover more human stories, like refugee camps and agrarian reform, but his bosses in New York wanted "bang bang!" A beautiful graduate of the Columbia School of Journalism arrived with her producer/boyfriend. She carried a camera with her at all times. The Contras attacked without warning. Managua was under siege. The reporter rushed out to cover the story. He was caught in the crossfire and killed. The play ended with the graduate student delivering a report on the *Evening News*, the reporter's body lying behind her. In death, the reporter had become the news. I called the play *Bang Bang Blues*.

In 1988, the play would be chosen as the US entry in Joseph Papp's Public Theater Festival Latino in New York City. In writing about what I'd witnessed, I managed to purge some of the demons. I began to heal. From time to time, the flashbacks of those days would return. From time to time, the nightmares would return as well. But with time I noticed they were fading. Fading, yes, but they would always be there.

It wasn't long before I came to be part of another war. I wouldn't suffer the same fate as the reporter in *Bang Bang Blues* who was shot in a barrage of bullets. Instead, I'd be shot down by a virus. I'd be diagnosed with HIV/AIDS. As I comforted friends who lay dying during those years, I couldn't help but think back to those other wars I'd been through. Then, I couldn't get the sounds of gunfire out of my head. This time the gunfire was silent but just as deadly. With time, new medications would be introduced that slowed down this malevolent virus. I was so grateful. Because of them I wouldn't end up like the reporter at the end of *Bang Bang Blues*. This reporter would rise again.

CHAPTER 8
IMELDA AND ME

When I'm called by God above
Don't have my name inscribed into the stone
Just say:
Here lies love . . . here lies love
Just say:
Here lies love . . . here lies love . . . here lies love.
—*Here Lies Love* by David Byrne and Fatboy Slim

THE CALL CAME IN to the NBC News assignment desk in Burbank. The weary assignment editor picked up the phone, and on the other end of the line he heard a clipped, authoritative voice: "Hello, this is Imelda Marcos. May I speak to Charles Gomez?"

There was a moment of silence. "Hold on." The assignment editor, stunned, shouted out, "It's Imelda Marcos. Where's Gomez?" I had already gone home for the day. When the editor got back on the line, he heard only an incessant dial tone. Imelda had hung up.

At home, I'd already begun packing. I'd received the call Imelda Marcos was trying to reach me. "You'd better get to Hawaii. She may want to talk." For weeks Imelda and Ferdinand had been exiled in a home in Honolulu after being forced from the Philippines. Everyone wanted an interview. A camera crew and a producer were already on the way to the airport. I was about to rush out the door when the phone began ringing. Thinking it might be the assignment desk with more info, I picked up. Instead it was my dear friend Sheila.

"Listen, I can't talk. Imelda just called the assignment desk and I got to get to Hawaii," I said breathlessly.

"You idiot, that was me," Sheila said, laughing.

"What, are you crazy?" I asked incredulously. "You've moved an entire network."

Sheila's unmistakable cackle thundered more loudly than before. It seemed it would never end. "I was kidding," she said finally.

"Well, I can't call them back and tell them my best friend was playing a practical joke. They'll be so pissed. I'm going to Hawaii and I'm going to get that interview one way or another." And with that I slammed down the phone and headed to LAX.

Months earlier in February 1986, Ferdinand and Imelda Marcos had fled the Philippines. Mass protests by the People Power Revolution had put their lives in danger. The US arranged for the infamous couple, charged with bilking the Philippines treasury of billions of dollars, to live in exile in Honolulu, Hawaii. The Marcoses, who had ruled since 1965, were ousted by Corazon Aquino, the widow of one of Ferdinand's fiercest former chief rivals, Benigno (Ninoy) Aquino. Aquino was assassinated on the tarmac of Manila International Airport in 1983 after landing in his home country following three years in exile. In the Philippines some remember the Marcos presidency as a period of economic prosperity. Others recall the lavish parties thrown by Ferdinand's glamorous wife, Imelda. She was known for her frequent state visits abroad, her shopping sprees and her fabled collection of thousands of pairs of shoes. But others remember Ferdinand's rule harshly. He was the tenth president of the Philippines from 1965 to 1986, and his regime was known for its corruption, exorbitance, ruthlessness and brutality.

The country was under martial law from 1972 to 1981. Ferdinand sought to clamp down on civil insurrections and the threat of a communist takeover following a series of bombings in Manila.

Human rights groups cited the abduction, torture and murder of over 10,000 Filipinos who publicly protested Ferdinand's policies. Besides the curfews, there was censorship. Private armies roamed the streets enforcing martial law. Thousands were thrown in jail and tortured.

By March 1986, network crews were scrambling to obtain the first interview of President Marcos in exile. I was dispatched for NBC News. Reporter Terry Drinkwater was sent by CBS News, and Judd Rose reported on the story for ABC News.

By the time my friend Sheila pulled her practical joke, I (as well as the other network reporters) had been making overtures to the Marcoses' staff in hopes of being first to hear their tales of woe about being forced to flee their homeland.

Staying at the beautiful Halekalani Hotel in Honolulu overlooking Diamond Head on a previous trip to Hawaii, I decided to send a dozen yellow roses to Mrs. Marcos as a way to get her to give NBC News the first interview. But I had committed a critical mistake. Later when I finally was able to speak to Mrs. Marcos herself, she told me that "yellow is the color of the jaundiced eye." I was confused by this statement, but I soon learned that yellow was the favorite color of President Corazon Aquino. What a blunder! I apologized profusely. She laughed nervously. "We have opposite points of view," she said softly, turning away from me in the living room of her rented Honolulu home.

So this time I sent gardenias. It seemed to work. Ferdinand Marcos eventually agreed to talk to NBC anchor Tom Brokaw. The Marcos interview with Brokaw wouldn't come until almost two months later. The Marcoses had decided to grant interviews to all the networks within days of each other so as to not show any favoritism.

By this time, I had made at least two trips to Hawaii, hanging out with the other network crews near the driveway of the Marcoses' rented home in the upscale Makiki Heights district. By now I had learned not to send yellow roses to Mrs. Marcos. On one occasion, I sent several fragrant roses. That prompted Mrs. Marcos to send a note to the hotel thanking me for the "kind gesture for a wounded soul."

The day of Tom Brokaw's interview with Ferdinand Marcos was a hot one in Honolulu. Fluffy clouds danced in an azure sky. A light breeze blew in off the Pacific, rustling the palms that swayed like green swings. The pink and violet bougainvilleas were in full bloom on the hedges outside the Marcos home. They gave off a sweet perfume one could smell from dozens of feet away. And if one breathed in deeply, gardenias seemed to be blooming close by as well. The unmistakable scent reminded me of the gardenia bushes my mother so proudly cultivated in the front yard of our Hialeah home. My daydreaming was interrupted by the sounds of cables being pulled across the backyard. We had gathered two hours before the scheduled interview so that the news crew could set up with the proper lights and necessary sound equipment. I was jolted by an apparition.

Mrs. Marcos strode toward us in a purple dress, its sleeves slightly puffed in the style of ornamental Philippine gowns called *ternos*. Her luxurious black hair was pinned back but swept up like a wave above her forehead, giving her a regal air. Although close to sixty by this time, her face was smooth like a plate. There were no wrinkles to mar the beatific visage. She seemed to be perpetually smiling, as if laughing at a private joke whispered to her by a confidant just out of view.

For a woman lauded for her fabled shoe collection, I noticed she was wearing only a modest pair of black patent leather small-heeled pumps. Somehow, I had expected rhinestones. By this time, news reports had trumpeted her reputed collection of some 3,000 pairs, a testament (one presumed) to her vanity and extravagance. And, indeed, news videos had shown the array of shoes lined up in neat little rows in their own spacious mini-suites within the marbled walls of the opulent Malacañang Palace, the official presidential residence in Manila, Philippines.

In the background, we spotted Ferdinand Marcos as he paced back and forth like a nervous soldier. He was wearing a dark three-piece navy suit. His eyes appeared watery, as if he had been crying.

But later I thought I heard him say the word "allergy" to an aide as he touched his brow.

Out of respect, I had dressed up for the interview even though I wasn't conducting it. I wore a double-breasted blue blazer and a wide burgundy-and-silver tie. I wore my long black hair over my ears, and in the back it flipped just a bit, prompting Marcos to smile and joke with Imelda, "Doesn't he remind you of German Moreno?" Moreno, I came to learn, was a beloved Spanish-Filipino television host, actor and comedian during the eighties, also known as "Kuya Germs" or the "Master Showman." A flamboyant showman known to dress in blue satin dress shirts, he founded the Philippines Walk of Fame in Quezon City, modeled after the Hollywood Walk of Fame.

"Oh yes," Imelda laughed. "He dyed his hair black, you know. You don't dye your hair, do you?" She giggled and tilted her head like a schoolgirl. As I looked at Imelda on that day, I found it hard to believe that this girlish woman was the ruthless person that had been portrayed in the press. Mrs. Marcos had been accused of plundering the Philippine economy, of being a clever and conniving kleptocrat. But on this afternoon, that Imelda was not in the room. Instead, here she was a self-effacing, charming and flirtatious hostess.

As the time of the interview neared, Imelda fussed around the house. At one point she attached a gardenia to a wooden religious statue who appeared to be the Christ child wearing a crown. She walked back my way, smiling, and suddenly began to engage in small talk.

"On one of the interviews, somebody banged the glass and there was a big noise," she said in a lilting voice. "Just as I was entering, they were asking a question about Mrs. Marcos's shoes. I went inside and there was a slam of the door. It was really the wind. Pop! And they said, 'Oh, Mrs. Marcos is angry because they are talking about the shoes,'" she continued, laughing.

At that point, my eyes went down to the patent leather pumps. "And you're wearing some very nice ones today," I offered. Her eyes lit up. It was as if her closest gay confidant had paid her a supreme compliment. She beamed like a teenager.

Looking down, she began wiggling her shoes in different directions as if to show them off to an admirer. "Oh, they are old," she said, tittering. "They're a little changed from how they were." Imelda had been caught off guard, and she seemed to relish the attention to her appearance. As the interview was about to start, she made a surprising unprompted disclosure. Perhaps it was something she had been thinking about all morning. And now that the ice had been broken, Imelda seemed eager to share a confidence.

"You know, the only thing I want to do is go back to the Philippines, of course," she said. And then she paused for dramatic effect. She blinked several times and her smile suddenly turned into the narrowest of frowns. Before she spoke, she opened her eyes widely as if she were uttering a truth she wanted to be heard loudly and clearly. "I'll cling to that soil. I'll cling to that land like a leech."

Little did I realize how prophetic Imelda's words would be. Three years later her husband would die in exile. And nearly six years after fleeing the Philippines in disgrace, Imelda Marcos would once again set foot on Philippine soil. She would eventually be elected a congresswoman of Leyte. And then she would run again, representing the second district of Ilocos Norte. And in May 2016, she would be reelected again for her third and final term.

But for now, Imelda, known by her admirers as "the Iron Butterfly," was here to cheer on her husband. She stood watching from the sidelines as he sat in a large cushy chair. She was fidgety, grabbing her dress between the fingers of her right hand as the interview began. Tom Brokaw led into his report: "He blames his loss of power on the Americans who flew him out of the country, and now he claims the new government has taken over his personal property."

Marcos began to speak, first softly, gaining force as he continued: "If I had not left Malacañang and been brought back to the US against my will, we would still be in control," Marcos said. "I had superior forces, dedicated men, when I was taken out of Malacañang, but that's neither here nor there. It doesn't matter anymore."

At this point, Brokaw mentioned his wife, though clearly uncomfortable bringing Mrs. Marcos into the fray. As he said her name, Mrs. Marcos gently bit her lip. "Can you tell us about Mrs. Marcos? She had friends all around the world wherever she traveled as she traveled in very high social circles. Has she been hearing from her friends?" As he asked the question, Mrs. Marcos seemed to want to smile and answer the question for herself. But she stood quietly and let her husband answer for her.

"Is that anything wrong?" Marcos asked defiantly. "She was First Lady of the Philippines. She symbolizes the women of our country. It's the only Christian nation in Asia." Marcos paused, appearing to catch his breath. "Like those shoes. Most of the shoes were donated and yet she's claimed to be a very extravagant housewife. In actuality, some of her shoes have been stolen by some members of the Cory [Corazon Aquino] group. And I understand also they are using our personal cars. Even Madame Cory was using my bulletproof ranger or the bulletproof car of my son."

The interview grew tense when Brokaw suggested that Marcos and his closest friends plundered the Philippines and took over whole industries before hightailing it to Hawaii.

"Oh, come on," Marcos countered. "Tom, you know very well that this is nothing but pure black propaganda."

The exchange clearly troubled Mrs. Marcos as well. As her husband was grilled she said softly, "You know that in that kind of government we have, there is no law. There is no constitution. There are no courts or judges. They can falsify. They can make up all kinds of evidence. I'd have no chance. So be it."

Brokaw continued to pressure President Marcos. "Don't you see the dilemma of reporters who are trying to find out the truth? It is your word against receipts, sworn testimony, against evidence from the palace, 3,000 pairs of shoes, luxurious homes everywhere and

$3 billion worth of property," Brokaw said. Marcos shook his head. "And you have no documents," Brokaw continued. "It's your word against all of that."

Marcos challenged lawyers to come up with documents in court proving he had all that money. "Beyond that, I have nothing more to say about those cases," he said.

Following the interview, Ferdinand and Imelda strolled the beautifully manicured grounds of their rented home. We took photographs of them as they pointed out toward the sea. And then Mrs. Marcos walked over to me and began to chat. I'm not sure what prompted her to want to speak, but I think Brokaw's interview with her husband had unnerved her and she wanted to get some things off her chest. She told me she left the Philippines wearing only one dress. She explained that the one she was wearing that day had been sent to her by her dry cleaner in the Philippines.

As for her husband's joking reference to opening a shoe shop she said, "Yes, Imelda's Shoes. Since my country is one of the biggest exporters of shoes, I would promote Philippine shoes." She then started to laugh—not a loud guffaw, but trilling laughter, the laughter perhaps of a young girl wanting to amuse her parents or adult company. "Also lingerie. We have a franchise on the biggest signature lingerie in the world." And then I asked Mrs. Marcos if she wanted to meet Mrs. Aquino. She paused for a moment before answering. "I would not have the guts, the courage to do what she did to get her job. It takes a lot of nerve and verve to do such a thing."

Fast-Forward, October 20, 2014

One of my best pals, Jorge Horan, and I sat transfixed watching an actress play Imelda Marcos at the Public Theater on Lafayette Street in New York City. Her name was Ruthie Ann Miles and she was the headliner in this electrifying interactive theatrical show called *Here Lies Love*. It was written by David Byrne and Fat Boy Slim, and it deconstructed the life journey of Imelda Marcos. As I watched Ms. Miles (she had an uncanny resemblance to the real Mrs. Marcos) I was struck by the similarities between this character who was playing Imelda and the flesh-and-blood persona I had once met, the real Imelda. Suddenly it all made sense. We watched as this young Imelda sang of her early years:

> *When I was a young girl in Leyte*
> *My dresses were hand-me-downs and scraps*
> *I'd see the people smile, when I would sing for them*
> *How happy they all seemed—when I would dance.*
> *We lived a stone's throw from the palace*
> *A simple country girl who had a dream*
> *The ladies passing by, a better class than I*
> *How much it meant to me to be like these.*

I understood now what was behind Imelda's meteoric rise to power and also her descent to disgrace. Before I met Imelda, she was only an image. She was a party girl dancing with a too-tanned George Hamilton or a perfectly coiffed First Lady attending a White House state dinner. By the time she arrived in Hawaii and I finally met her, the sometimes corrupt and bloody path she and her husband forged would forever change the history of the Philippines. Like Eva Peron in Argentina, Imelda Marcos had propelled herself into a larger-than-life position known as much for her excesses as her so-called love of beauty. And here was Ms. Miles singing before a scrim simulating a Manila rainfall, reminding us that behind the image of the extravagant dragon lady with the multitude of shoes was also a gentle girl who believed in much simpler truths:

> *The most important things are love and beauty*
> *It doesn't matter if you're rich or poor*

To prosper and to fly, a basic human right
The feeling in your heart that you're secure.

But beauty and human rights weren't always pervasive in the Philippines of Imelda and Ferdinand Marcos. As a young reporter, I remembered vividly the 1983 news video of Marcos rival Ninoy Aquino returning to the Philippines after years in exile. Sitting in his plane as it was about to land, Aquino uttered a fateful prophecy: "My feeling is we all have to die sometime. If it is my fate to die by an assassin's bullets, so be it. But I cannot be petrified by inaction or fear of assassination." Moments later we hear a series of shots as Aquino is executed walking across the tarmac. The image of his bloody, lifeless body shocked television news audiences around the world. Needless to say, it shocked me as well.

The subsequent outrage against the Marcoses fueled the unrest that would eventually force their departure. Investigations never uncovered who was responsible for the assassination of Ninoy Aquino.

As I sat watching *Here Lies Love*, there was a fictionalized scene where Imelda comforted Aquino in jail before he left for exile in the United States. She sang to a statue of the Christ child, very much like the statue I saw Imelda attaching a gardenia to in Honolulu.

"Santo Nino, Santo Nino, take good care of him," she sang. And she told Aquino, "Ninoy, you were my first love. But you said I was too tall. The heart gets stronger and grows colder, for the Rose of Tacloban." And then, soothing his brow, Ms. Miles sang: "You'll be safer in America. There are those who would see you dead." And as I watched I was transported back to that hot afternoon in Hawaii as Mrs. Marcos spoke of the courage of Corazon Aquino. And I wondered if she was also thinking of the courage Benigno Aquino had shown in those frantic moments before a gunman loyal to her husband's regime executed her one-time love on the hot asphalt of an airport tarmac.

Rewind, December 1986

It had been many months since reporters caught a glimpse of Ferdinand and Imelda Marcos in Honolulu. They had gone into seclusion after moving to yet another home on a hilltop overlooking Diamond Head. On the evening of December 9, Tom Brokaw once again reported on the latest developments from the Philippines. The government of Corazon Aquino had worked out a sixty-day cease-fire. She had made it one of her top goals when she replaced Marcos ten months earlier. Brokaw also reported that Marcos had won somewhat of a legal victory in the US. A federal judge in Los Angeles ruled Marcos acted properly when he took the fifth amendment almost 200 times during questioning in an Aquino lawsuit aimed at recovering the Marcoses' fortune.

But this time Brokaw wouldn't interview Ferdinand and Imelda. This time the task would fall to me. That impromptu trip I had made to Hawaii months before as well as sending the bouquets of flowers had finally paid off. I got the coveted sit-down interview with Ferdinand and Imelda. I called my mother the night before I was scheduled to interview them. Mami knew I was in Hawaii, a paradise that she loved. My mother had visited Honolulu a few times with friends from a church group, always bringing back gorgeous orchids she would plant in her backyard.

"Mami, I'm going to be talking to Mrs. Marcos," I told her.

"Oh, that is wonderful, Charlito. Don't forget to show *los zapatos*," she said, laughing. Even my Cuban mother knew about Imelda's famous shoes.

Certainly Mami didn't approve of the Marcoses' corrupt regime. She was oblivious to a report by the Presidential Commission on Good Government that Ferdinand and Imelda Marcos followed a decadent lifestyle. They were accused of embezzling and absconding with billions of dollars from the Philippines between 1965 and 1986.

My mother was enamored with Mrs. Marcos's glamour, and on more than one occasion she told me she'd love to try on a pair of Imelda's shoes. "I bet we wear the same size," she said with a wink.

My report started by showing the Marcoses' opulent Honolulu retreat in exile. Its rent was being paid by Marcos loyalists in the United States. I explained that Marcos and his wife had kept largely out of view. In the last months, Marcos had spent hours talking to his lawyers about the dozens of lawsuits accusing him of stealing billions from his homeland. I also reported that Marcos had just finished writing a book about his time in exile.

Ferdinand Marcos escorted me into a living area where he sat on a sofa. I asked him about recent demonstrations in the Philippines by his supporters and whether he was encouraging them to protest.

"I told them point blank, I do not agree with any effort to destabilize the Aquino government," Marcos told me. "Between Cory Aquino succeeding and the communists taking over, I'd rather have Cory Aquino, and I have tried to help."

I asked Marcos whether he was fully comfortable in the United States.

"I'm not," he said emphatically. "No, I'd rather be in the Philippines. I don't want to go to any other country than the Philippines. Why, I feel like a caged animal. I have lived a very active life."

And then I asked Marcos: "If Aquino allows you to return to power but not as a statesman, would you return?"

Marcos paused before answering. "On a promise I would not try to destabilize the government, I would probably accept it," he said.

My news report went on to describe how lavishly the couple lived. "They're surrounded by fine furnishings, good food and a household of servants including one who swats the flies away. Despite the comforts, the loss of power, prestige and status have had a profound impact on the couple." Producer Art Lord and I sat at a huge table covered with a decorative tablecloth. The room smelled of orchid plants and the faintest hint of lavender. My mother would be in heaven being so close to dozens of orchids. Suddenly Marcos spoke: "It's not just a sense of loss. It's a sense of death. Complete extinction," he said, his eyes misting. "This is what I feel and sometimes she feels it too."

At this point the camera panned to show Mrs. Marcos (dressed resplendently in red) seated to my right. She gestured emphatically. Her voice trembled as she spoke: "This is worse than death because you're even deprived of basic human rights. Of country, of citizenship, of freedom and honor," she said. "If this is life, I'd rather die anytime. I'm going to go back even if I have to face a battery of bullets." In truth, Imelda never faced a firing squad or a battery of bullets. She was welcomed back warmly to the Philippines by loyalists six years after being forced to flee.

Fast-Forward, November 4, 1991, *New York Times*

Nearly six years after fleeing in disgrace with crates of gold and pesos, Imelda Marcos set foot on Philippine soil again to face court charges of graft and tax evasion, and perhaps to run for president. She was greeted here with tight security as she arrived with all the flamboyance that had made her a symbol of the excesses of her husband, the late President Ferdinand E. Marcos.

Eventually Mrs. Marcos would succeed in returning the body of her husband to the land where he ruled for twenty years. And she would rule as a congresswoman, once again basking in the limelight she had so adored when her husband was one of the most powerful rulers in Asia.

In 1988, I returned to New York to once again work as a news reporter for WWOR-TV. Imelda Marcos's celebrated shoe and clothing collections were auctioned at New York's Christie's on February 11, 1988. The auction drew large crowds but not necessarily high bids. The furnishings and shoes were from a luxury apartment once owned by the Marcoses in the Olympic Towers on Fifth Avenue.

The proceeds were used to finance land reform in the Philippines.

According to the UPI, four pairs of shoes were purchased by the curator of a museum in Nova Scotia. Imelda's shoes went for bargain prices at $66, $77, $88 and $90, respectively.

The UPI went on to report that "a fifth pair, a silver-gold rhinestone-tipped pump, was purchased by a New York City man who asked to remain unidentified. The man told the auctioneer he wanted the shoes for his mother." That unidentified man was me. I had asked Channel 9 to cover the auction for the evening news broadcast. But what I never told my bosses is that in the middle of the auction fever, I had raised a paddle and impulsively purchased a pair of Imelda's shoes myself.

Two months later, my mother and I attended a glittery Cuban wedding in Miami. It was the kind of wedding where the female guests wore foxtail stoles in the middle of summer and sported gaudy dresses of gold lamé and animal prints. And it was the kind of wedding where many women wore twinkling chandelier-type earrings that cascaded to their shoulders. As my mother and I strolled down the aisle to what sounded like a celestial choir of angels, I noticed the guests in their church pews ever so slowly cast downward glances. For there on my mother's feet were the sparkling gold-and-silver rhinestone heels once worn by the First Lady of the Philippines Imelda Marcos.

My mother, who always had a flair for the dramatic, relished the moment. The shoes fit her perfectly. It was her Cuban Cinderella moment. I could not know then that many years later I would hear a young woman playing Imelda Marcos sing that "the most important things are love and beauty. It doesn't matter if you're rich or poor. To prosper and to fly, a basic human right, the feeling in your heart that you're secure." At that moment my mother was secure in her beauty. A Philippine woman had given a Cuban woman a gift.

Whatever her excesses, Imelda Marcos had managed to bring my mom a moment of unexpected joy. Somehow, I felt Mrs. Marcos would approve. History had come full circle. So, on that day, light from the church's stained-glass windows illuminated my mother as she walked slowly down the aisle to her seat. She was the center of attention. And even the most exquisite stained glass could not compete with the light that twinkled that afternoon from a pair of shoes that once belonged to an "Iron Butterfly" from a place far, far away.

Fast-Forward, November 9, 2019, *New York Post*

The Marcos family is poised to take aim at the presidency once again in the land where Ferdinand and Imelda imposed 20 years of autocratic rule—and looted the treasury to fuel their legendary extravagance.

Their hopes ride on an affable 62-year-old (Ferdinand Romualdez Marcos, Jr.) who has waged a three-year court battle to be declared the nation's rightful vice president.

CHAPTER 9
HEART ATTACK

My heart will never break, but it will stop beating.
—Anthony T. Hincks, Author

THE SURGEON SLICED OPEN my chest. He held my heart in his hands.

I had suffered a major heart attack. I came to the hospital expecting to have a stent placed in my heart. By the time it was over, I had undergone quadruple bypass open heart surgery. I was now in the company of Bill Clinton, David Letterman and Regis Philbin. They all underwent coronary bypass surgery.

Doctors put me in a medically induced coma for four days. At one point the chief surgeon told my brother that it might be a good idea to say his goodbyes. My heart was in danger of rupturing. My surgeon used the word "exploding." As the real-life drama played out in intensive care, my closest social media friends took to their Facebook newsfeeds and timelines. They spread the word. They notified their friends and followers. Soon there was an outpouring of genuine concern, prayers and affirmations multiplied in post after post. It was like receiving a collective virtual embrace. Strangers who remembered me from my days in television news sent positive "vibrations" my way.

As I lay intubated in a coma, a machine doing the breathing for me, my friends provided Facebook with frequent and sometimes breathless updates. My brother, Willie, said my face looked ashen. A former cop, he told me later that he had only seen that gray color on the faces of those close to death. He flew in from Weston, Florida, to be at my side. And as I walked the fine line between life and death, I later learned, Catholic Masses were being held for my recovery.

How did I arrive at this moment? It all started as I rode in a car with friends to Fire Island. I was suddenly hit with what I thought was a severe case of heartburn. A friend suggested I pop some Tums. But Tums wouldn't take care of what I had. The pain wouldn't go away. Besides Tums, I took aspirin after aspirin. Still no relief. When I arrived at our Fire Island home, my housemates insisted I join them in the pool. So, despite my condition, I dove into the cool waters. But that didn't help either. Something was wrong, dangerously wrong.

Feeling feverish and listless, I took the first ferry back to the city. I was rushing home because I had signed up to participate in the annual AIDS Walk New York. I had raised $1,500 for the Keep a Child Alive Foundation and the GMHC (Gay Men's Health Crisis). I didn't want to disappoint the many friends who had supported me by making pledges. Feeling fatigued when I got home, I gulped down aspirin and some over-the-counter flu remedies. By the next morning I felt a little better, and off I went to the 6.2-mile walk. I was short of breath, but I attributed that to my chronic asthma. I crossed the finish line huffing and puffing.

"Are you sure you're alright?" a friend asked.

"Absolutely," I replied. The worst was yet to come.

The next night I attended a play with friend Chita Rivera, but I could barely breathe. Every time I tried, it felt like someone was hammering my chest. After the show, I said to Chita, "Do you mind if we don't have dinner? I feel I'm coming down with something." She took my hand and said, "Of course. Feel better." She gave me a hug and I raced home.

When I got there I felt worse. I started popping aspirin. Still no relief. My hands were clammy and I felt a dull pain near my heart.

I felt as if I were suffocating. I hopped into a cab straight to St. Luke's Roosevelt Hospital. Tests concluded I had indeed suffered a massive heart attack. Three days later a cardiac surgeon appeared at my bedside. He looked just like Robert Young in the TV show *Marcus Welby, M.D.* The surgeon explained that an angiogram (a test that uses X-rays to take pictures of blood vessels) showed that I had suffered severe heart damage. I'd need emergency open heart bypass surgery. And it had to be done the next morning. Was I hearing right? I had expected a stent or two to be placed in my arteries, not to be opened up like a can of sardines. He said the operation would involve taking a healthy blood vessel from another part of my body and using it to bypass the blocked arteries.

The doctor left the room and suddenly I started bawling like a baby. One of my dearest friends, Matthew, had been waiting just outside. When he rushed in and saw the state I was in, he threw his arms around me and reassured me that everything would be all right.

The next day I emerged from the six-hour surgery and was wheeled down a long, winding hallway. I heard a strange sound like someone gently strumming their fingers over a xylophone. It turned out to be the sounds from the machines I was hooked up to keep me alive. I could make out tiny twinkling lights above me like stars in the night sky. I felt at that moment that I hadn't survived. Was I witnessing my own death?

"I didn't make it," I said to myself. "No, it can't be. I have too much left to do." I had to finish my book. I had to ask the man I loved (Matthew) to marry me. I had to see Mami and Papi one more time. I had to tell my father how much I loved him and that I hoped he didn't feel ashamed that I was gay and living with AIDS.

The lights above me kept twinkling like a hospital version of the Milky Way. And I still heard the xylophone in my mind. I closed my eyes and a tender scene played out. I saw Papi holding Mami's withered hand as she watched cartoons on TV. I saw Papi prop up my mother's favorite stuffed monkey toy on a pillow. He had cared for his beloved Angelina all these years as Alzheimer's ravaged her, leaving her a shell of the beautiful woman she once was. She could barely speak now except for gibberish punctuated by words in Spanish. It was a language Papi seemed to understand. And together they both spoke it, a language of love. Dear God, I prayed to live to see them again. I wanted to live so that one day I could find a love like theirs.

Doctors say that people placed in medically induced comas can still hear. Through half-shut eyes, I saw my brother, Willie. He put his face next to mine.

"Charlie, it's going to be alright. Joy [my sister-in-law] and Summer [my niece] send you their love. I am here now. It's alright. You can come back to us," he said. With those words, a calm came over me. If my brother was here whispering in my ear, perhaps I was alive after all. Instead of moving through a tunnel of darkness, I felt I was running toward a light. I fell into a sleep, a long deep sleep.

As I lay in a coma, Willie walked over to the nurse's station to get more information on my condition. He was accompanied by Matthew and another friend, Daniel. The surgeon, still in scrubs, overheard them talking. Walking over, the surgeon began to speak. It was like a monologue delivered by a character in a one-man show:

I operated on your brother. I held his heart in my hands. Did you know that your brother had a heart attack in 2003? It was a major heart attack that caused a lot of irreversible damage. Apparently, they treated it medically and just sent him on home. When he had his most recent heart attack, the heart sustained even more damage. He took Tums for something he should have known was a heart attack. Instead of seeking medical attention, he walked 6.2 miles in a walkathon. He waited until the next day before coming to the hospital. We did a quadruple bypass on his heart. Then, I discovered the walls of your brother's heart between the areas that had been

*damaged were paper thin. Your brother's heart could explode.
I had to put a patch over it to bolster it. The rupture could
be a few minutes from now. It could be a few hours. So, you
should go in there and say your goodbyes.*

My brother, Matthew and Daniel couldn't believe what they were
hearing. Daniel stood stone-faced because he was the friend who
suggested I take antacids to relieve my chest pains. Then the doctor
offered a ray of hope. "Every twenty-four hours without an incident
means that the heart is trying to heal. Mr. Gomez could still make it."
My brother thanked him and went to call his wife and my father to
tell them the news.

The next morning, Matthew posted developments on
Facebook. "[We] are posting to inform you that Chuck's situation is
heartbreaking and the next forty-eight hours are critical. Please take
a moment now to say a prayer and send positive energy. Hold him in
your thoughts like a wounded dove that needs your love."

The reaction was overwhelming. Hundreds of people, some I
didn't even know, began offering prayers and healing energy. Friends
in turn shared the postings. My heart attack had gone viral. "Prayers,
prayers, prayers, prayers," wrote Virginia Hogan Spitzer. "Prayers
from the West Coast," wrote Tommy Hickey from Arizona. From
Caracas, Venezuela, to Rome, Italy, Facebook friends sent their
messages of hope. "Bombard Chuck's spirits with prayers and positive
thoughts," wrote Sheila Stainback. One post by Matthew two days
after the surgery elicited dozens of responses, positive affirmations
of hope. My friend, Shelley Ross, urged her followers to increase the
money donated for my AIDS Walk above the $1,500 mark. Michele
Gillen, a longtime friend and journalist from Miami, wrote in the
comments section, "Just spoke with him before the [AIDS] Walk. I
called to tell him how proud I was and impressed with his amazing
[blogs] for *The Huffington Post*. At the end of the day he is a journalist
and those words he shared are his legacy."

As I lay in that coma flooded by so many positive thoughts and prayers, it was almost like I could feel their power. They gave me strength. And indeed, if one believes God or a higher power can answer our prayers, then Facebook's timeline had become my lifeline. But still my brother and friends worried that I might not make it. Outside my room, Matthew and Daniel fought back tears, but my friend Sheila wouldn't have it.

"I refuse to accept that Chuck might die," she said. "Let's believe he'll come out of this." Four days after I was placed in a medically induced coma, I began to blink. "Come back to us," my brother had whispered into my ear right after the surgery. And I did. Sheila got it right.

The road to recovery wasn't easy. No one told me that when I "came back" I'd imagine seeing huge ants crawl across the floor and believe one of my nurses was a voodoo priestess chanting to spirits. I had ICU psychosis, a condition in which hallucinations were common. They were caused by the week of heavy sedation. One time I imagined the cleaning lady was about to attack me with her broom. Another time I told Sheila that a Latino nurse was accusing me of coming on to him sexually and threatening to alert the media. "We won't let that happen," was Sheila's calm reply. It was better than hearing "You're nuts!" My brother, Matthew and Daniel laughed up a storm after hearing about my delusions. Luckily my psychosis only lasted a few days.

After two weeks, I was sitting up, eating in bed and learning to walk without a cane. A skilled team of physical and occupational therapists helped me with my agility and endurance. Slowly, I got better. The ashen-faced patient doctors had once given twenty-four hours to live was finally on the mend. Longtime friends came to visit. My spirits were lifted. And Michele was soon sitting next to me on my hospital bed. She looked me in the eye and smiled.

"Chuck, you must write about your life-and-death experience," she said. With that, she pushed a pad into my lap. I began to write.

As she stood next to me encouraging me, with each sentence I wrote I felt stronger. Indeed, I felt reborn.

I was learning that recovery was a long and tedious process. Before the heart attack I was a muscular 185-pound man. Now I had slipped to below 150 pounds, and in photographs taken in the hospital I appeared gaunt and hollow-eyed. My mind told me that it was time to return to the gym and to my muscled glory days. In reality, I could barely walk without straining to breathe. The fingers of my left hand were numb, and I couldn't pick up simple objects. I was transferred to the physical therapy wing. Every day, I worked with an occupational therapist. I relearned how to climb stairs without getting winded by taking deep breaths. "Breathe in as deep as you can," my therapist urged. But every time I tried, it hurt. It was explained to me that after heart surgery, breathing and coughing could be painful. But coughing was necessary to expel mucus. I was given a hand-held device to encourage deep breathing. It measured the volume of air I could hold as I took deep breaths through the device.

With my breathing under control, of course I turned to my appearance. Bypass surgery had taken its toll, and the face that looked back at me in the mirror scared me. I called my longtime friend and hairstylist Susie Lew. "My hair is all white and long and I look like a werewolf," I told her in a panic. Susie showed up in my hospital room with a robe, scissors and a comb. She laughed uproariously as she entered.

"Time to make Chuckie-Poo beautiful again," she exclaimed in a heavy Brooklyn accent. And she took out the dye and began her magic. I told Daniel to run to the drug store and get a brush and more combs. I ordered my brother to close the door.

"I don't want the nurses to think I'm gay," I said.

"You've got a plastic hairnet on your head, your hair is covered with shoe polish, you're wearing a smock and you're worried that they might figure out you're gay?" he responded. Susie and my brother laughed so hard that nurses walking by stopped in their tracks to stare at the makeshift salon. "Ooooh Lordy," one nurse said. "So that's how it is? We've never seen that here before," said the other. When Susie finished her ministrations, the werewolf was no longer a beast but a beauty (well, if not a beauty, not an old guy with white hair and overgrown salt-and-pepper eyebrows).

I invited my friends to visit. Sheila showed up with a colorful bouquet of flowers. And on the same day, Chita and her assistant Rosie showed up as well. Laughter filled the room.

"I thought he looked bad that night," Chita exclaimed.

"You mean, like someone who was having a heart attack?" Sheila asked.

"Exactly," Chita replied. The famous Sheila cackle echoed through the room. It was the same laugh I heard so many years ago in the first newsroom where we worked together. It was great to laugh about life again.

Chita sat on my hospital bed and pulled something from her pocket. It was a small brown cloth stamp attached to a brown string, like a necklace. "This is a scapular of Our Lady of Mount Carmel," she said, putting it around my neck. "Wear this, Chuck, and you'll be protected always." I was overcome. I hugged her tightly and thanked her.

After about ten days, I was finally going home. It had been almost six weeks. It was not only the beginning of a struggle to recover; it was the beginning of trying to understand what brought me to the brink of death.

When I left WNBC in 1998, I was consumed with self-loathing. The stigma surrounding HIV hadn't disappeared. So I set about changing my outward appearance. I believed that if I presented an image of a robust, muscled man, no one would suspect I had HIV/AIDS. Even within the gay community, there were those who distanced themselves. There were so many times I'd disclose my status only to be rejected. The fear was real. Some gays referred to those of us with HIV/AIDS as "Disability Queens." I wanted to defy them. And so, I overcompensated. I hired a series of trainers and went to work changing my body. The gym was my church, and I worshiped at the altar of physical perfection. Within a year the difference was noticeable. My shoulders broadened and my biceps (or "guns") had grown considerably. When I walked down the street, I was no longer the emaciated AIDS victim. I had turned my midlife crisis around. But still I wanted more.

I joined a muscle gym in Chelsea that's now out of business. It was *the* gay bodybuilding mecca. The gays and "Muscle Marys" (as they were derisively called) paraded past the weight machines in a daily display admiring their reflections in the floor-to-ceiling mirrors. Like Narcissus staring into a pond, they stared into the glass lovingly. There was a saying at the gym: "If you don't weigh at least 200 pounds of solid muscle, you should leave!" At 5'7" and 155 pounds, I hardly met that ideal. But slowly, as I began to gain more weight and stepped up my nutrition, I transformed. But I knew that to reach the next plateau, I needed to step up my game. And stepping up meant taking steroids. Many men with HIV/AIDS had low testosterone levels. So it wasn't unusual for doctors to prescribe "test" to correct the imbalance. But it was never enough. That's when I got into trouble.

You didn't have to be a genius to figure out who was selling underground steroids. You could hear the whispers on the workout floor and see the "deals" going down in the locker room. One guy who trained Mr. Olympia was the favorite go-to dealer. He was a balding, short man with Popeye-like muscles who spoke with a heavy Spanish accent. Soon I was supplementing my regular testosterone intake with at least two other steroids (Deca Durabolin and Primabolin). A nurse taught me how to inject the combination of steroids (to burn fat and maintain muscle tissue) right into my butt. Over time steroids increased blood pressure and could lead to heart disease. When my doctor raised concern over my blood pressure numbers, I kept my mouth shut.

In 2003 during a routine electrocardiogram, my doctor detected something unusual. He said that I had suffered some kind of heart episode. He sent me to a cardiologist, who confirmed I had arterial stenosis. Stenosis is the constriction of an artery. Stents and bypass surgery are common treatments. But my cardiologist at that time said nothing about stents. He wanted me to go the non-invasive route. And so, I took the heart pills he prescribed. At the same time, I continued sneaking in my steroid cycles. A cycle is the period of actual steroid use. By 2012 when I had my second heart attack, I had sustained severe and irreversible damage. My cardiologist told me there was no way of knowing if taking steroids caused my second heart attack. But certainly it couldn't have helped.

Although I injected steroids so no one would think I had HIV, there was another reason. I thought my muscular appearance was a way of attracting men. I had become a victim of gay vanity. And indeed, I would show off whenever I could. At my peak, I weighed over 185 pounds. On the beach on Fire Island I reveled in posing like a modern-day Charles Atlas. I showed off the obligatory six-pack wearing a tight white Speedo. But by 2012 that image had disintegrated. The heart attack deflated me. I had lost more than twenty-five pounds, and my muscles were history. In the hospital my brother made me promise to never take steroids again. I never touched a steroid after that. And then my brother said that in order for me to get better, my roommate had to go.

B. and I had lived together almost twenty years. He held me in his arms when I tested HIV positive. But matters had deteriorated between us. We went from companions to good friends to barely speaking. His drug addiction got worse, and because of it, he lost a string of jobs. I too had turned to drugs after learning of my AIDS diagnosis. But I turned things around. With B. it was another story. He held on to a part-time job, but just barely. He hadn't paid rent for years. I asked him to leave many times, but he always came up with an excuse. So, while I recuperated, my brother told B. that he had a week to pack his stuff and get out. B. agreed.

Rewind, April 2011—Journal Entry

I got to St. Vincent's Hospital and made my way to B.'s cubicle in Intensive Care. I ran to his bed. I looked into that beautiful face. He was sweating a lot. I caressed his left arm and gently whispered, "Sweetie, can you hear me?" His eyes popped open.

"Chuckie, what's going on? Where am I?" I told him that he was in Intensive Care. I said that it looked like he might have overdosed in the bathhouse. "Oh no, how embarrassing. We've got to get out of here."

Fast-Forward, June 2012

B.'s clutter had turned our apartment into a flop-house. Garbage bags were filled with drug paraphernalia, bondage gear and baggies filled with crystal-meth. I threatened to throw it all away. But instead of confronting him, I withdrew. I gave him a half-hearted ultimatum to leave the apartment. At the last minute I always caved in to his pleas to stay.

The walls hadn't been painted in almost ten years. The apartment had the feel of a cave. With him gone, my brother and friends decided to clear the apartment of the trash, repaint and redecorate.

Back at the hospital before I was released, I still thought of B. I remembered the good times, but the bad times overshadowed them.

Rewind, September 2011—Journal Entry

When I woke up and walked into the living room, I was greeted by a drug scene. Several candles were lit and placed on our mirrored coffee table. Next to the burning candles were two little vials filled with liquid. Glass pipes littered the floor. Tiny plastic bags filled with white powder were all over the table. A young man who looked like he could be Latino was passed out in his underwear on the sofa. New Age music played on the stereo. As for B., he was sitting on the floor naked, his back propped up against the sofa, staring into space. I was furious.

"B.," I shouted. No answer. Finally, I heard a deep gurgling as he suddenly began to scream. "Aaaaaarh!" Then louder: "Aaaaaarh." And then, for what seemed like an eternity, he began screaming gibberish. I was so scared. B. was in the throes of an apparent overdose.

Fast-Forward, June 2012

When I got home after almost five weeks in the hospital, I walked into an apartment I didn't recognize. It was like an episode of a TV show that sends a family on vacation while interior decorators magically conduct a makeover. The dreary-colored walls now glowed in beautiful shades of lime and burnt orange. All the furniture except a few chairs and a blue chaise lounge was gone. My brother and his "team" had come up with a dream apartment.

My recovery was slow. I underwent months of further rehabilitation, including cardio training and exercises involving light weights. I tried to increase my heart capacity and increase the percentage of blood that flowed through my body after my heart contracted. Doctors called it "the ejection fraction." Why was this important? Unless I could increase the blood flow, I would have to be outfitted for a pacemaker/defibrillator. In the meantime, my cardiologist recommended I use a portable defibrillator. I felt that my life had been turned upside down within the space of five weeks, and now this strange black box, attached to a wraparound cloth girdle, was a constant reminder of how things had changed. But if this little black box would keep me alive, it was well worth the inconvenience.

A week later my friends accompanied me to Fire Island wearing my new and very fashionable (at least to me) contraption. It looked like I was carrying a purse or a "murse" (a man bag). I got a lot of strange looks. But six weeks after my heart attack I was back in my house on the ocean. "You're the only gay guy I know who could have a heart attack, recover, get back on his feet and back to Fire Island to party," said one of my Brazilian housemates. "You're Super Queen."

I had been going to Fire Island since I was twenty-one. The Pines had always been home to "the boys of summer." But this boy was well past his prime. The image I had carefully cultivated crumbled like a sandcastle. In its place was a painfully thin man in his late fifties wearing a box on his hip and a smile on his face. That Saturday afternoon my housemates accompanied me to tea dance at the Blue Whale. The gay tea dance went back to the *dansants*, a French tradition. It was usually held during summer months from late afternoon to early evening. Gay tea dances started in the late sixties in Cherry Grove, also in Fire Island, as a way of creating an alternative safe haven for the LGBTQ community. And so, on this afternoon my housemates surrounded me as we boogied to blaring disco music. A familiar Donna Summer tune blasted from the speakers:

She works hard for the money
So hard for it, honey
She works hard for the money
So you better treat her right

A mirror ball twirled above me. I raised my arms in the air and wildly flailed them back and forth. Instead of feeling self-conscious, I felt grateful to be alive!

But returning home from the Pines, I faced a new reality: the reaction of others I thought were my friends. I ran into a former gym buddy on the street. We used to be workout partners, spotting each other as we bench-pressed. But as I walked up happily to greet him, he dourly gave me the once-over and walked by me like he didn't even recognize me. Suddenly I felt worthless. No longer muscular, I was no longer visible. I had to change my self-image.

I turned to my writing to help me sort through a series of conflicting emotions. How did I see myself? Did I feel damaged? So I decided to write about what I was feeling. I filled page after page. I wrote about my heart attack, but also about other things. I wrote about my father. I wrote about having AIDS. And soon a memoir began to take shape. You're reading it right now.

My heart attack taught me so much. It took a life-threatening wake-up call to put my priorities in order. Superficial acquaintances, toxic friends and roommates were gone. I had survived for a reason.

I decided to call my father in Hialeah. Papi's distinct voice bellowed on the other end.

"Ah-lo," he said.

"How's Mami?" I asked.

"She's sleeping now," he said. I told him that I loved him and couldn't wait to see them in Miami.

"I promise to come soon," I said. And then I asked the man whose approval I always sought a question. "Papi, now that it's been a while since my heart attack, what do you think I should do?" I heard a long pause.

"*Ve a la iglesia*," he said. (Go to church.) Papi volunteered at his parish. Now he wanted me to do the same. And so the next day I went to Holy Cross Church and asked the pastor what I could do to give back.

"Volunteer at the food pantry," he said. So now every two weeks I do just that. We fill plastic bags with canned goods, cereal, pasta, milk and sometimes frozen chicken and fish for the disadvantaged. Sometimes I see entire families, including children, pushing carts as they march in to get their food. "Thank you for being here," many tell us. We thank them back and hand them their plastic bags filled with canned foods, cereal and pasta. At another table they are handed fresh produce and sometimes yogurt.

What I and my fellow volunteers get back is so much more than what we put in. Now my satisfaction comes from helping others, not from superficial displays of vanity or posing on the beach.

I'm no longer one of those boys of summer. Gay Peter Pan died with my heart attack. Neverland is gone. It turns out that what matters most isn't the approval of strangers. What matters most is the love and acceptance of family and friends and helping others.

On Thanksgiving Day I kept my promise to Papi. I came to Hialeah to see him and Mami. I walked into her bedroom, the portable heart monitor attached to my hip blinking its green light. As I entered the room I saw my brother, my niece and her husband gathered around my mother's bed. I walked over to her, looked into her drawn face and began to cry. She looked so frail. She looked so helpless. I knew at that moment that Mami didn't have long to live. And then I noticed she was clutching something to her chest. It was the stuffed monkey with the large brown eyes Papi had given her so long ago.

I leaned over to kiss her. Suddenly, so many memories flooded back to me: I saw Mami whispering to me at Lourdes that the Virgin Mary had appeared to her, reassuring her no harm would come my way. I felt Mami's warm embrace as she told me "*Tenga fe.*" And I could see Mami hovering over me as I was having an asthma attack at three years old. I knew that she kept these memories in her heart as well. And although Alzheimer's had robbed her of so much, her eyes spoke to me, telling me she recognized me as her son that afternoon.

Yes, a surgeon sliced open my chest. He held my heart in his hands. I was given a second chance at life. I was given another opportunity to see Papi and kiss Mami as she held the stuffed monkey toy she loved so much.

My heart attack wasn't an ending. It put me on a new and different path, and with every heartbeat, I'm reminded of that again and again.

CHAPTER 10
CUBAN SUN RISING

The light illuminates the city's face. Havana, her cloak in tatters, her visage emaciated, greets me. I feel a pang of sadness for what has been allowed to dissipate in this once splendorous land, the tropical paradise of our collective dreams.
—Charles Gomez

FRIDAY, JANUARY 29, 2016, 5:58 a.m.

A morning litany jolts me from my sleep. *"Oye acere, porque tú sabes."* (Hey, come on, because you know.) *"Ay hermano. No seas así."* (Oh brother. Do not be like that.) *"Pero no te vuelvas maricón!"* (But do not become gay.) Cuban phrases from my parents' homeland carried by the wind. From Infanta, the street where I'm staying, I keep hearing snatches of conversations from revelers not yet ready for a Thursday night of partying to end. The Havana apartment I've rented is four stories above the din. The voices get louder. *"Pero como vas a decir eso."* (But how are you going to say that?) *"Puta!"* (Whore!) *"No, la puta eres tú!"* (No, the whore is you.). These are the same voices that at night are like lullabies that gently put me to sleep. I get up and walk to the tiny pink bathroom sink to throw cold water on my face. *"Hoy tengo que madrugar para ver el sol"* (Today I have to get up early to see the sun), I whisper to myself. I translate internally.

As I get dressed I look at the three framed images of Cuban faces and entwined lovers hanging above my bed. They are by the Cuban artist Victor Manuel. A brown curtain with embedded abstract designs flutters to my right. I get dressed and walk into the living room. The walls are painted coral. Two aluminum rocking chairs face two smaller chairs covered in wicker. A Havana salon. From the solitary window I look at the terra-cotta roof of a building across the way. It is still too dark to make out details, but as I look down at the sidewalk below, I see a man slowly walking in the shadows. I go to the kitchen refrigerator to drink from a bottle of water. I ponder a surreal still life as I walk by. On a shelf stands a wooden torso. It starts at the neck and ends at the hips. Both arms are cut off. She's a voluptuous woman with large breasts that turn toward the sky. The nipples have been sculpted perfectly so as to look like bullets shooting upward. Cuban idiosyncrasy on display.

6:07 a.m.

I leave the apartment and descend a curved stairway four floors to the street. It's still dark. I head up Infanta toward 23. I see a group of young people huddled on the concrete ramp that slides out from the Ministry of Foreign Commerce. I hear the strains of a guitar followed by a male voice gently singing: "*Porque somos así. Porque el amor es así.*" (Because that's the way we are. That's the way love is.) In the indigo darkness, I can hardly make out the man behind the morning serenade. But then, suddenly, I see him. He's a Cuban not yet out of his twenties, dressed in black from head to toe. And he's wearing a cowboy hat. Across the street, a man in a red uniform sweeps the floor of an outdoor cafeteria. *Whoosh. Whoosh. Whoosh.* The sounds accompany the cowboy's lament. As I walk to the corner, the smell of urine mixed with salt air overwhelms me. But as I walk toward El Malecón, the seawall, the acrid smell is replaced by the sweet smell of the sea. "*Sin ti, no tengo alma,*" sings the cowboy. (Without you, I have no soul.) As I walk, his voice begins to fade. On the highway, two cars whiz by. Behind me the towers of the famed

Nacional Hotel, a tie to Cuba's nostalgic past, rise from a rocky cliff. I cross the street.

6:10 a.m.

As I approach El Malecón, huge waves crash over the seawall. I am alone. I walk closer to El Malecón and look to the sky. A ribbon of pink and lavender is tied around the horizon. It's still dark. Against this backdrop I notice the flickering light from El Morro Castle. The incandescent beams crisscross the sky. The fortress guards the entrance to Havana Bay. It was originally under the control of Spain. It was built in 1589 after raids on Havana's harbor by pirates and colonists. In 1762, the British attacked Havana and took over El Morro. A year later it was returned to Spain. Since the sixties, thousands of Cubans (men, women and children) have escaped on rafts to the US with El Morro's light illuminating the beginning of their perilous journeys. Not all make it. Some lose their lives at sea.

6:12 a.m.

I'm jolted from my daydream by a sound behind me. I turn and see an old man casting a fishing line into the turbulent waters in front of me. He is a fisherman. His skin is ebony and his hair is the color of freshly fallen snow. I take a pic with my iPhone. A narrative takes shape in my mind. I see it on a page, a paragraph with certain words capitalized for emphasis:

> *Just before dawn in HAVANA as the morning mist dances in an INDIGO SKY, an old fisherman approaches EL MALECÓN (the seawall), line in hand. He is hoping to catch an elusive prize. But the waves crash over the seawall, crushing the hopes of the fisherman as the CUBAN dawn APPROACHES. The seas are too rough. The waves WASH*

over the wall. And the spray SPLATTERS his face. And so he WAITS and WONDERS. Across the sea, another world, another seawall, another fisherman. Casting his line, hoping for the best.

And from where I'm standing, a few feet away, I can see the fisherman's eyes. They carry the memories of many mornings just like this one. I'm reminded of Hemingway's *Old Man and the Sea* and the Cuban fisherman Santiago: "Everything about him was old except his eyes and they were the same color as the sea and were cheerful and undefeated."

As the old man flings his line, he opens his mouth wide for several seconds as if summoning a fish to bite. But the waves are too high. The man closes his mouth. A look of disappointment crosses his face. He looks at me quickly. Turns away, then turns back and mutters: "*No muerden.*" (Not biting.)

6:15 a.m.

At that moment a huge wave crashes over the seawall. I manage to jump back. It's a glorious wave that sends a geyser of water into the sky. I take a photo. The fisherman is caught in the spray but barely moves. He looks into the sea and stares long and hard as he pulls the line like a puppeteer.

In these moments before the dawn, I look up and see a full moon still in the sky. I turn away from the fisherman. I make out a young street sweeper in sneakers without shoelaces. He gets closer. "*Mucha basura,*" he says to me. (Lots of trash.) I look toward the sea again, then up to the sky. God dabs his palette with a silky brush. But instead of paint, he uses different hues of light. He splashes them against the sky: maroon strips turn into a bluish lavender and then into shades of coral and pink. God flings his wrist like the fisherman flinging his line. From his brush, dabs of mango-orange light scatter across *el cielo* (heaven). The light becomes brighter. Then I see it. Cuban sun rising.

The light illuminates the city's face. Havana, her cloak in tatters, her visage emaciated, greets me. I feel a pang of sadness for what has been allowed to dissipate in this once splendorous land, the tropical paradise of our collective dreams. Crumbling façades in pastel hues look like they may simply disappear into the sea, the sea that separates us. And I feel for the Cuban people. The revolution hasn't been easy for them. Shortages still abound. They've lived through the economic crisis of the "Special Period" when the Soviet Union dissolved. There were shortages of energy resources like gasoline and diesel fuel. And there were extreme reductions of rationed food. People had to live without goods and services that they took for granted. After 2000, Cuba-Russia relations improved under President Vladimir Putin. But most Cubans still struggle to make ends meet.

6:20 a.m.

As I stand by the seawall, the spray from a wave splashing my face, I'm reminded of why I've come to Cuba. I'm here to try to convince Papi to return for a visit—to connect with his past. On this trip I hope to retrace his steps. I'll take photographs of the church in La Víbora where he married Mami. I'll visit the home he lived in when he was nine years old. I'll see for myself the streets he played on. I'll go to the home where my brother and I stayed when we came with our mother to Cuba in 1959. Being here exhilarates me. As I watch the sky brighten and the sea churn on this dawn, I feel like a son of Cuba. The pieces all seem to fit. This magical place is why I am the way that I am. In the US I feel there is something missing. But in Cuba, on this morning, I feel complete. I look toward the sea. Its color is not yet blue green. As the sun's rays pierce the horizon, the color of the sea below is a blue violet. It's the way the great Cuban writer José Lezama Lima described it. Instead of *el mar* (a masculine reference), he described the Cuban sea as *la mar* (decidedly feminine). "The violet sea," he wrote, "longs for the birth of the gods, for to be born here is an indescribable feast." Although I was not born in Cuba, I am part of it as if I had been. I haven't been left out of the feast.

6:30 a.m.

I walk home. I pass a gas station and a cafeteria. Cars whiz by me on El Malecón. Havana has awakened. As I get closer to my building I see the guitar player I heard earlier walk by me with his entourage. I ask him, "What songs were you playing in those moments before the dawn of another Havana day?"

"All of them," he says, smiling. "All of them."

Havana is a once-beautiful gem that has lost its luster. The architecture hearkens back to Spain of the 1500s, a Moorish-inspired style of graceful archways, semi-enclosed *portales* (porches), and large airy windows adorned with wrought iron gates. A lot of the architecture is also in the Baroque style of Italy in the seventeenth century. But buildings now collapse from lack of maintenance. Havana faces the sea, but strangely enough it's practically devoid of ships because of US sanctions. I ponder all of this as the guitar player passes me. His songs are of love, but if he were to write a song about Havana, I imagine it would almost certainly have to include a sad refrain or two.

1:25 p.m.

I start walking up La Rampa toward the Havana Libre Hotel. The breeze off the seawall is particularly strong. Waves crash onto the street. I see a line of vintage cars. Avocado green. Maroon. Pink. Red. They're parked for the tourists. I look up to see the towers of the Hotel Nacional. Suddenly a stout woman walks by me with her friend.

"Oh my God, that wind from El Malecón is lifting my dress," she says, laughing. "It's going to knock me over." Her friend is wearing an orange blouse that reminds me of the color of an overripe mango. "And it doesn't do anything for my hair," she says. "But it's really this permanent Cuka gave me that is driving me crazy." She points to her burnished mane of tight ringlets. "It makes me feel like a real witch," she trills. They titter like canaries, *chee-chee-chee*, their high voices mixing with the sounds of the honking horns and the *wheesh-wheesh-wheesh* of the whistling Havana wind, an impromptu Cuban orchestration that brings a smile to my face.

1:36 p.m.

A black woman in a Madonna-like ponytail wearing tight leggings and a turquoise blouse cuts in front of a motorcycle. I notice an old woman with a scarf around her neck standing next to a shopping cart filled with candy, chocolate and popcorn. "*Caramelo*" (candy), she sings like a wannabe Celia Cruz. "*Caramelo a peso.*" (Candy for a dollar.) I continue walking up La Rampa, and I feel the sidewalk rising like a hill. A huge ceiba tree towers before me, and its green leaves flutter past my face like confetti. I look to my left and see a *ventana Habanera* (Havana window). I'm captivated by the beautiful detail, the window shaped like an archway on an aqua marine–hued edifice. It's not too far away from the sun-kissed azure waters off El Malecón, waters that seem to smell of sweet perfume. To me the window evokes Art Deco and Spanish Colonial at the same time. And the gentle dancing curve of the molding above the window frames is so beautiful, almost achingly so. I notice tiny shattered windows within the arch. They seem to serve as a metaphor for the damage and faded beauty of Havana, pointing to another time—to the Havana of coquettish Cuban señoritas in ruffled gowns, of troubadours in slicked-back hair shaking maracas and singing seductive serenades of love.

1:40 p.m.

A long line stretches from an ATM. Next to the ATM a sign reads *13 de Octubre Dia del Trabajador Azucarero* (October 13, Day of the Sugar Worker). I pass another shopping cart (this one's pink) filled with popcorn and candy. But there's no one standing beside it. It's abandoned. I wonder why. I keep walking. I pass the Ministry of Public Health. Suddenly I'm confronted by what looks to be a flea market. My eye is drawn to a vintage Chevy made out of wood and a sculpture of a voluptuous naked Cubana, her hands stretched behind her head in posed rapture. I buy the car for Matthew and a bracelet for Sheila.

2:00 p.m.

I continue on La Rampa and notice the sidewalks seem to be made from cobblestones. I notice young people texting on their cellphones. Across the street in bold red letters I make out the words *VIVA CUBA*. I turn on my tape recorder and start to speak: "Old cars as far as the eye can see." I read a license plate, "C171292," and a red Buick whizzes by. "The women in tiered skirts looking like shells, colorful leggings, actually quite fashionable." Now I'm at Twenty-Third and L, the center of everything. The Lara Theater is showing a movie called *La Cosa Humana* (*The Human Thing*) directed by Gerardo Chijona, starring Hector Medina and Enrique Moreno.

I'm caught by surprise when a tall handsome man in his early forties interrupts my running commentary. "It's the oldest theater we have in Havana," he says. He explains to me that he is a masseur and would like to give me a massage. I wonder if he's a sex worker. He has a place nearby, he tells me. I contemplate the little stubble of beard growing in a patch directly below his lower lip. He reminds me of a goat. I gently turn him down.

2:15 p.m.

I walk across the street. A sign is planted in the ground, surrounded by bushes. It features a drawing of José Martí, a renowned Cuban poet and activist, next to a drawing of a man who looks like Stalin. "These are virtuous times and they should be our foundation," the sign reads. I notice a large park sprawling for several blocks. I enter slowly and see the word *Coppelia* in metal letters on a curving brick wall. *Coppelia*. Suddenly it rings a bell. My Cuban friend Adoldo told me about it. It was the brainchild of Fidel Castro's secretary Celia Sanchez.

I make my way to a long counter shaped like an *S* and sit down on a stool. Next to me, dozens of Cubans hunch over plates of ice cream. I strike up a conversation with a man and a woman. They explain that anything more than a scoop of ice cream is considered an *ensalada* (a salad). So, if I want three scoops—say, of vanilla ice cream—I must order an *ensalada*. The man says I should also order *dulces* (little rolls with syrup fillings). I agree and order *dulces* with my *ensalada*. I pay in Cuban pesos and my entire dish costs the equivalent of less than one American dollar. Finally, the ice cream is placed in front of me and I dig in. It's heavenly! There's something special about sitting next to Cubans eating ice cream on this sunny Havana day. I'm not a tourist as I sit at this counter. I am a Cuban. I feel giddy.

A Night Earlier, January 28, 2016, 10:05 p.m.

I walk toward El Malecón. It's a clear Havana night and above me a small moon floats in a velvet sky. I follow streams of young people walking toward the sea. It's a Havana hangout where the Cuban millennials gather. And on this night the millennials are joined by this baby boomer. I sit on the seawall as the waves lap up behind me. Beside me a pretty girl in a baby-blue blouse and white shorts sits with a friend. Beside them appears to be a gay couple gesturing flamboyantly. I notice there are plastic cups beside them. A red drink has spilled. Wine, perhaps?

Across the street I spot the *gasolinera* (gas station) doubling as an outdoor restaurant. I remember when I visited in 1999 that young people, just like those sitting beside me, packed the restaurant. Everyone was riveted to a TV set watching the 1997 movie *Titanic*. Their eyes opened wide as Leonardo DiCaprio screamed "Rose!" and Kate Winslet screamed "Jack!" over and over again as waters filled the sinking ship. What was the Cuban fascination with a movie like the *Titanic*? Was Cuba a sinking ship? The moonlight bathes the *gasolinera* now. It's lit in shades of cerulean and cobalt and midnight blue, too. At this moment it's the most beautiful gas station I've ever seen.

10:15 p.m.

The pretty girl in the baby-blue blouse is now talking. Her graceful hand with long slender fingers (might she play the piano?) slices the air and then turns upward as she asks her friend, "*Vas marchar con las antorchas?*" (Are you marching with the torches?) Ah, the torches. It all makes sense now. About an hour ago I had noticed the streets were closed off near the University of Havana, down the street from the Havana Libre Hotel. I had asked a cab driver why. "*La misma mierda,*" he answered. (The same old shit). He explains that tonight at 11:30 students will walk down the steps of the University of Havana carrying torches to commemorate the birthday of José Martí, the renowned Cuban poet, activist and the so-called "Father of Cuban Independence." "But it has nothing to do with Marti," the driver sniffs. "It's all about Fidel and Raul." (He's referring to Fidel and Raul Castro.)

The young man on El Malecón answers his friend. "No, what for? All those people screaming. It's so crowded. Let's just drink," he says. They laugh. I walk back home and decide to turn in for the night. As I try to sleep, I'm suddenly awakened by a thunderous noise. I hear chanting and singing. The sounds get closer. "*Viva Martí!*" I hear. "*Viva Raul! Viva Fidel!*" I get up and hastily scramble down the stairs. The cheers and the chants grow louder. I fling open the door to my building on Infanta. And then I see them. Hundreds of torches light up the sky. They are carried by thousands of young men and women. Some wave Cuban flags. "*Viva Martí!*" A group of youths is holding a banner that reads *Patria y Humanidad* (Country and Humanity). As I watch intently, I'm moved by this apparent display of unity. Is it all about nationalism and support for the Castro regime? Were they ordered to march?

Two Nights Earlier, 8:08 p.m.

In the verdant neighborhood of Miramar, the unmistakable sounds of Cuban jazz emanate from a popular nightspot named El Diablo Tun Tun. On a stage bathed in lavender and blue lights, a pint-sized singer in a mustache and scruffy beard strums his guitar. I make my way into this crowded room filled with well-dressed Cubans, their eyes glued on the stage. A man by the name of Ramón commandeers me to a table and introduces me to everyone. Ramón is related to the man renting me a place to stay. There's a doctor and his wife, a woman who doubles as a backup singer for the *trovador* (troubadour). I also meet a mother and son visiting from Bilbao, Spain. I'm referred to as the "journalist from New York." My eyes are drawn to the stage and I suddenly feel Ramón gently moving my shoulders back and forth as the band plays. The singer's name is Ray Fernandez, and he croons folksy laments that at times poke fun (and in some cases even dare to question) the Castro government. He calls his music *nueva trova*. It's a movement in Cuban music in which the lyrics of songs are usually political. The crowd (lots of sexy señoritas and men in button-down collared shirts) sings along to the lyrics. They cheer when Fernandez mentions then-president Obama and his efforts to bring about political rapprochement. I keep thinking to myself that at another time, Fernandez might have been yanked off the stage. But the Castro regime seems to be allowing or at least tolerating a small amount of dissent from artists like Fernandez.

9:00 p.m.

As the concert ends, Ramon convinces me to join the group as they continue to party on this Havana night. We jump into cars and head for a local club. We walk to the grounds in the back of a lounge and suddenly we are facing the ocean. The Havana breeze washes over us, blowing our hair. We all look like scarecrows, happy scarecrows. We order drinks. We are joined by a couple, well-known Havana ballet dancers. I learn they are newlyweds. He's a tall strapping type and she's a short blonde dynamo. Together they make a striking pair. As we sit and talk, I feel so fortunate to be hanging out with "regular" Cubans. This is not a stop on a tourist tour; this is the real deal. Our last stop is the home of the dancers in a section of Havana known as Vedado. We scramble out of our cars and I can't believe my eyes. We are in front of what can only be described as a mini-mansion. This is where the dancers live. And on the bottom floor there's a restaurant that serves tapas such as Cuban *croquettas* (delicious breaded concoctions stuffed with ham or cheese). We sit at a long table, and from my vantage point I see apricot-colored silk curtains billowing in the delicate Havana breeze.

February 1, 2016

The tourists are out in throngs. I watch them walk down the cobblestone streets and listen to street bands playing traditional Cuban *sons*. The *son* is a genre of music that originated in Eastern Cuba in the late nineteenth century. It blends Spanish and African rhythms to create folkloric melodies. It's considered the root of today's salsa music. *Sons* speak to the heart of all that is Cuban. The tourists pose for photographs outside the Cathedral of Havana and snap pics of local curiosities like a colorfully dressed old lady puffing away at a Cuban cigar. I notice two other women posing for photos.

They are black and wear beautiful satin costumes in colorful shades of yellow, purple and blue. They sit holding baskets of pink and red carnations. They wear multi-colored beaded bracelets and plastic hoop earrings. And the tourists snap away.

I watch as the hordes with the cameras gaze at the intricate, curved stained-glass windows above graceful archways in the plazas. I stand behind them as they listen to the ubiquitous *guayabera*-clad Cuban street musicians. I hear *los cantantes* (the singers) warble their *son Cubanos* to the sound of the intoxicating Afro-Cuban percussion. The musicians shake maracas and strum guitars with nimble fingers while others beat on bongos Desi Arnaz style. The tourists cheer and beg them to keep playing. I resent them. I feel the tourists are invading "my" country. But I'm American, so why do I feel this way?

January 30, 2016, 9:00 a.m.

I walk a few blocks from where I'm staying to the Hotel Nacional de Cuba. It's Cuba's most famous luxury hotel. Built in 1930, the Hotel Nacional has been a meeting place for presidents and statesmen, movers and shakers, gangsters and businessmen, movie stars and showgirls and, of course, tourists from around the world. On this glorious Havana day, I stand awestruck, staring at the long driveway graced with towering palm trees leading to the main entrance. The majestic hotel reaches toward the sky, its two colonial steeples framing it on both sides. No matter how many times I visit the Nacional, I'm stunned by its beauty. Walking into the lobby I look up to the vaulted ceilings. The architecture is a mixture of Spanish Colonial, Baroque and neo-classical. Tourists buzz around the lobby like bees. A uniformed doorman asks me, "May I help you?" I explain I'm here for the breakfast. "Right this way," he says to me as if I'm the most important person in the world.

A chubby blonde with a gleaming smile in a too-tight pastel-colored uniform leads me to a table. "Feel free to have anything from the buffet," she says cheerfully, tossing her hair. I watch her walk away, shaking her derriere from side to side *a la Cubana*. I look toward the buffet area. A breakfast feast has been laid out for hotel guests or anyone willing to shell out $13. I count thirteen separate tables laden with delicacies. There are eggs, sausages and bacon. There's a buffet table for cornflakes and oatmeal. And another for breads and pastries. I notice another large table displaying a variety of fruit, including fresh guava, papaya, mamey, mango and bananas. One always hears of food shortages in Cuba, but if the Cuban people are allowed only a finite quantity of food each month, at hotels like the Nacional there appear to be no limits.

9:30 a.m.

I finish breakfast and walk out a huge door leading to the grounds in the back. A pathway leads to the Atlantic Ocean and El Malecón. It's like an oasis in a tropical paradise. Huge palm and ceiba trees adorn a plaza graced with a gurgling fountain at the center. Beyond that I make out the sapphire blue of the Atlantic Ocean. Where I'm standing is steeped in history. Spain used the land now occupied by the Nacional for the construction of various fortifications to protect Havana from constant attacks by privateers and pirates. Havana at one point had been captured by the English. It wasn't until 1902 that Cuba finally achieved its independence from Spain and became a republic. I walk down a pathway, past the fountain, and stare into the sea. On this balmy Havana morning the breeze blows my hair. I ask a guard to take a photograph. I notice a cannon and a plaque. The plaque reads, "From this spot on the night of June 13, 1898, this Krupp Cannon of 280mm from a distance of 8,000 yards twice bombed the USS *Montgomery*, a ship that was part of the American fleet during the blockade of Havana during the Spanish-Cuban-American War. Dedicated at The Hotel Nacional on April 25, 1956."

I decide to leave the Nacional, and as I walk down La Rampa toward El Malecón, a tall imposing man walks toward me. He is broad-shouldered and as handsome as a Hollywood leading man. "Taxi?" he asks. He points to a two-toned (green and gray) 1948 Chevrolet parked feet away. Cubans call their old American cars *almendrones*. There are two types of *almendrones*. There are the cars that get you to spots around the city at fifty cents for a shared ride. Then there are the *almendrones* that take tourists out of town to sightsee or to beach resorts. They can cost the equivalent of up to fifty American dollars per day.

I explain that I am going to La Víbora where my father once lived. I want to retrace his steps. I want to take photographs of the place where Papi lived, and the Iglesia de los Pasionistas de la Víbora where he and Mami married. We agree on a price (roughly the equivalent of US $30).

My driver's name is Orlando. He's been driving a cab for twenty-one years. He asks me about my background and my family. Within minutes I feel comfortable as if I've known Orlando all my life. He jokes in the easy manner of most Cubans, the way my father and my grandfather joked. He makes fun of the way people look. He gossips about other drivers. He calls one older driver untrustworthy. He tells me he's a former Ministry of Interior official who rats on colleagues. He talks and talks—another favorite Cuban pastime. Cubans call such banter "*Radio Bemba.*" *Bemba* refers to lips, lips that love to spread stories. It's a Cuban thing. Orlando talks honestly about the current political climate, about the US opening diplomatic ties and about the Castro brothers. Years ago when I visited, drivers would never speak so openly, fearing that "the walls had ears." But in the last sixteen years, the fear seems to have lessened.

We drive along El Malecón. Leaving central Havana, I stare at El Morro. Huge waves crash on the rocks below it, against the backdrop of an azure sky. On the way I notice homes in an alarming state of disrepair. On one the paint fades to ugly shades of yellow and gray. Other homes are in ruin, a few orange bricks here and there peeking from crumbling structures. As we enter La Víbora, Orlando pulls over and asks an old lady on the street, "Where is Los Pasionistas?" She gives us directions and we continue driving. Finally, the church comes into view. Orlando parks the car and I walk out, looking at this place which has so much history for my family.

I take photographs of the ornate, spindly church steeples. I pause before the long polished aisle leading to the altar. Two ceramic altar boys dressed in red-and-white vestments stand like soldiers. I look up at a beautifully carved vaulted ceiling. Glimmering glass chandeliers hang from above. Rays of light stream through the large glass windows behind the altar. To my left I see a woman who appears to be in her seventies standing before a large statue of Jesus on a cross. Her hand holds the figure's knee as she looks solemnly into Jesus's face. To the left is a statue of Cuba's patron saint, the Virgin of Charity. I look back toward the altar. In my mind it's suddenly 1951. I envision my mother in her lace wedding dress walking ever so slowly toward my father to the strains of the "Ave Maria."

I get in Orlando's car and we head to the neighborhood where my dad lived as a boy. We turn on Avellaneda. It is a short block dotted with homes made out of brick and cement. Finally, we park in front of 210 Avellaneda. It is a large plot concealed by covered gates. This is where my grandfather's brother, Catalino, lived with his wife, Adela. Next door was where Papi lived with Pipo, and my dad talked of remembering a house made out of wood where he played. As I get out of the car, I notice a man in his eighties standing outside a gate across the street. I ask him about the wooden house.

"José Antonio would know about that," he says, revealing a smile with a missing tooth. "But he's at work now. He came to this neighborhood in 1976 and that wooden house was still here then."

I tell the old man that my father left Cuba in 1945.

"Oh," he says, "after the people who lived there left, Felipe moved in with his family."

Felipe? Could it possibly be the same Felipe who Papi worked with in the *bodeguita*? Could it be the same Felipe who taught Papi to rub oil on coffee beans to make them appear fresher to customers?

"Felipe passed away some years ago," the old man says sadly. The man explains that Felipe's children live just blocks away. "When you get to San Delgado, turn right, cross San Catalina, and the house is right there next to the park," he says. With my iPhone I take photographs of the houses so my brother can show them to my father. Next to 210 is 206 Avellaneda. The house is painted in shades of coral and brick and covered with a white gate one can see through. I believe this is where the *bodeguita* was where Papi ground coffee beans for Mami. Next to it there's a small white house with the numbers 204 nailed to the wall. Through a gate I make out a porch with a pink-and-green tiled floor. A fifties-style outdoor chair is placed next to an aluminum rocking chair. This is the house where Papi lived right before he left for the US in 1945. I imagine my grandmother helping Papi pack on the night before he was to leave for Miami.

Our last stop is the home where my brother and I stayed with my mom during our brief visit some five decades ago. As I ride in the car with Orlando over potholes in the street, I become the Charlito I was when I was just six years old. It is the summer of 1959 and Castro has invited the militiamen who fought with him in the mountains to come into Havana. From the porch of Josefina 18, we wave, hold tiny Cuban flags and cheer as the men drive by in caravans. Castro has still not declared that his revolution is a socialist one.

As Orlando stops in front of the home, I instantly recognize the porch. In that moment I am Charlito waving at the *milicianos*. I run to the porch and shout through a gate: "*Hola*, is anyone home?" Soon a smiling rotund woman in her sixties with curly hair, wearing a floral housedress, bounds out.

"My name is Charles Gomez and I'm the son of Guillermo," I say excitedly. "Do you know a woman who lived here whose name was Orfelina?"

"Of course I know who Orfelina is. She was my aunt and godmother." I almost can't believe my ears. What she is telling me confirms that we are related—a distant cousin, but a relative nonetheless.

"I am Tania and I am the daughter of Victor and niece of Roberto, Adelina and Orfelina. I'm their direct niece and also a first cousin to Gladys," she says.

I immediately recognize the name of Gladys, a cousin. I didn't expect to find a relative, a connection to Papi's past. Tania begins to reminisce, her eyes opening wide, her hands fluttering like a butterfly.

"Aunt Adelina *cocinaba riquísimo* [cooked deliciously] and her *ropa vieja* [shredded beef], yucca and black beans and rice were exquisite," she purrs. "Come into the house and I'll make you a *cafecito* [Cuban coffee]." She opens the gate.

It is preserved exactly as I remember it. The floor is still adorned with the same Spanish tiles. I stare at the same kaleidoscope patterns featuring triangular leaves within circles. Tables are adorned with ceramic figurines like the kind my mother kept at our home in Hialeah. To the left is the television set where my brother and I watched cartoons. I can hear the high-pitched voice of *La Cucarachita Martina* as she meets her beau, the big-eared cartoon mouse. I am in Cuban heaven. As I stand here in this Cuban home, I feel I finally make sense to myself in a way I didn't before. The sights and sounds go right through me, triggering a feeling of aliveness I can't begin to explain.

Tania returns with the *cafecito* and it is delicious. It is so sweet it wrinkles my nose and puckers my lips. I look up and catch a glimpse of the long, forest-green hallway (the color of my bedroom in New York) I walked down every morning when I stayed here so many years ago with Mami. On a refrigerator I spot a magnet of a butterfly next to the words *Te Quiero* written in a cursive style.

I ask Tania if I can see the rest of the house. "Of course," she says. I turn on the video camera on my phone and hit record: "We're walking through the house where I stayed in 1959," I say. "There's the bathroom. This is the hallway, and in the backyard my mother was at a sink." I aim the phone. "It was right here," I say.

Suddenly Tania cuts in. "That's exactly where the sink was. And it's only been a month that we started making these repairs," she says.

I continue my tour of the house, iPhone recording every moment. "To the left is where I stayed with my brother, and here's the living room." From there I move to the porch: "This is the porch that I stood on with my brother as we watched the *milicianos* come by in 1959, preserved perfectly." I stop recording and Tania and I hug once more. We exchange phone numbers and emails and promise to keep in touch.

"I love you," she says.

"*Te quiero tambien*" (I love you as well), I reply. I walk to the car, and before I step into it, I turn around and look toward the house that holds so many rich memories. Tania and her husband, Alejandro, wave, and in my mind, they're waving in slow motion. With each movement of their hands, decades seem to flash by.

They are decades marked by different dreams and different destinies. My father left Cuba to live his American dream. Tania and Alejandro stayed behind, living out their own destiny under the Havana sun. But Papi, Tania and Alejandro share the same homeland that defines them. It's the Cuba of our collective dreams, the Cuba that binds us and unites us. Although I hadn't met my cousin and her husband until this trip, I feel they are a part of me in some inexplicable way. And when we embrace to say *adios*, it's as if I have always known them somewhere deep in my heart.

CHAPTER 11
CUBA IS CALLING

No matter where I am
Cuba is calling
It's inside me
It won't let me get away
With every breath I take
Cuba is calling.
—Tropicana, the Musical

AS I WALK INTO my apartment from picking up the mail, the Cuban standard "Guantanamera" wafts from the stereo speakers. It's a song about a girl from Guantánamo, Cuba, and it was written in 1929 as a patriotic song. In 1966 the American group the Sandpipers had a hit when their version of "Guantanamera" reached the top of the Billboard charts.

On my way to the dining room table, I pass a lithograph of a Havana archway topped by multi-colored stained glass by the Cuban artist Humberto Calzada. These are the echoes of Cuba reverberating through my living room on this humid summer day. I sit down and sort through the usual catalogs and junk mail. Suddenly something catches my eye. It's a letter addressed to me with Papi's unmistakable cursive writing, the letters all slanted to the right. The *G* is florid and almost feminine, the bottom curved in an oval like an exquisite Spanish guitar. Where did Papi learn to write like that? From some nuns in Havana? The return address reads *Palm Avenue, Hialeah, Florida.*

"*Yo soy un hombre sincero de donde crece la palma,*" sings the voice coming from the speaker. (I am a sincere man from where the palm trees grow). The envelope is somewhat bulky. What could possibly be inside? I tear it open. But instead of moola, I find a carefully folded newspaper clipping. Hmm, what is Papi up to?

I unfold the article. It's two pages long. There in the Spanish edition of the *Miami Herald* is a story about the first cruises to Cuba in almost sixty years. At first the Cuban government balked at allowing Cubans who left Cuba years ago to travel on the historic cruises. But all that has changed. A photograph shows a large ship in turquoise waters, the name *Adonia* emblazoned on the side.

I'm astonished. Almost a year ago, I tried to convince my papi to come with me to Cuba. "I'm not going there," he said dismissively. "Go to Cuba by yourself." And I did. While there I took dozens of photos, including ones of La Víbora, the deteriorating neighborhood Papi had left when he was just seventeen. My brother, who didn't live far away, drove to Papi's Hialeah home. He showed my dad the pictures I'd sent on my iPhone. "You know, Charlie," Willie told me, "you could see his face light up when he saw the pictures."

But now with this clipping it's clear that Papi wants to return to Cuba. I call my brother excitedly and tell him the news.

"Willie, he's trying to tell us he wants to go."

There's silence on the line.

A year earlier when I told my brother about my planned Cuba trip, he scoffed. I asked him if he might want to go with me. "Why would I ever want to go? I didn't lose anything over there," he replied. My mind flashed to memories of our trip in 1959. A faded black-and-white photo Mami gave me shows us smiling with a *miliciano* (militiaman) who had fought with Fidel in the mountains. My brother's words brought me back to earth. "I didn't lose anything over there," I kept hearing. Another voice whispered to me too: "But think of everything you could find there." And so, I held out hope for Willie as well as my dad.

"*Guantanamera. Guajira Guantanamera*," sings the voice that fills my ears. To my surprise, Willie doesn't shoot down the idea this time.

"Well, I'd have to call up to see how much it would cost. But if we do go to Cuba, a cruise would be the best idea because that way Papi would be the most comfortable and safe too."

I'm elated. If we can pull this off, it will be the trip of a lifetime: my brother and I accompanying my father to Cuba after more than six decades. My excitement is tempered by a pang of sadness. Mami died almost two years ago and won't be traveling with us. We will have to take her in our hearts.

Within an hour or two, my brother calls up with tentative dates and prices. Now we have to call up Dad.

"Papi, Willie and I called the cruise line and we can travel to Cuba," I say. "Don't worry about the cost. It's our gift. Will you go?" It doesn't take him long to say, "*Sí, sí.*" The dream is finally coming true.

"*Guantanamera, guajira Guantanamera.*"

September 17, 2016

I am in the bedroom of my father's Hialeah home. With my tiny Sony camera I videotape him pushing a suitcase on rollers. From the closet he methodically pulls out guayaberas (lightweight Cuban shirts with two breast pockets and two pockets over the hips) and places them on the bed. They are in pastel hues, and one is embroidered with the seal of Havana. "I got one for each day of the trip," he explains. He leads me to the hallway outside the bedroom. The wall is covered from floor to ceiling with framed photographs of our relatives: the Gomez and Gonzalez families. "There's Pipo with Peter," he says, pointing to a black-and-white photograph of my deceased grandfather and his son Peter. Papi calls it his "Wall of Honor."

"*Vamos al comedor,*" he says. (Let's go to the dining room.) It is the night before our cruise. But instead of being giddy and excited, Papi appears somber, as if there's something weighing heavily on his mind. From a large manila envelope, he pulls out a number of photographs. "I found this envelope on the bottom of the closet," he says. "I've never seen them. Look, up here, it's your address from New York. You mailed them back to Mami."

The photographs represent a treasure trove from our past. There are photos of my brother and me on horseback, photos of us bathing in the surf in Cuba. "*Mira*" (Look), my father says excitedly. He begins sorting through photographs from his wedding. "How can it be that after so many years I've never seen these?" he asks almost angrily. In the photos, my mother stands looking like an angel. She wears a beautiful satin-and-lace wedding gown. In one, a woman named Hilda stands beside her. She looks like the matron of honor. "It's the first time I see this picture of Hilda," he says like a little boy finding a long-lost toy.

Finally, from the envelope he pulls out a large photo that is folded in half. When he straightens it out, it shows my mother standing alone in the voluminous gown, staring into the camera.

"I don't remember ever seeing this photograph either," he says. It's colorized and my mother's lips are ruby red. And so are her cheeks. She smiles slightly like a Cuban Mona Lisa. "China," my dad whispers—a Cuban term of endearment referencing the Chinese who had slipped into Cuban society so many years ago.

An image flashes through my mind: my grandfather rocking me in a chair singing a lullaby in Spanish. It's about a Chinese man who comes to Cuba and falls in love with a beautiful Cuban woman. "*Cubana de mi ilusión, vivi siempre con mi. Que con mi yo quiero gozar de tu amor.*" (Cuban woman of my fantasy, live forever with me. With you I want to relish our love.)

My father looks at the photo and gently rubs his finger across it. "*Tu mami*," he says softly. (Your mother.) In rubbing the photograph, it's as if he's gently caressing her face.

As I sit there with Papi, I realize that we're embarking on a journey filled with expectations. My dad's returning to Cuba hoping to capture a special magic. Will he feel like that adolescent boy working in his pipo's bodega? Will he feel the same joy he felt when he ground coffee for my mother? Will he remember gazing at her admiringly? Will he remember pushing his brother's stroller around the block at a feverish pace so he could get back to playing ball with the neighborhood boys? Or will the Cuba he visits turn out to be a shell of the homeland he once knew?

My brother is going to Cuba hoping to relive another kind of magic. He'll become seven years old again. He'll remember the dawn, remember waiting to hear the sound of horses clip-clopping down Josefina Street as a vendor shouts, "Fruits, vegetables, milk!" The sounds will startle him, causing him to dress hurriedly. It's the summer of 1959. He's in that home in La Víbora, Havana. He's back again.

I have different expectations. I was a little boy who felt odd back then. I felt unsettled wondering where I fit in. I'm going back to meet the boy I once was, the shy kid in the shorts and striped shirt. I'm going back to tell him everything will turn out all right someday. And I'm going to be with Papi—to see Cuba through his eyes. He loves Willie, but he loves me too. I still can't help wondering who is Papi's favorite son.

Our expectations aren't ones we've expressed to others or even to ourselves. But Cuba has shaped all of us in one way or another. Our father's journey back to his homeland will bring us together. It will unite us in a way we can't even begin to imagine.

Papi is going back to Cuba despite friends who caution him, "You'll be helping the Castro regime." My father isn't afraid.

"Let them think what they're going to think and say what they're going to say," he says. "I'm going with my sons to see Cuba because I don't have a lot of time left on the planet." I think Papi's wrong. He's going to outlive us all.

Fast-Forward, Two Months after Our Trip to Cuba
Fidel Castro dies at ninety. I call to tell Papi the news. His

response: "I thought he'd die a lot sooner." I ask him about the celebrations in Little Havana. "No one should celebrate someone's death," Papi says. "Death is in the hands of Jesus Christ, not us."

Rewind, Hialeah, the Night before We Leave for Cuba

"Now I want you try on the guayaberas I have for you in the closet," Papi says. Some are plain, others more elaborate with floral designs. A Cuban friend explained to me that any floral design indicated the shirt was made in Puerto Rico. According to him, Cuban guayaberas have a very simple pleated design. He said that Puerto Ricans copied our guayaberas just like they copied our flag. As my dad sorts through the guayaberas, I can hear my friend's voice in my head. "The Cuban flag features a red triangle affixed with a single white star against blue and white stripes," he would say. "The red signifies the blood shed during the Spanish-American War when Cuba fought for its independence. In the Puerto Rican flag, the star is set against a field of blue, to indicate the sky," he said. "Blood is more significant than sky."

The voice in my head is drowned out by Papi's. "Try on the mediums. You said you wore mediums, right?" My dad wears his guayaberas with a pride that makes me smile. And it makes me wish I could take them a tad more seriously. Guayaberas symbolize Cuban tradition, and it seems right my dad wants me to be traditional on this most important of family trips. So, I try on the guayaberas. The shirts are heavily starched and smell of cologne. First, I try on the baby-blue long-sleeved one. Too tight. I can barely button it across my chest. "You're too big," my dad starts shouting. For my father and brother (and perhaps for me as well), shouting instead of speaking in a normal tone seems to be a Cuban trait.

"Try the yellow one," he bellows. I try on the yellow guayabera. Again, I can barely button the thing across my chest. "But you're not a medium," my dad screeches. "Who told you you were a medium?"

I explain to my dad I wear a medium for a lot of my shirts. "You're a large! You're a large," he screams.

"OK, Papi, I'm a large, OK!" And so, I'm not destined to wear my dad's special guayaberas on this trip. I'll have to wear my own. Shorty's screams still ring in my ears.

September 19, 2016

We sail all night, and when we wake up it feels almost like Christmas morning. Anticipation. Excitement. Like that time so many years ago when Papi and Mami hid wrapped toys in the hallway of our Allapattah house thinking we'd never spot them. But on this morning, instead of presents, Cuba will be our gift. What is it about Cuba that is so distinctive that we can't wait to set foot on its soil? Is it about the music? The Afro-Cuban jazz, salsa, rumba, cha-cha-cha? Or is it the *son cubano* combined with that unmistakable Afro-Cuban percussion? Or *guaguancó*, that sub-genre of the Cuban rumba that puts together percussion, singing and dance? Is it about singer Celia Cruz or Benny Moré, the famed Cuban tenor, songwriter and bandleader?

Could it be about the food? The white rice and black beans? The succulent pork? The extraordinary seafood? And then there are those culinary influences from Spain and Africa, from the Yoruba tribes that were brought to Cuba as slaves. Is it about the mixture of races? The Spanish influence along with contributions from Taíno Indians and Africans? And let's not forget the Chinese.

It can't be that because many Latin countries have the same mixture of races. What is it about Cuba that's so special? Could it be the heat that sizzles year-round and makes natives run for cover in shady plazas at noon? Or perhaps it's that certain something in the air that sends *señoritas* into the streets wearing wildly patterned leggings and tube tops hugging hourglass figures. Could it be Santeria, that mixture of Catholicism and the Yoruba religion? It's the religion that created orishas and gods like the father of the earth, Babalu Aye.

Remember Desi Arnaz (*I Love Lucy*), who popularized Santeria in the US by banging on conga drums with his hands and wailing "Babalu"? In *Tropicana, the Musical* there's a song that explains Cuba's allure. It is sung by the Tropikettes, the spirits of three Tropicana showgirls who are transported magically back to Havana for one special night:

> *Cuba is a feeling.*
> *Cuba is a fragrance*
> *Cuba is a canvas of colors,*
> *A rainbow in every hue.*
> *It is everything*
> *The sea and sky above*
> *It is in our hearts*
> *This place that we all love.*

This is the Cuba we set sail to see. Outside our cabin, as the *Adonia* floats on calm waters, I notice a pinkish glow brushing across the pastel-blue sky.

"*Papi, hoy vemos a tu Cuba,*" I say as we dress. (Today we see your Cuba.) As he gets ready in the bathroom I hear him say, "*Ay, que bueno.*" (Oh, how good.) I don a beige linen shirt and white linen pants and a white hat. I'm trying on this day to look very much like a character out of Graham Greene's *Our Man in Havana*. My brother and Papi dress in blue shirts that match the color of the sea. My brother's looks more Hawaiian than Cuban. Shorty throws on a brownish straw hat with a blue band. My brother's hat is white like mine. Papi smiles as he carefully places the necklace with a huge cross around his neck. He kisses it quickly for good measure. And so, the three amigos scurry to the Conservatory, the ship's restaurant, to grab our morning coffee. It isn't café Cubano, but it will have to do.

Even though it is barely dawn, dozens of fellow passengers gather in the Conservatory as well. We see a couple from New Jersey we befriended.

"When are you going to get your straw hat?" my brother asks.

"Nope, nope, not me," the husband replies.

"Oh, he just hates them," his cheerful wife adds. As we sip our coffee, we still can't see Havana in the distance. Papi's unusually quiet this morning. It's as if he's struggling to come to terms with setting foot on Cuban soil for the first time in so long. Now, at eighty-eight, Papi tells us he's on *"tiempo prestado"* (borrowed time). But time's been good to our father. We walk out to the deck and gaze at the shoreline. And then, like a glittering necklace, the Havana skyline sparkles in the distance. My dad raises his hand to his forehead as if he's shielding his eyes. His Cuba is finally on the horizon. He looks out and doesn't move. He's transfixed as his beloved homeland comes into view.

It takes close to an hour for the *Adonia* to pull into Havana Harbor. And from the right deck we can make out the buildings lining the Port of Cuba and parts of Old Havana. Papi becomes excited when he sees Regla across the bay (one of the fifteen municipalities or boroughs of Havana). He gazes at the sixty-six-foot-tall Christ of Havana that protects Havana Bay. When he visited Cuba in 1958, the statue had just been erected.

"Mira, el Christo," he says, excitedly pointing toward the statue. On this clear morning we can see el Christo covered in scaffolding for repairs.

"What are you feeling, Dad?" I ask.

"Sadness," he replies.

"But why sadness?" I ask.

"Because it's been too many years that I've been away." I notice a tiny tear rolling down his face. "I never thought I'd ever see this again," he says. He points again. His gold rings glisten in the sun. *"Gesu Cristo,"* he keeps repeating. "I'm thinking of Mami. I know she's with me here now looking at all this too."

An image flashes in my mind. Mami sitting in the front passenger seat of Dad's car. I'm eleven or twelve. I wonder what Mami's thinking.

Why has she locked herself in our car? I see her from the kitchen door. She sees me staring. I look afraid. She turns away, raising her hand. She looks like she is swatting away a particularly persistent fly.

I'm jolted back to the deck of the *Adonia* by the sound of my brother snapping away on his Canon camera. *Click. Click. Click.* I ask Willie what he's thinking.

"Well, it's a freaking experience," he says. "We haven't been here since, what, third grade."

My dad interjects: "Sixty-five years."

My brother nods. "And for him it's been almost sixty-five years. He got married to Mom in 1951. It's just beautiful." Suddenly Willie stops speaking as if he's trying to remember something important. The brim of his white hat flutters slightly, like the sheets on Mami's clothesline blowing in the breeze in the backyard of our home in Hialeah. I look at Papi as he gazes at Havana sprawled out before him. I put my arm around his shoulder and squeeze tightly. We feel the warmth of the Havana sun.

"Did you see El Morro?" my brother asks. Of course I do. He's talking about Morro Castle, the famous fortress guarding the entrance to Havana. My dad has a large painting of El Morro hanging on his living room wall.

Soon we are led from the ship through customs. Tour guides from Havanatur (an international tour operator) await us. Papi looks around, still dazed by his surroundings. Is this really Cuba? Is he really here?

"Now we start," the guide tells us as we're led to a section of Old Havana close to where the *Adonia* is docked. "We're going to build a touristic area right here in the future," the middle-aged guide explains. We enlist another guide, a young blonde woman, to take a picture of the three of us, our first photo of our return on Cuban soil. My father stands between us, his hands crossed below his protruding tummy. I have my hands on Papi's shoulder. My brother places his arm around Papi's back. My father looks somewhat like a pint-sized version of Papa Hemingway. His mouth is slightly ajar in an expression that looks like disbelief. Behind us in the distance El Morro looms, the same El Morro from Papi's painting.

My father's eyes open wide on this scorcher of a day as he takes in the sights. It's as if he's seeing Havana for the first time. Willie says, "He's like a kid on Christmas morning." I watch as Papi stares at the bubble gum—colored vintage cars whizzing by, juxtaposed with old-fashioned horse-drawn carriages. From inside, delighted tourists snap away at us! Across the way we see a balcony from which a clothesline has been fastened. Underwear and panties billow in the Havana breeze. I think of Mami carefully squeezing wooden clothespins to hang our underwear on the clothesline in Hialeah. Peeking from behind the fluttering laundry, a little girl in blondish Afro-puff pigtails smiles a mischievous gap-toothed grin. The female tour guide holds my father's hand as we walk on the cobblestone streets through Old Havana. Papi looks like a little boy being led by his mother.

We pass three middle-aged black women sunning themselves, dressed in colorful folkloric garb. An older woman in heavy makeup and eyelashes as long as a peacock's feathers is dressed in blue ruffles. On a corner she puffs away at a Cuban cigar. Beside her is a cobalt-blue aluminum glass filled with dollar bills (Cuban "CUCS") left by tourists. CUCS stands for Cuban Convertible Currency. It was originally created to be used in the tourism industry and for luxury items. In 2016, it's used solely by tourists at an exchange rate of roughly USD $1 equaling one CUC.

We stroll through an elaborate labyrinth of streets, ending up in front of the Cathedral of the Virgin Mary of the Immaculate Conception. The cathedral is famous. For centuries it's been the center of Havana's social life. Cubans gather in the cathedral's plaza to greet each other, to gossip and even to fall in love. To say it's breathtaking is an understatement. It's a Baroque-style church dating back to the 1700s. My brother takes a picture. Papi looks up at its steeples, his mouth open in awe.

"*Aquí recojiamos al Padre Gasolina*," he says. (Here is where we picked up Father Gasoline.) Papi explains that Padre Gasolina was an old Catholic priest. He was given his nickname because he loved alcohol. My dad says he'd ride on the bus that Pipo owned and commandeered from La Víbora where they lived. The rickety bus picked up passengers all the way to the Havana Cathedral. There they'd pick up Father Gasolina after a night of carousing. Papi helped him climb up the bus. Then my grandfather would drive Father Gasolina back to his church on a hill in La Víbora. He was so drunk my grandfather would ask Papi to help the inebriated priest walk up the dozens of steps to the rectory. Then it was time to say good night to Father Gasolina.

At every turn, another recollection lights up Papi's face. He begins to reminisce.

"I went to Catholic school with the nuns right around here."

He recalls coming into town with his friend Felipe when he was fifteen. He tells me how he felt looking up at this ornate cathedral, counting the scrolls and columns. And as he stands there gazing at the cathedral so many years later, he finds himself counting the columns once more. Papi remembers how he felt as a boy walking into this huge church, dwarfed by the huge vaulted ceilings, humbled by the holiness of it all. He's the skinny kid who stared at those impossibly beautiful stained-glass windows as they lit up this corner and that one. Sometimes the light filtering through the stained-glass windows cast a brilliant beam that lit up the statue of the Virgin of Charity. The light. *The light.* Another recollection: the Night of the Lights.

The light in the cathedral takes Papi back to the night of September 4, 1944. He's a teenage boy working at the military hospital of Columbia in Marianao in Havana. Papi's godfather, Achille Morerra, had connections with a guy named Benitoa. He got Papi a job as an electrician's assistant.

President Fulgencio Batista is in power. But not for long. Ramón Grau San Martín, a physician, has just been elected president. That night the hospital gets word that Batista is on his way. It's 2 a.m.

and still no Batista. So Papi dozes off. Suddenly he's awakened by a loud voice: "*Guillermito, el general está entrando*," he hears someone scream at him. (Guillermito, the general is coming in.)

Papi, all 5'2" of him, scrambles on top of a large empty oil barrel just as Batista and his military escorts whiz by. Papi reaches the large switch that turns on the lights for the grounds of the military hospital. The light. The light. Reflector after reflector lights up the night sky in the brightest spectacle Papi has ever seen. Papi is momentarily blinded. He shuts his eyes tightly. Suddenly he hears a voice. It is the booming voice of President Batista himself. When Papi opens his eyes, Batista is smiling broadly. Papi is scared to death. Did he do something wrong? Batista, with his slightly slanted eyes widening under perfectly shaped eyebrows, chuckles as he addresses some soldiers.

"You see this boy here. He knows what he's doing," Batista says. "I'm going to pay for his studies so he can become an electrician. See to it." Papi studied for a year, but by 1945 he was on his way to the US. Fifteen years later, 1952, Batista rose to power again as Cuba's US-backed dictator. He would flee the island and go into exile as Castro and his revolution declared victory on January 1, 1959. But Papi would never forget the Batista who smiled kindly on him that night, that "night of the lights" more than seven decades ago.

Then it's time for the tour guides to lead us through a narrow twisting and turning path to Hemingway's haunt, Bodeguita del Medio. The bar with a restaurant, the birthplace of the mojito cocktail, is tucked away into a small nondescript building. One has to walk up a narrow stairway to reach the top floor. Once we get there my brother points out to Papi all the signatures that are scrawled on the walls. They're left by tourists just like us. There are a few famous names as well: poet Pablo Neruda, Gabriel García Márquez, Salvador Allende, Nat King Cole, and of course Ernest Hemingway. As I hurriedly jot my name on the wall ("Charles Gomez was here"), waiters guide our *Adonia* group to waiting tables. Papi and Willie drag behind, but finally they're seated on a long wooden bench.

A small band strikes up a Cuban song. It reminds me of the kind of storytelling so prevalent in our country music as a young Cuban man plays the guitar, a dark-haired woman plays the bongos and a blonde short-haired woman sings in a joyous, mellifluous voice. Papi looks thrilled as someone hands him a mojito with just a little rum and he moves his head back and forth to the music. "I'm flying with an eagle to where my love is," sings the blonde woman as she shakes her maracas. *Chi-kee-chi-kee-chi-kee* they sound.

As she warbles, the waiters bring us a typical Cuban feast: boiled rice, black beans, pork roasted in its own juice, pork rinds and toasted fried plantains. Papi eats heartily as I videotape all the fun. *Chi-kee-chi-kee-chi-kee*—the maracas' sound. My brother and Papi sit by themselves as I eat at another table. To me it underscores a subtle family dynamic I always feel but never bring up: My dad and my brother are like two peas in a pod. They share a macho sensibility. Mami and I were the outsiders. We were fragile with an underlying strength. Growing up I always thought of Papi and Willie as bullies. They made me feel insecure. They were strong and boisterous. I was quiet and withdrawn. The dynamic played out in obvious and subtle ways: making fun of me, knocking my common sense, criticizing my smarts.

I learned to compensate, by becoming book smart, by excelling in school. My mother rewarded me with attention and love. She protected me. She sensed I was gay even before I did. And she still loved me for it, or despite it. Although we never talked about it, what was left unsaid between mother and son spoke volumes. But I always felt Papi was troubled by the fear that his son might turn out to be "that way." I felt this way as a kid of six when I first visited Cuba with Mami and Willie, and I felt it into my adulthood. If I mentioned these feelings, my brother might scoff. He always felt that I was the favorite son; I had my doubts. But something Papi said when I visited him on Thanksgiving a year ago made things better. We bonded and he made me feel as if I mattered.

As I sit here at La Bodeguita del Medio with the smell of pork wafting through the air, I think about Cuba and how it's so much a part of all our lives. I think about how much I tried to convince my papi to come here. Now that he's returned to his homeland, I can see by the joy dancing in his eyes that he's so happy that he did. This morning he looked out at Havana from the ship and said that he felt Mami was with him. And if she is with Papi, she is with us as well, smiling down on us from heaven. I feel her presence as the band begins to play one of her favorite *boleros* (ballads), "Bésame Mucho":

Bésame, bésame mucho
Bésame como si fuera esta noche la última vez
Bésame, bésame mucho,
Que tengo miedo perderte, perderte después.

When I was about twelve, I remember Mother singing along with this song when it came on the radio. It was actually a Mexican song written in the forties when Mami was a teenager, but Cubans had adopted it as their own. Mami would sing it as she mopped the floor with the unmistakable smell of Lysol (or, as she called it, Lie-so):

Kiss me a lot
As I'm afraid of losing you forever.

The sound of applause jolts me back to reality. They're clapping for the singer. We leave La Bodeguita del Medio to continue the tour. Outside the restaurant a singer catches my father's eye. He's a blind man playing a guitar. He sings a song popularized by the Buena Vista Social Club, an immensely popular Cuban band. My father touches him on the shoulder, obviously moved by this afternoon serenade. He drops a CUC or two into his bucket.

Walking through Old Havana we pass tourists eating at sidewalk cafés and women hawking T-shirts and souvenirs from tiny shops. And the streets are lined with art. I notice the faces of several black woman painted on canvas. They are wide-eyed, the Cuban version of

Keane paintings. The black women look identical except for the color of their scarves and the flowers affixed to their hair. Art and music. In Havana they seem to be everywhere. We look up and see beautiful windows decorated with stained glass that catches the sun and turns them into prisms. I look up. As we round the bend to another plaza, I ask our tour guide, a Cuban gentleman in his fifties, what he thinks of my father coming back to Cuba after six decades. The tour guide looks directly at my brother. "I think it's great you've come back."

My brother is stunned. "No, I'm not the father who's come back," he stammers. "This is my father." He points at Papi and laughs. Several people on the tour start laughing as well. "And that's my brother," Willie says. "He only looks younger because he puts shoe polish in his hair." More laughter. For the record, I don't use shoe polish.

As we walk, I smell the delicious aroma of Cuban food cooking from one of the *paladars*. The *paladars* are restaurants in people's homes that have sprung up all around Havana. For less than five bucks you can eat like a king. Suddenly the smell puts me back in Mami's kitchen. I'd stand beside her as she conjured up meal after meal. She was a Cuban magician. Her magic was in *la cocina* (the kitchen). When my brother, his wife, Joy, and daughter, Summer, came over, she'd cook her special recipe of *arroz con pollo* (chicken and rice). It seemed to melt in your mouth. I found out many years later that it had to do with liquor. That's right. The chicken was tasty because of the booze.

My sister-in-law, Joy, tells me, "She always made it when we came to Sunday dinner. She had no recipes written and couldn't tell me how to make it, so I watched her and wrote down exactly what she did."

According to Joy, Mami used three pounds of chicken cut into pieces, half a medium onion diced, half a green pepper diced, lots of fresh garlic that was smashed, the juice of two fresh limes, one teaspoon of ground cumin, one bay leaf and salt and pepper to taste.

Mami would simmer all the above ingredients for about twenty-five minutes. Then she added the good stuff. She'd pour in one cup of

Edmundo dry white wine, eight ounces of tomato sauce, one cup of beer and one teaspoon of yellow food color. Then she'd add enough water to equal twice as much liquid as what was used when the tomato sauce and wine and beer were added. She'd then bring all of this to a boil and add two cups of uncooked rice and cook for about fifteen to twenty minutes on low heat. The result was Cuban heaven. *Ay, que rico*! (Oh, how rich!)

Visions of wolfing down Mami's *arroz con pollo* cha-cha-cha through my head as I walk through the plaza of San Francisco. We watch as a flock of pigeons take flight. They soar past delicate archways framed with rainbow-colored stained glass. We keep walking until we arrive at a beautiful building painted in a vivid pinkish-peach hue. It is the Ambos Mundos Hotel. It's here that Ernest Hemingway stayed in room 511 from 1932 to 1939. And it's here where he began writing *For Whom the Bell Tolls.*

As soon as we walk through the lobby, we step back in time. *"Papi, aquí se quedó Hemingway,"* I explain. I tell him this is where Hemingway once lived. A woman is playing a flute to the tune "As Time Goes By." Intermittently she stops to shake two maracas. One is blue, the other red.

Papi smiles and moves his head to the melody. When the song's over, the audience applauds. I imagine Ernest Hemingway standing in the lobby and listening to the song as well. I imagine it's at the end of a day after hours spent writing. "As Time Goes By" was written in 1931 and Hemingway stayed here from 1932 to 1939, so it's certainly possible. In Havana on this sun-kissed afternoon anything seems possible.

Back on board, Papi has more energy than I do. The Old Havana tour has exhausted me. I plop down on my cabin bed. "Look at him," Shorty says, laughing. "I'm older and look at me." I lay down, trying to go through photos I've taken on my iPhone. Tomorrow we go to Papi's old neighborhood to visit the church where he married Mami and the home my brother and I stayed when we visited in 1959. "Look at him in that guayabera," my father says, laughing, looking at my brother. "He can't fit into it. Look at him, that chest! He looks inflated." They share a big laugh

Suddenly I'm that five-year-old in Crandon Park Beach standing in the water behind my brother as Papi takes a picture. I was a chubby kid with a flabby chest, and I felt so self-conscious. Was I like a girl with small breasts standing there hoping no one noticed? Why did I look like that? I remember Mami saying she was hoping for a girl when she was pregnant with me. Had I turned out to be a little girl after all? All these feelings come rushing back to me in the roar of Papi's laughter. And then I hear my brother laughing too, and I'm that little boy uncomfortable in his own body.

I'm too ashamed to be me. I realize that instead of making fun of me, I want my father to love me. I want Papi to love me not as much as Willie but more than Willie. I want to be the favorite Cuban son.

September 19, 2016, 11:00 p.m.

We are in line for the Tropicana Night Club. My brother takes pictures. Papi stands in line beaming as other passengers from the trip greet him. He's become a celebrity of sorts on the *Adonia*. I videotape it all. Then I run over to a large statue of a ballet dancer bathed in pink and purple light. She's the symbol of the Tropicana. She's been standing here in this exact same pose since 1939.

"So, what do you think of my dad?" I ask a woman traveling with us on the trip.

"I think your dad is an amazing man. You don't always see kids [she calls us kids] traveling with their folks and taking them somewhere," she says. "It's just fantastic. What an adventure. I look at you and you have so much emotion." My dad stands there smiling from ear to ear.

"It brings back a lot of memories," he says like a shy little boy.

"When I saw you this morning on the ship I told my husband, 'He's Cuban going back for the first time.'"

The line snakes slowly to the entrance, and finally we're seated in a large theater-like space. Normally the show takes place out in the open under the stars. That is Tropicana's tag line: *Paradise Under the Stars*. But it's a Monday night, so they move tonight's show under what is called Los Arcos de Cristal (the Arches of Glass).

Our tickets for the show cost over one hundred dollars, five times the average Cuban monthly wage. My brother and my father are seated at a table further away from the stage. I sit just a little closer. I think about all the Cubans who can't afford to see a show like this. It saddens me that the rations they buy through the system (every fifteen days) are barely enough to purchase milk, rice, beans and sugar for a family. Cuba imports about 70 percent of its food, and 80 percent of it is rationed to the public.

It's showtime!

The showgirls don't emerge so much as they explode on stage. "*Para mi Cuba, yo tengo un son*" (For my Cuba, I have a son), they sing wearing gold lamé G-strings and bikini tops. It's all topped off with huge headdresses that resemble bows on steroids. I heard austerity measures forced the costume designers to come up with tissue and fabric made to look like feathers, a far cry from the late fifties when ostrich plumes were imported from Las Vegas or Paris.

Papi sits entranced, sipping on his rum drink, his eyes popping out as he watches this parade of pulchritude. There's a lively number danced to the traditional "Guantanamera." It seems especially appropriate given my father's visit. A singer croons "*Ante que me muero, me quiero hechar un verso del alma*." (Before I die, I want to sing a special verse that comes straight from my heart.)

The real crowd favorite is when the showgirls saunter out wearing what appear to be huge chandeliers on their heads. It's surreal. By the time the closing number explodes on stage, everyone, including Papi, is on his feet. "Tropicana, oh Havana, por Havana," the showgirls and chorus boys sing as they snake down the aisle grabbing patrons to dance with them. I'm so caught up in the spirit that I join one of the showgirls dancing in the aisles. After a few minutes, I return exhausted to my table. I look over and see such a look of contentment on Papi's face. It's been a long time since I've seen that expression. He no longer looks worried and tired like he did when I visited him in Hialeah for Thanksgiving.

September 20, 2016

Hemingway bought his home in the working-class town of San Francisco de Paula in 1940 for only $12,500 and promptly named it *Finca Vigía* (Look-out House). Papi is excited to visit it.

"He wrote his books here," he says. Papi is right. At Ambos Mundos Hotel Hemingway wrote *For Whom the Bell Tolls*. But here at Finca Vigía, Hemingway wrote one of my favorite books, *The Old Man and the Sea*. He was inspired by a fisherman who lived not too far away in Cojimar and fished the waters off Havana.

The tour guide, a young Cuban woman with copper-colored skin and a ready smile, tells us that Finca Vigía sits on 140 acres. "Before he passed away, Hemingway willed the house to the Cuban people," she says. "There were rumors that Castro took it away when he took over, but that's not true. It was turned into a museum." She explains that when Hemingway won the Nobel Prize for Literature in 1954, he donated the proceeds to the basilica of Cuba's Virgin of Charity in Santiago, Cuba.

The guide tells us we aren't allowed to enter the house but only photograph it from the door. It seems that tourists stole books and knickknacks as keepsakes, so the Cuban government closed it off. I walk up to the front door and videotape the living room. It's kept as it was when Hemingway lived here. There are comfy chairs, coffee tables and side tables made out of wood, lots of books and deer heads mounted on the wall. Meanwhile my brother goes behind the property and takes photos of Hemingway's fishing boat, *Pilar*. He also takes pictures of the graves of Hemingway's beloved dogs. I ask Papi how he likes Finca Vigía.

"It's very beautiful. I am going to stay here during my next vacation," he jokes.

We walk back to the bus and wait for the other folks. Papi engages the bus driver.

"The Cubans want to be our friends," Papi says. "I find the youth to be very warm and open. Slowly maybe things will change."

The driver agrees. "We want change. It will come."

My father hugs him. "We have to give love. Love will change things." We drive to a restaurant in Cojimar that Hemingway is said to have frequented. On the walls are photos of Fidel and Hemingway. As we await lunch, a band incongruously begins to play the Eagles' "Hotel California."

Above our table on a wall of photographs, one in particular catches my eye. It is a photo of Gregorio Fuentes, Hemingway's boat captain and friend for more than twenty years. More importantly, Fuentes was the inspiration for *The Old Man and the Sea*. After lunch the bus takes us to a monument honoring Hemingway in Cojimar. Across from it is an imposing fortress built by the Spanish colonialists in the middle of the eighteenth century. We drive back to Havana, eagerly looking forward to the rest of our afternoon.

We're about to visit La Víbora, where Papi lived from the time he was nine to when he left Cuba for the United States at the age of seventeen.

We're dropped off near La Floridita, the home of the daiquiri, and we walk through Old Havana to meet up with our driver, Orlando. Orlando was my chauffeur when I came to Cuba a year earlier. He's already driven me to La Víbora, so he knows the quickest way to get there. We meet at the Plaza of San Francisco, and although it's been almost a year since he saw me, he spots me right away. I introduce him to Willie and Papi and they immediately click. Orlando is Cuban through and through. It's the way he speaks, the way he jokes and the way he knows how to weave a story. Orlando is like a relative I've always known.

We climb into his two-seat 1948 gray-and-green Chevy, a shiny vintage vehicle he keeps in tip-top shape. Around Havana the Chevrolets, Buicks, Fords, Plymouths and Studebakers from the fifties are familiar sights. Some look shiny and new. But others are held together with hope and a prayer as well as some odd parts and scrap metal. When Castro came to power he banned the import of American cars and mechanical parts. And so Cubans had to be resourceful. Sometimes you'll even find a Russian engine in a 1950s Chevy.

As we drive closer and closer to La Víbora, the buildings change. They have greatly deteriorated. Some are falling apart, missing parts of their structure. La Víbora gives off a Beirut vibe, as if it is a war zone that has been neglected for decades. As we drive, I turn around and notice Papi is shaking his head.

"It's horrible," he says. "This doesn't look like La Víbora I knew." We pass the church on a hill where Father Gasolina lived. We get closer to Los Pasionistas de la Víbora where Mami and Papi got married. In the distance we see its steeples soaring into the sky.

"Can you see them, Papi?" I ask. We drive in silence, and within moments we are there. I jump out of the front seat and open the door so Papi can get out. He emerges in slow motion. It takes him a minute or two to get his footing.

"Let's go, Papi," I say. My brother stays behind taking more photographs. My father looks up to the triangular steeples. They are elaborately carved with inlaid crosses and tiny archways.

All around the church, the streets look like they're filled with rubble. The homes nearby look destroyed.

Papi takes his time walking up the steps of Los Pasionistas. "Where is Willie?" he asks, turning around.

"Don't worry, Papi. He'll be right behind us," I say. "Let's go in." I walk behind Papi as he gets to the center aisle. It stretches before him to the altar in the distance. He walks slowly, looking right and then looking left. After what seems to be an eternity, he arrives within feet of the altar. He makes the sign of the cross and sits in a pew.

By this time, my brother has walked in. We watch Papi pray and suddenly we embrace. We feel what Dad is feeling. It's all come full circle. This is the place where it all began. And, more than ever, I feel Mami's presence. Is she hovering above us looking down like an angel? Is she holding to her heart the framed photograph of our family I brought to her in the hospital hours before she left us?

My dad finishes lighting the candle and walks toward the back of the church. There he encounters two old women. They tell him they take care of the church.

"Everything has changed in Cuba," one tells my father, "but the church stays the same." The caretaker has told Papi that parishioners in Germany have contributed to the upkeep of this church. But he also says there used to be ten priests. Now there are only two.

My dad makes the sign of the cross on one woman's forehead. He explains he is a Eucharistic minister. Suddenly the woman appears to break down.

"This place has no solution," she says. "Nothing changes here. Nothing. Every day it gets worse and worse and worse."

Papi tries to comfort her, but it's useless.

"They say things are getting better. You hear it over the television: things are better," she says, fighting back the tears. "But it isn't better. It isn't."

My dad consoles her. "We have to pray a lot," he tells her. "We just have to keep on praying." They hug and we leave the church.

In the car on the way to the house on Josefina where my brother and I stayed in 1959, my father says very little. "The church looks the same," he says softly. "But it's not really the same." He talks about Mami and how she'd volunteer at the church carnivals they called *tombolas*. "But the ladies say they stopped having them," he says sadly. "Nothing here seems to be as it was before."

In a minute we are in front of Josefina 18. I scramble out of the car and shout toward the open door, "Tania, Tania, are you here?" Tania is the distant cousin I visited when I came to Cuba in January.

Her husband, Alejandro, comes running out. He explains Tania isn't home because she had to teach a class.

"But you're invited to come in." Alejandro hugs us and Papi as if we are long lost brothers.

My brother walks inside the home for the first time since 1959. Suddenly he walks out to the porch. He looks like he's possessed. He waves his arms frenetically. "The store's over there," he says. "It's across the street. That's where I used to buy the *pirulis* [lollipops]. They used to put money in my hand and pin a note to my pocket which listed what I had to buy. I'd cross the street to the drugstore," he remembered. "Once I got there, they'd take the note off my chest and give me what was on the note." By this time my brother was speaking so fast I could barely understand what he was saying. "Once, I brought back brown sugar and it stained my shirt and Mami made me take it off so she could wash it in the sink."

My brother leads me across the street to the drugstore, which looks like it's been abandoned. Inside is a dusty cash register just as he remembered it. "And look, there's a scale," he says. "That's where they used to weigh the candy." Tears form in his eyes and he's almost unable to speak.

Back at the house, Papi is talking rapidly to Alejandro. In typical Cuban style, he's talking so fast he's swallowing words and rolling his *r*'s frenetically, like a *campesino* (farmer) slicing through a sugar cane field in high season. Papi tells him the house has changed a lot since he visited it back in 1958. Papi remembers that it used to be open in the backyard and filled with trees. Now a small structure has been built on the property. By this time, my brother has walked to the backyard as well.

"Charlie, look," he says. "You see that building back there? That's where Claudio lived." Claudio was a boy about our age we had befriended on our visit when we were kids. In the morning we used to throw *piedresitas* (little rocks) at his window so he'd wake up.

My brother is talking like an overexcited seven-year-old. That's almost how old he was when he burned up our house in Little River.

Alejandro asks us to stay late so that we can see Tania. We explain we have to get back to the ship because it leaves in two hours. Papi looks sad.

"There is so much history here, so many memories," he says. With that, he embraces Alejandro. We say goodbye and Orlando drives us to Papi's former home on Avellaneda. In two minutes we're there.

Orlando parks the Chevy in front of 206 and Papi shuffles out. Time stands still. In 1926 Catalino Gonzalez, Papi's step-grandfather, built the first wooden home on this dusty block that my father's looking at now. Papi stands on the same crumbling sidewalk he played on as a kid. Suddenly sights and sounds come back to him in a jumble.

"I can hear your mima screaming at me to play with baby Eddie," he says, "and I can almost see my tia Adela." She's regaling him with stories from the days when she was spry and ornery. He finds himself reminiscing. If his mother was lady-like, Tia Adela was a Cuban Annie Oakley. But instead of a rifle she wielded her machete.

Shorty squints into the afternoon sun. A blue-and-gray *zunzún* (Cuban hummingbird) flutters its wings above him. Papi squints some more, looking at the row of houses (at least one demolished and rebuilt as a two-story structure), and suddenly the faces of the family he so loved flash before him. There's Eliseo, Adela and Catalino's son, the first of the Gonzalez family to seek his fortune in the US. And he sees Rogelio, Evelio, Catalino Jr., Berta, Juana and Nicolas, Adelina, they're all there. Have they come to welcome him? His smile fades into the tightest of frowns. Papi realizes he's the last member of his family still alive.

And now, at this moment, as the sights and sounds play out before him, he can hear Adela laughing. In that voice, that deep, clear voice, she's telling him the story of the intruder again. One hot Havana night, Adela's alone in the Avellaneda home. She's writing a letter to her son, Eliseo. Suddenly she hears a strange sound. At the top of the tall doorway, where there's a moveable glass opening, she notices two hands with wiggling fingers trying to make it over the door. Adela's eyes widen and she springs into action. Without stopping to think, she grabs the glistening machete standing in the corner. And with one quick movement, *whish*, she slices off the wiggling fingers above.

The sound of a man screaming bloody murder pierces the darkness. "Ayyy, ayyy," the man wails. The intruder flees into the Havana night. Safe once more, Adela puts the machete back in the corner where it belongs. No one messes with Tia Adela!

Papi's daydream is interrupted. He's not fourteen years old anymore. He's eighty-eight, and more than seven decades suddenly condense into this one moment, a moment he never thought he'd live to see. The *zunzún* flies back across the sky.

Papi walks slowly to the childhood home he lived in all those years. He doesn't recognize it. It's no longer white but painted in shades of mango orange and canary yellow. A heavy gate has been erected outside it. The first thing he notices is that he doesn't see the door to the *bodeguita* where he ground coffee beans for my mother as a teenager. In its place is a window.

"There was a door there," he says, pointing. "They've changed everything. When you opened the door, there was a large room and then a bathroom off to the side. When my mother left this house, she sold it to a priest."

My dad decides to walk down the street. To his left is a structure that has been burned to the ground. "That's where the other store was," he says sadly. He walks back to 206 Avellaneda. A heavy woman wearing a tube top and a short skirt chimes in.

"There used to be a barber shop here," she says, pointing to the spot where the *bodeguita* once was.

"Yes, a barbershop," my father says.

Papi remembers the barbershop where a man named Amado cut my brother's hair and mine too. He'd snip away like a gardener snipping a hedge. Pieces of curly hair would tumble to the floor. Amado's finishing touch was to shape my hair into a little ball on top of my head. He called it "*la bolita.*"

Orlando looks at his watch indicating it's time for us to head back to the ship. My father looks one last time at the old neighborhood. The faces of his family and friends slowly fade as he steps into the back seat of the Chevy. He peers from the window one last time. Is Tia Adela waving *adios*? *Adios*, Avellaneda, *adios*.

On the way back to the ship, my brother asks about *el Parque de los Chivos* (the Park of the Goats). "Gladys used to take us there," he said. "We would ride the goats around the park." I have Orlando drive us to an abandoned amusement park a few blocks away.

"No, this isn't it," Willie insists. "It was a park that had a fountain in the middle." Orlando drives around some more and we finally reach the park my brother remembered. It's now an empty lot covered by brown grass. The fountain has disappeared. The goats are nowhere to be found.

Back on the ship, I ask Papi what he thought of seeing his beloved La Víbora.

"The neighborhood is so different," he says. "It has changed completely. It's deteriorated. Some of it is destroyed. I feel sad. But this is part of life," he says. "We can't expect everything to stay the same. It's like our lives. We are here temporarily. We're born to die."

But the church in which he was married brought him joy. "They've kept it up so beautifully," he says. "Even the original organ still works." He thinks Mami would have been so happy to see it again. "I could see her walking toward me all over again. And she was smiling. She was smiling at me."

At sunset the *Adonia* sails away from Havana. We pass El Morro Castle against a pinkish-blue sky. On the other side of the ship we watch as the glittering necklace of the Havana skyline slowly disappears from view. The sky grows darker, which only makes the lights from the Nacional Hotel in the distance shine brighter. They flicker like tiny flames from the votive candles inside the Cathedral of Havana. But as we pull away, the lights dim until finally the Nacional disappears from view. On deck men and women wave in slow motion at the faraway buildings. I'm reminded of cousin Tania waving goodbye to me from the porch of her home in La Víbora. Havana is gone, but the sights and sounds of this enchanted city linger in our memories and in our hearts.

In the next two days we travel to Cienfuegos on the southern coast of Cuba. We take pictures of the statue of Cuban statesman José Martí in the plaza. We listen to a choir of men in suits and women in pastel gowns sing for us in an old theater. They don't sing Cuban standards but songs dearer to the hearts of American tourists:

When I fall in love, it will be forever
Or I'll never fall in love
In a restless world like this
Love is ended before it's begun.
And too many moonlight kisses
Seem to cool in the warmth of the sun.

We take photos of those vintage cars kept in perfect condition. We gaze at sublime stained-glass windows above graceful archways leading to perfectly manicured courtyards adorned with gurgling fountains. We tour architectural jewels like the Palacio del Valle with its Romanesque steeples soaring into the sky in the Punta Gorda of Cienfuegos.

We sail to Santiago to visit the basilica of Cuba's patron saint, the Virgin of Charity. Papi takes out a dozen bottles and dutifully fills them with holy water to later give to his friends in Hialeah. He walks slowly to the altar and prays to la Virgencita in her golden robes. He caresses his crucifix. He prays for his sons. And he prays for Mami, too. In a town square we listen to a steel drum band. Too impatient, Papi heads back to the bus to look for a tiny wooden statue of the Virgin Mary he misplaced. I videotape the band. They play Mami's favorite song: "Ave Maria."

And now they're playing "The Girl from Ipanema." I notice a very old Cuban woman dancing to the beat under a gray-and-black umbrella on the porch of a nearby home. Suddenly she puts the umbrella down and breaks into a Cuban rumba. She moves her legs back and forth nimbly, lost in the music. And as I record her impromptu *baile* (dance), I'm reminded that Cuban rhythm isn't just for the young. It is for those who carry the beat within them regardless of age.

By now the old woman is laughing as she's dancing. And across the street I hear others laughing as well. The Cuban spirit is infectious. As I walk away, she's still dancing. With every step she takes, Cuba is calling. Back on the bus, Papi finds his statue of the Virgin of Charity. He's made the pilgrimage to see la Virgencita in Santiago, the holiest pilgrimage any Cuban can make. Before going back to the ship, we stop at a souvenir stand. Papi negotiates with a Cuban for some more trinkets. As I record the exchange, the vendor notices me.

"Hey, this guy wants to take your picture."

Papi explains that I'm his son.

"Here you have another son in Cuba," the vendor says. "Your father's made a family here. We Cubans are your brothers and you are ours as well."

Back on the *Adonia* we set sail to Miami. Papi gazes at the majestic purple mountains of Oriente as they loom in the distance. "What a beautiful country my homeland is," he says. "Thank you, *hijos*. I never thought I'd live to see my Cuba once last time."

With that, the three of us embrace. Cuba has united us. I hear the sounds of the ocean as our ship rocks back and forth. I press up against Papi and I feel his heart beating next to mine. It's like a soothing lullaby, and when I close my eyes I drift back to my special time with Papi on Thanksgiving in Hialeah a year ago. The memories are sweet ones. We became closer than we'd ever been as Papi shared stories of his childhood in Cuba, stories I had never heard before. And when he told me about the first time he laid eyes on Mami, his eyes filled with tears. And mine did too.

My mother died on Thanksgiving two years ago, and so on our return to Florida we decide to go to her gravesite. Willie drives us, and at the cemetery we meet my niece, Summer, and her husband, Joe. My brother brings shears and trims the grass around Mami's tombstone. Papi places a bouquet on her final resting place. Then we join hands as Summer leads us in the Lord's Prayer. As I clasp Papi's hand, I remember something Summer said about Papi. She said he told her, "You know, people say it's wrong to be gay. If you're gay, people can't say it's wrong. God made them that way."

My father never shared these thoughts with me. He learned I was living with HIV from a column in *The Miami Herald*, May 2000.

Two years ago, Gomez left his job at WNBC in New York to work full-time on Tropicana, a project that evolved from a one-act play he wrote and staged in 1989. It was a critical time for Gomez. Battling HIV, he often felt too weak to work. But months later as he dug into the project, he gained strength, both physical and spiritual.

I asked Papi if he had read the column.

"Yes, and I wasn't too happy with what they wrote," he replied. Although I had told my mother three years earlier, she never broke the news to my father. "People die from this virus, don't they?"

"Sometimes, Papi," I said, "but I have it under control. Don't worry."

But we had never talked about the fact that I was gay. I knew he always sensed it. He sensed it that time I couldn't screw on the garden hose back when I was eleven. He felt it when I wore the red AIDS ribbon on my tux the night I won an Emmy Award.

And Papi sensed it another time, when he added my partner's photo to his "Wall of Honor." It was the same wall where he proudly displayed his relatives' photos. They were snapshots from another time, faded reminders of his parents, his uncles and his cousins. They had all fled Cuba for a better life in the US. And there right next to them was a photo of my partner and I smiling—next to all the Cuban sons and daughters who were gone but not forgotten. We had earned our place on the Wall of Honor. I was so touched, not to mention so proud. What I hadn't realized was that as my father grew older, he had become more tolerant. All these years I had worried that he was ashamed of his gay son. Now I learned that my fears were unfounded. Was it too late for us?

On the last morning of my Thanksgiving visit, I sat at the dining room table sipping a *cafecito* and writing in my journal as I always did growing up. I still had so many unanswered questions for Papi. But before I could ask them, I suddenly felt Shorty's hand on my shoulder.

"*Oye, Papito.*" (Hey, Daddy.)

He said, "It's great that you spent so much time with me. I hope I didn't annoy you too much."

I shook my head, "Of course not, Papi, I loved every minute."

He squeezed my shoulder tightly. "You know, it doesn't matter who you love. God made you *como eres* [like you are]. You've been through so much. I always prayed for you, and your mami did too, that you would be alright." Papi's voice began to tremble, and I could tell that he was close to crying. He paused a moment and said, "Son, I'm proud of you. I've always been proud of you."

Finally. They were the words I had waited a lifetime to hear.

EPILOGUE

IT'S YEARS IN THE future. Papi has passed. An old man lies in a hospital bed. I watch from the other side of the room. My brother and Joy leave. Now Summer walks in with a photograph in a silver frame and some beautiful flowers. Are they gardenias? She throws herself over the old man's bed. She's crying. Suddenly she softly sings a song, but I can't make out the words. I notice that the picture she's brought is of our family, just like the photo I left for Mami on the day that she died. Summer whispers to the old man to rest, that she'll be back in the morning. She rushes out of the room. It's only now that I realize I'm the old man in the bed. I hear ghosts whispering to me, and I can barely hear what they're saying. They're the ghosts of Papi, Pipo, Catalino, Everardo, Eliseo and all the Cuban sons who came to this country so long ago. They're calling me like Cuba is calling me. They want me to join them now. I feel strong arms lifting me. I'm a Cuban son. *I'M A CUBAN SON RISING.*

ACKNOWLEDGMENTS

THERE ARE SO MANY to thank for helping me on this incredible journey. In no particular order: Matthew Carnino, Vanderbilt University News Archives, *Miami Herald* Archives, WBBM-TV, CBS News, NBC News, WWOR-TV, Guillermo Gomez, Stanley Siegel, Bob Bergeron, Susan Meiseles, Dennis Leyva, Sheila Stainback, Tom Santopietro, Alan Markinson, Richard Blanco, Paula Madison, William Gomez, Joy Gomez, Bonnie Erbé, Ike Seamans, Larry Doyle, Kathy Hersh, Manuel Alvarez, Mario R. de Carvahlo, Michele Gillen, Jane Kashlak, Carl Hersh, Shelley Ross, George Lewis, Cristina Garcia, Pam Stack, Anne-Marie O'Connor, Dr. Daniel Swistel, Dr. Dayana Eslava, Krishna Stone, John Koehler, Patrick L. Riley, Tami Ansoorian Buenick, Charlotte Perry Aguilar, Conchita Sarnoff, Vivien Lesnik Weisman, Antonia Zapata Romo, Daniel Greenstone, Saundra Santiago, Matthew Schwartz and Joshua Dewane.

CPSIA information can be obtained
at www.ICGtesting.com
Printed in the USA
LVHW091747300920
667545LV00007B/74

9 781646 630523